T0274074

Winner of the John Burroughs Medal for Na

National Outdoor Book Award Winner

℘

PRAISE FOR *HALCYON JOURNEY*

"In a world that is rapidly losing its birds, we need reminders of how glorious they really are—their songs, their colors, their eagerness for life. *Halcyon Journey* is a lively, joyous celebration of kingfishers and rivers, by a writer whose love for birds sings on the page."
—Kathleen Dean Moore, author of *Earth's Wild Music*

"The kingfisher has long deserved a queen from our own kind, and here she is: Marina Richie. This sharply observant author has written a book that can draw us all into the fascinating and secret lives of the fresh-water king. My own cherished moments in seeing these birds along rivers will forever be enhanced by the stories told here and the insights revealed."
—Tim Palmer, author of *America's Great River Journeys,*
Rivers of Oregon, and other books

"Marina Richie's unsentimental yet passionate quest to know the belted kingfisher delights the senses, with descriptions of the natural world that are both photographic and poetic. Getting to know this elusive and storied bird produces an unexpected suspense—not only for the author reflecting at the midpoint of her life, but for all of us and our common planetary fate. With sustained and sustaining attention, this 'citizen scientist' shows us what it means to be present in our lives and in the world."
—Suzanne Matson, author of *Ultraviolet*

"In this crazy world, it's good to have a teacher, a spirit guide, a guardian. Marina Richie has found hers in the blue ball of fire called the kingfisher. In *Halcyon Journey* we join her quest to know this bird through startling science, resonant field observation, and a storyteller's knack for putting us breathless into the presence of this divine bird."
—Kim Stafford, author of *Singer Come from Afar*

"Much is still unknown about the belted kingfisher, surprisingly—hence the gift of this beautifully written book, which offers the best of citizen science and lyrical observation. If curiosity is the definition of love, then this is a true love story, for it is born of pure inquisitiveness. From Montana to South Africa, from the Smithsonian to a creek, from studying flight to nesting to migration to myth, this story soars with Richie's graceful observations of the bird and eloquent words on the page."
—Laura Pritchett, author of PEN USA Award winner *Hell's Bottom, Colorado*

Halcyon Journey

IN SEARCH OF THE BELTED KINGFISHER

Marina Richie

Illustrations by Ram Papish

Oregon State University Press   Corvallis

Library of Congress Cataloging-in-Publication Data

Names: Richie, Marina, author. | Papish, Ramiel, illustrator.
Title: Halcyon journey : in search of the belted kingfisher / Marina Richie ; illustrations by Ram Papish.
Description: Corvallis : Oregon State University Press, [2022] | Includes biblio-
graphical references and index.
Identifiers: LCCN 2022010798 | ISBN 9780870712036 (paperback) |
ISBN 9780870712043 (ebook)
Subjects: LCSH: Richie, Marina. | Belted kingfisher—Montana. | Bird watchers—
Montana—Biography. | Natural history—United States.
Classification: LCC QL696.C72 R53 2022 | DDC 598.072/34786—dc23/
eng/20220315
LC record available at https://lccn.loc.gov/2022010798

∞ This paper meets the requirements of ANSI/NISO Z39.48-1992
(Permanence of Paper).

© 2022 Marina Richie
All rights reserved
First published in 2022 by Oregon State University Press
Third printing 2024
Printed in the United States of America

Oregon State University
OSU Press

Oregon State University Press
121 The Valley Library
Corvallis OR 97331-4501
541-737-3166 ∙ fax 541-737-3170
www.osupress.oregonstate.edu

I dedicate this book to my father David Richie (1932–2002), who taught me to appreciate the wonder of birds.

Contents

Coming Home

HALCYON JOURNEY

Rattlesnake National
Recreation Area

Rattlesnake
Valley

Rattlesnake Creek

Nł?ay Sewłkʷs

North Hills

Tom Green Park

Bugbee
Preserve

Greenough Park

Mount Jumbo
Nmɫɫe

Missoula
Nł?ay

N

Clark Fork River   Nmesuletk

Introduction

Some journeys are meant to be hard. Belted kingfishers are loners, territorial, and wary. They are fiendish to study. Yet, a difficult quest promises both allure and reward. The heartbeat of this story pulses along Rattlesnake Creek in Missoula, Montana, where a pair of kingfishers still court, nest, and tend their young to the music of rollicking currents. Over the course of seven years, from spring 2008 through the summer of 2015, I followed with curiosity as the birds continued to baffle, elude, and enlighten.

In certain tribal stories, the belted kingfisher is a messenger, helper, or protector. To tap into those powers takes more than one season. Each year, I recorded behaviors in the company of naturalist friends. By the forested creek's edge, I would find the convergence of Greek and indigenous myths, kinship with wild inhabitants, and personal transformation.

Traveling far to investigate clues to the mystery of why the female is more colorful than the male, I met several members of the greater family, from the ringed kingfisher on the Mexico border to the giant kingfisher in South Africa. Seeking the dazzling bird of Greek myth, I prowled Hampstead Heath in London and found the common kingfisher in a dreamlike setting.

On the east coast, I pulled out trays of study skins in an eerie back room of the Smithsonian, paddled below hovering belted kingfishers in a North Carolina bay, and sought wintering birds by Chincoteague National Wildlife Refuge over the solstice. Returning to Rattlesnake Creek, I opened my eyes anew to one species on a small stretch of stream in the context of an interwoven planet.

Flying with practiced ease above North America's streams, rivers, lakes, ponds, and coastlines, belted kingfishers are the supreme avian anglers. They may be only a tad bigger than robins, but their beaks are blades, and their obsidian eyes miss nothing.

Whether hovering or diving from a branch, a kingfisher's headfirst plunge to snap fish near the surface is swift and precise. Touching down by cities, towns, farms, and wilderness alike, belted kingfishers flourish only where water is clean, in places with plentiful fish, perches, and coveted earthen nest banks. Even their plumage matches the sheens of water and stone—dusky blues, grays, whites, and, for the female, a dash of cinnamony red to form the namesake belt.

In the first days of my pivotal decision to track the kingfisher, on a windy spring afternoon beneath Bozeman's Bridger Range, cheering for my son's team from the soccer field sidelines, I'd confided to a fellow parent: I'd made a discovery—a revelation that added a mythic appeal to an already charismatic bird.

"Cool, you've found the feel-good bird!" the parent said, with that knack he had for clinching the spare phrase, a skill he applied to his prose and a side job of pruning trees, lopping off limbs with editorial precision.

Those prescient words would ring true in ways I had not considered. Like the elusive quality of idyllic halcyon days, the secretive nature of kingfishers would prove instrumental to my happiness. Running, stumbling, tangling through wild rose and hawthorns, shivering, and staying put for hours, I'd savor every hard-fought glimpse. A surge of feeling good resulted from tenacity, like a marathoner crossing a finish line, another personal goal I finally achieved in September of 2015.

That's one kind of feeling good. Another stemmed from immersion in my home creek with the kingfisher as a guide. Dabbling toes in the frigid wilderness-fed waters, my senses awakened to the syncopated glugs, sprays, froths, and singing of an enlivened stream.

Hiding in a camouflaged blind, I merged with the alders, cottonwoods, and pines. When a Swainson's thrush landed within grasp and opened his beak to sing, I nodded to yet another sign of my bird-loving father's presence, as if we could still revel in the soloist poet of the wafting, spiraling-away verse. In the company of creekside inhabitants, sorrows and losses cascaded into the clear waters where bull trout finned upstream to spawn.

In the intervening years, I've integrated new science, more indigenous stories, and insights gained from reflection and observations, including one memorable evening on the Oregon coast. As golden sun rays lapped upon a sandstone outcrop that stood between me and a vigilant kingfisher, the receding high tide yielded just enough room to edge around the corner within view of a nest hole excavated by the diligent parents. One cautious step at a time, I ducked below leathery green leaves of a salal bush. In my black down jacket, gray pants, and rubber boots, I hoped to blend in like a cormorant. Instead, I faced the full fury of an indignant queen fisher. Her crown was a feathery two-part crest, her throne a lichen-draped branch, and her decree a volley of reproving notes.

I gazed with longing at the burnished coppery red belt on a moon-white chest and yearned to plead my case: "I'm your subject. I will stay right here and fasten myself to this sandstone cliff like a barnacle. I won't be in your way."

But no. She breezed off to cross the bay that opened to the Pacific. I backed away into the linger of light, leaving the nesting kingfishers in peace.

Listening to National Public Radio in June of 2021, I heard the Pulitzer Prize–winning poet Yusef Komunyakaa describe his calling: "It feels like one has been chosen as a caretaker of observation."

For all who witness the intricacies of nature, we are the caretakers of observation, too. As the climate and extinction crises accelerate, the clarion notes of kingfishers convey a ratcheting up of urgency. With care comes responsibility to act on behalf of all forms of life that cannot speak for themselves.

My offering here is at once an ode to the halcyon bird and a call for protection of their watery homes, from headwater springs to ocean confluences and all the interconnected wilds, from ancient forests to wildflower meadows and beaver-created marshes.

Since making the pivotal choice to trail a tricky bird with a flair for fishing, I've learned much, during what has become a lifelong apprenticeship. Seeking kingfishers near rippling or tranquil waters, worries tend to mist away.

Living now in Bend, Oregon, I listen for the reverberating notes that ricochet across the jade green currents of the Deschutes River in a mellifluent staccato always taking me home. Veering quick and low to the sun-sparkled whitewater, a kingfisher flicks droplets with pointed wingtips. Star spreader. Joy splasher.

First Year

CHAPTER I

Hole Quest

The belted kingfisher is a striking and picturesque feature of the landscape whether in action or at rest. The mountain trout stream would lose much of its charm without the rattling call of the lone fisherman and the flash of his broad, blue wings, as he follows the course of the stream, flying well below the treetops until he glides upward to alight on his accustomed perch, there to tilt his short tail nervously up and down and raise and lower his long crest a few times, as he sounds his battle cry again.

—Arthur Cleveland Bent, "Belted Kingfisher," *Life Histories of Familiar North American Birds*

Leaning over the balcony railing of the second-story bedroom, I listened to the surge of Rattlesnake Creek flooding two blocks away. Close by, a yellow warbler sang the morning into buttery sweetness. Robins caroled. Magpies squawked. But the ringing staccato of the bird I longed to hear would never mingle with backyard birds. Instead, the belted kingfisher would be pelting downstream on strong wings, always looking for fish.

Minutes earlier, I'd read the dictionary word of the day:

Halcyon \HAL-see-uhn\, noun: 1. A kingfisher. 2. A mythical bird, identified with the kingfisher that was fabled to nest at sea about the time of the winter solstice and to calm the waves during incubation. 3. Calm; quiet; peaceful; undisturbed; happy; as, "deep, halcyon repose." 4. Marked by peace and prosperity; as, "halcyon years."

❧

As the dawn chorus flooded every awakening fiber, I repeated two words as if turning stones in my freckled hands. Halcyon. Kingfisher. Halcyon. Kingfisher.

A flame flickered. It was May of 2008, and by the end of November, I would turn fifty. I ought to have been content living and writing in the vibrant university town of Missoula, Montana, with my book-loving, soccer-playing, eleven-year-old son, a science teacher husband, a golden retriever-ish dog, and wildness in view. Still, the momentous birthday loomed with a sense of disquiet. Caught up in to-do lists, writing deadlines, and carpools, the days were clicking by without a sense of purpose.

I found my center on all-too-short forays outdoors. Running on the nearby North Hills, I watched ravens tumble in winds that whisked the bunchgrass. At the creek's edge, senses flared like a white-tailed deer and the hollow knocking of a pileated woodpecker resonated deep in my rib cage. What if nature as escape could instead become my raison d'être?

One bird and one word stirred like an insistent breeze, summoning me to follow. Halcyon stems from the Greek *hals* (sea) and *kuo* (conceive). To conceive is to create. Where better to feel the creative spirit than in the watery haunts of kingfishers? Tracing the halcyon definition to an ancient Greek myth, I read of two lovers, Halcyon and Ceyx, transformed by the gods Zeus and Hera into kingfishers destined to nest annually over the winter solstice. Then, Aeolus, god of the winds and father of Halcyon, would calm the rough waves for fourteen days, seven on either side of the solstice. Sailors called this interlude the halcyon days, bracketed by storms.

Since childhood, I'd dreamed of feathers, light hollow bones, and lofting above the earth on wings that would never let me fall. Pursue a bird of happiness and transformation? I was in.

The bird of myth, the common kingfisher, may live far away in Europe and Asia, yet right here, North America's belted kingfisher bears the colors of water and the royalty of a frisky crest that riffs in the winds. The scientific name is *Megaceryle alcyon*. The genus means big blue, and the species name *alcyon* is the Greek spelling of halcyon.

I chose the belted kingfisher on a spring morning of revelation. I made my promise to shadow this jay-sized bird that knows the headfirst dive into fish-filled waters, the brush of sky on crest feathers, and the shelter of an earthen nest burrow. At once powerful and agile, the kingfisher flies high above the trees or low to the currents. By attending to this bird, would I find the halcyon rhythm of my home watershed?

Little did I know that this quest would extend from one to multiple perplexing seasons, lead to publishing a new scientific finding, and propel me on far-flung journeys sleuthing answers to a mystery. Tracking this loner of a bird would prove far from easy. The kingfisher remains the artful dodger, skilled in vanishing acts.

ꝏ

Soon after that word-of-the-day morning, I'd driven five hours east to Billings, Montana, for a writing assignment at an Audubon nature center close by the longest free-flowing river in the lower 48 states—the Yellowstone. My raincoat leaked in the downpour as I stumbled along a trail to the cottonwood-lined river—swollen, chocolate brown, a hundred yards wide, and spilling over the banks.

I saw her. A female kingfisher perched on a fallen tree moored in the center of the river. Her crested head was the blue of washed denim, tousled and sodden. White neck feathers formed a gleaming ring above a slate-blue band that dipped to a point on her snowy chest. Below that, a rusty red belt clasped in mid-belly and draped down both flanks, partly hidden by closed wings of blue-gray hues.

Only the female wears the namesake belt, and that could be meaningful. In contrast, a male shows a single bluish upper band, like a prim bandana on his white breast. In the bird world, males are almost always more colorful than females when there's a difference between the two. The rare gender reversal drew me in like the myth. Could I chase clues to this puzzle that scientists had yet to solve?

A male flew in, a pinwheel of whites and thunderous blues. His flurry of notes pattered like rain. She preened her wet feathers. He landed and then lifted off, each downward wing stroke scooping the heavy air. She followed him skyward, wheeling to expose white underwings with the reddish plumage extending into her armpits, like the work of a slapdash painter.

Circling once, they descended in unison to the same driftwood that parted the currents. He looked upriver, and she swiveled her head to glance downriver. Out in the middle of the turbid Yellowstone River, the pair seemed unperturbed by the torrent—or were they? Perhaps their hearts beat faster in each other's presence, like two people on a park bench in the rain, wildly attracted to each other.

ॐ

My kingfisher desire felt more potent than any prior bird crush. My first spoken word was "duck." Since then, I'd earned a dubious reputation for tripping over tree roots, drifting onto the shoulder while driving, and interrupting conversations to point out a lone hawk floating the cloud river. Yet, never had I fallen for one bird over others. Reading more about kingfishers, I presumed I was not their only lover, even if published literature was sparse.

Across the world, 120 species illuminate a surprising array of habitats, extending from waters to rainforests and even the outback of Australia. They dwell on every continent except Antarctica. More than half the species are at risk, from critically endangered to vulnerable. So far, the belted kingfisher is not one of them, but populations are declining—like so many birds in my lifetime.

Most kingfishers are not fish eaters. Some perch and wait in forests to drop down on terrestrial prey. Many are known for brilliant colors. No matter how far afield, identifying a bird as a kingfisher is easier than you might think. Like flipping through an album of family relatives, you can spot their oversized heads, prominent dagger bills, and spunky panache.

The belted kingfisher reigns over the waters of Canada and the United States, joined only at the southern border with Mexico by ringed and green kingfishers and, occasionally, an Amazon kingfisher. Their nesting range sweeps across Alaska and Northern Canada and southward through much of the United States. In winter, they seek ice-free waters, and some will migrate to Mexico, the West Indies, Central America, and even to northern Venezuela, Colombia, and Guyana.

ॐ

Throughout the summer of 2008, I dipped into kingfishers in the field like an explorer readying for the expedition. When friends invited me to raft the Blackfoot River above the confluence with the Clark Fork River six miles east of Missoula, I jumped at the chance to seek a kingfisher nest overlooking the currents that reverberate with the crystalline prose of Norman Maclean in the book *A River Runs Through It*. In the film bearing the same name, the bird song of the river repeated throughout is the kingfisher, which sounds not like the purr, whiz, whir, or scream of a fly reel, but the quick ratcheting of a heavy spin reel—with a birdy musicality.

Sure enough, as we floated under a bank where cliff swallows flitted from mud nests fastened to rock overhangs, a calling kingfisher dashed away from us. Steely-blue wings shimmered with a dusting of white flakes. A pair of sandhill cranes flapped up from a meadow with prehistoric grace. Common mergansers pitter-pattered on scarlet webbed feet across the river surface to lift off. A western tanager's two-note whistle signaled his radiant presence of orange, yellow, and black plumage. A lone osprey and then a bald eagle slid overhead. Red-tailed hawks etched invisible circles in an achingly blue sky.

The day was like the one Oregon author Kathleen Dean Moore described in her book of essays, *Riverwalking*:

> If so, a good river must be essential happiness, happiness distilled and running between high banks, because on a river tranquility and excitement alternate every half mile, every tight, cliff-bound curve, every quiet pool where white flowers float on the reflection of the sky.

Like halcyon days bracketed by storms, a good river accentuates the fleeting quality of happiness. There's no complacency. What else makes a good river? Birds of all sizes, songs, and shapes, and among them, the kingfisher presides. This is the bird that scours the currents, launders the sky, and rinses the forest with every cleansing wingbeat.

What then makes a good lake? Spending a weekend at my neighbors' cabin on Flathead Lake, seventy miles north of Missoula, four of us boarded the same craft whereon a kingfisher that morning had surveyed the bay from the top of the mast. To sail on the largest freshwater lake west of the Mississippi can feel like heading out to sea. Leaving the cove and rounding the point, our sails billowed as we bucked whitecaps. Drinking the elixir of wind, we skimmed fast and light—like a kingfisher.

❧

Snowflakes as big as nickels descended in a blinding storm flung from a lowering cloud, a typical March squall on the Clark Fork River. By that following spring, I'd become obsessed with finding a nesting pair of kingfishers to observe for a season. I hoped to locate an active earthen burrow beside Rattlesnake Creek, which flows into the Clark Fork in downtown Missoula. If not, I would seek a nest within a twenty-five-mile radius of home.

At the river's edge, I brushed fresh snow from a beaver-chewed cottonwood stump that was knee-high and the width of my fist. Just then, a kingfisher jarred the muffled world with a squirrel-like chatter of repeated notes forming a triplet, *rat-a-tat . . . rat-a-tat . . . rat-a-tat*, rising to an emphatic crescendo. Then he was in view, only fifteen feet away on an alder branch bending over the river. Gripping a writhing fish in his bill, the kingfisher wing-sprinted off to the far side of the river. The departing trilling call whorled with the snow. Writing the date in my pocket journal, I paused. Of course, the halcyon bird appeared on my father's birthday, the eighth of March, when he would have turned seventy-five.

The storm lifted. The inky cloud that had enveloped Missoula's downtown riverfront in an ominous embrace soon wafted away. While early spring weather tended to be as unpredictable as an evasive kingfisher, I may have found a favored fishing spot.

As March advanced with snowmelt, slush, and buttercups, so did my sense of urgency. Reading accounts over the winter of early twentieth-century women naturalists in long skirts parting thickets to find riverside nest banks inspired me to head out the door as often as possible. I hoped to become as savvy as Neltje Blanchan, who offered this kingfisher tip from her 1926 book simply titled *Birds*:

> The bird knows every pool where minnow play, every projection along the bank where a fish might hide, and is ever on the alert, not only to catch a dinner, but to escape from the sight of the human being who intrudes on his domain and wants to "know" him.

As I waited again by the beaver-chewed stump, a male kingfisher swiveled midair to touch down on the same perch. If I could, I'd reach out to give his disheveled crest a ruffle as I did with my son's unruly strawberry-blonde hair when he'd allow me.

His stocky body seemed to elongate as he tipped his head to scrutinize the dark waters, intent on the river below. Then, he plummeted like a blazing spear, a smooth entry from one medium to another, only to splash his wings on the fluidity of water and launch back to the branch with a trout grasped in his beak. *Thwack!* A sideways strike of the wriggling prey. Two more thumps, a dexterous flip in the air, and the headfirst swallow.

Dropping to hands and knees, I crawl closer. Emitting a conflagration of notes, the kingfisher pummels away to the far side of the river. In his wake, a thumb-sized, downy gray feather clings to a twig. I place the feather between two blank pages of my notebook. A spattering of whitewash (the uric acid that is bird poop) on the rocks confirms the bird's regular presence. However, I see no sign of a promising vertical stream bank anywhere up and down the river trail, where I often pedaled my bike and jumped off to scramble down banks for a better look.

This transition from winter to spring was edgy and volatile. The courtship of birds, the budding of trees, and the startle of wildflowers also came with storm, flood, and wind. This search for kingfishers often took me right into the fury.

Anglers ought to know about the wiles and whereabouts of the kingfisher. After all, some stay in the Kingfisher Lodge, cast from a Kingfisher drift boat, or buy their gear at the Kingfisher Flyshop in Missoula. I owned a fly rod then and had not given up the fly-fishing idea entirely. Trifling with this graceful form of angling, I had waded into brooks and tangled my fly in willow bushes on the backcast. When I informed my fishing friends that I was on the prowl for kingfishers, most brightened at the mention of their name.

They also assailed me with questions like, "Do kingfishers eat anything besides fish?" Yes, I told them with the expertise of the textbook researcher. When waters are too muddy, they've been known to eat crayfish and amphibians. In a pinch, the opportunistic birds might snack on insects, reptiles, young birds, small mammals, and berries.

Asking fishermen where I might find a nest resulted most often in baffled looks. They didn't know. Wouldn't a kingfisher build a stick nest like an osprey, bald eagle, or great blue heron? A few had witnessed kingfishers gusting in and out of the holes the birds had excavated. None knew that the female typically lays six or seven eggs in a football-sized chamber at the end of a three- to six-foot-long tunnel. The quail-sized eggs are elliptical and glossy white. The parents tend them well in the protective darkness, and all chicks usually survive to fledge.

I shared that statistic with an avid fly-fisherman as we ran at a fast clip along the Clark Fork River Trail one brisk afternoon. My speedy friend never slowed. Instead, he tugged on his ball cap, puzzled.

"So many chicks. Why aren't there a lot more kingfishers out there?"

Scientists conjecture few young birds live past their first tough year without parents to feed or shelter them. The juveniles are on their own only a couple weeks after fledging.

৪০

After reading that kingfishers at Montana's northerly latitude (44 to 49 degrees North) paired up in early April and laid eggs by mid-May, I knew I had no time to lose. April had arrived. As if on cue, the phone rang with a hot tip from my ornithologist friend Chris Paige that would take me a half-hour drive south along the north-flowing Bitterroot River, a Clark Fork tributary merging on the western edge of Missoula.

An hour later, bundled in fleece jackets, we were watching a belted kingfisher plying the breeze. Each wingbeat blessed the currents with a feathery touch. So often, I'd missed this view by a split second, hearing the receding rattle call. I noted the flash of a reddish belt—the first female of the spring I'd seen. She navigated the tight airspace above a sluggish arm of the river, veering between cottonwoods and willows overhanging a slough the width of an irrigation ditch.

The presence of a female was a good sign, as were the propitious riffles on the water surface. Anglers know well that a riffle, a diminutive rapid, is an excellent place to find fish, and where there are fish, there could well be kingfishers.

Sunlight skipped across the Bitterroot, which sighed, twisted, and turned. Unfettered by dams, the river continues to meander, cut new channels, and create quiet sloughs. On that day, the waters ran low and clear. Soon, the annual floods would rage as temperatures warmed and snow melted high in the Selway-Bitterroot Wilderness to the west and the Sapphire Range to the east. The tranquil scene would roar with high brown waters bearing sediment, churning logs, and the cottonwood seeds of new life.

Chris and I followed the crumbling cutbanks below a pasture. We checked under overhanging roots in the ten-foot-high bank, searching for possible nest holes. In some places, whole slabs were calving where the river had undercut the bank, leaving the topsoil exposed like a snow cornice. I'd never examined the banks a river carves, other than to lament problems often associated with slumping soils. When property owners cut down riverside trees and shrubs, they tear the natural fabric of roots. Cattle grazing on the river's edge leads to trampled banks. As the currents strike a weakened bank, whole walls may crash into the water.

However, long before people cleared trees and grazed livestock, kingfishers found natural cutbanks with root-free soils above the high-water mark. The problems we cause come from too much, too often, and too cumbrous an impact.

Molding coffee-colored soils in my hands, I was the potter finding her clay. The riverbank met some criteria for nesting kingfishers, but there were signs of slides and crumbling. We moved on, picking our way over cobblestones between the slough and the main channel. Chris and I were a couple of golden-red-haired women trailed by golden-red dogs, hers a purebred lab and mine a happy hybrid mix. A goose-shaped cloud masked the sun and skimmed away. We basked in a glisk of warmth.

A handful of cedar waxwings flustered so close we could almost touch their sleek and tawny songbird bodies. Surrounded by their black-masked faces with stylish head tufts, hints of scarlet on their wings, and yellow tips on tails, we listened to their high-pitched keening.

At last! A male kingfisher chattered from a cottonwood branch: *Kik Kik Kik Kik Kik!* The rapid concatenation of high-pitched notes reminded me of the river's power to grind rocks to pebbles and, at last, to sand.

His crest rumpled in the breeze as he sighted down his spear-like bill to the river below. Humbled by the morning's bounty on a day of mercurial sunshine, I gave a silent thanks to this male and the female, both gifting us with their presence. But to think I could sashay in and find their nest within a sheltering bank on this day or any early foray proved naive. Why hadn't I chosen a water-loving bird with an obvious nest, like an osprey's crisscrossing sticks on a treetop?

The male kingfisher flapped away in a burst of taunting laughter. After a few minutes, we sat down on a granite boulder smoothed by water flow. Our dogs settled at our feet. We lingered in companionable silence until our fingers and lips turned blue in the chill. No sign.

Like the elusive nature of halcyon, happiness has a way of slipping through your fingers. Still, chickadees harmonized with blackbirds, a spirit-lifting *dee-dee dee* and *konk-la-ree* chorus that sounded a lot like "lucky, lucky, lucky me!" Immersed in riverine beauty, I felt the invigorating thrill of all that lay ahead. Would I be able to shadow this canny avian guide through the maze of riparian forests to a coveted nest?

In at least one way, my father Dave Richie reminded me of a kingfisher. He, too, could not resist the magnetic draw of what lay beyond the next bend of a trail, whether land or water passage.

My father's career in the National Park Service took our family of five from suburban Arlington, Virginia, to Mount Rainier National Park in Washington. It was there at age eight that I fell in love with the West. We lived in Longmire, below the immense snowy dome, in a log home enclosed on three sides by Douglas-firs and hemlocks pinnacling the sky.

On an epic hike to Eagle Peak in the Tatoosh Range with my brother David (then Davey), thirteen months older than me, our father never doubted we could ascend almost 3,000 feet in three and a half miles, luring us with Kendal Mint Cake every few switchbacks. On the way down, we glissaded a snowfield. I wore pink shorts, and the ice burned the backs of my legs.

Within the mossy light of evergreen ancient forests, I chased my younger brother Rob (then Bobby), who was four and once skidded to a stop within steps of a newborn fawn. We were a trio of nature children of the sixties—Davey, Bobby, and Debbie (my given name is Deborah).

We left Mount Rainier all too soon for the Columbia River of Eastern Washington, where Dad served as Lake Roosevelt National Recreation Area's superintendent. There, we dove into a life punctuated by rodeos, powwows, boat rides, and skating on icy lakes in the grassy hills of the Colville Reservation, the home of twelve tribes, including the Chief Joseph Band of the Nez Perce. Instead of beholding the cloud-capped Mount Rainier, we stared at Grand Coulee Dam, a brutal reminder of our ability to choke rivers and to send salmon toward extinction. This worst of the Columbia dams blocked salmon from reaching 645 miles of river above the huge cement plug, and the associated tributary streams where the fish once spawned.

I don't recall being aware of the tragedy. I do remember forming a kids' conservation group dubbed the Columbia River Rats, and the thrill when my *Ranger Rick's Nature Magazine* kit arrived with buttons and stickers proclaiming us junior rangers. I wonder, did a kingfisher fly by our group of nine-year-old kids by the river, making our grand plans on behalf of the earth?

Then, my father had a brief change of heart about his career during the Vietnam War era, resulting in a brief hiatus from the National Park Service. We moved east to Pennsylvania, where he taught history at Westtown Friends School, which he'd once attended. I come from a long line of pacifist Friends (Quakers) on the Richie side. High school seniors with low draft numbers would gather in our living room to debate whether they would go to jail, flee to Canada, or apply for conscientious objector status. I'd try to absorb the unfathomable, but my sphere was climbing trees, playing ice hockey on Westtown Pond, kicking soccer balls with my brothers, and studying birds.

In fifth grade, I devised a science fair project in the backyard of our rented farmhouse. First, I placed handfuls of sunflower, safflower, thistle seeds, and cracked corn on our rickety wooden picnic table, on the grass, and in hanging feeders. Next, I drew a chart with my ruler. Every morning for a month, I rose at dawn to look out the kitchen window and record the birds that arrived, noting what they preferred to eat and their behaviors. Who liked to be on the ground? On the table? Which birds chased the others away?

I took black-and-white snapshots and wrote in careful pencil the names of each species: chickadee, robin, tufted titmouse, blue jay, cardinal, house finch, and goldfinch. My chart matched birds with their preferred foods and feeding locations. I added comments about which birds were pushy, scared off, or tolerant. For my effort and handwritten report with photos, I earned an honorable mention in Westtown Friend School's fifth- and sixth-grade science fair. I was ecstatic.

℘

From those first endeavors at bird study as a fifth grader, I'd become a journalist well-versed in the interview. Now, having done the background research, it was time to contact the few scientists who knew and cared about the belted kingfisher. I'd decided to become another kind of authority, not a PhD ornithologist, but a citizen scientist devoted to a mysterious bird.

My first call was to Dr. Michael Hamas of Central Michigan University, author of the original 1994 belted kingfisher account in Cornell Lab of Ornithology's "Birds of the World," a well-respected online (and, originally, print) source, which is now frequently updated with the latest science. That account still begins with these enticing words for all who want to discover something new: "The Belted Kingfisher, one of the most widespread land birds in North America, remains poorly studied." He completed the first in-depth investigation of the belted kingfisher in 1975 at the University of Minnesota for his doctoral dissertation on ecological and physiological adaptations. His university website page showed a dapper man with a dark mustache, like the fictional detective Hercule Poirot. I picked up the phone and he answered on the first ring with an affable greeting. Within a few minutes, I was addressing him by his nickname, Mic.

"What's most amazing to people about kingfishers is they nest underground," Mic said. He credited a college ornithology field trip for piquing his curiosity when they came to a burrow in a most unexpected place—on the steep incline of a sandpit a half mile from water.

Mic advised that I stick to creeks or riversides. Once I'd found a bare vertical stream bank safe from floods, the soil couldn't be too rocky, vegetated, or root-filled. Another factor? Seclusion. Kingfishers aren't above picking disturbed sites like road cuts or gravel and sandpits, but they are private birds. After I had located a nest, the excitement would begin. Mic described seeing a kingfisher kicking soil out from the tunnel "like a garden hose spraying dirt instead of water."

Kingfisher feet are tiny compared to those of other perching birds, yet the fusion of the two outer toes creates a handy shovel. As one bird takes a turn digging, the mate outside often chimes in with encouraging rattles. If alarmed, the call may shift to a harsh scream, and both will fly off.

"Those birds are up early in the morning. They're very skitty," Mic cautioned. "They do not like human presence at all. I have sat in a car that served as my blind at 4:30 in the morning with towels on the window to obscure all movement. It's a lot of luck to observe kingfisher behavior."

A few years after that college field trip, Mic published a 1974 note in *The Auk* (then the quarterly journal of the American Ornithologists' Union, now the American Ornithological Society) that documented an uptick in nest sites in north-central Minnesota, where earthen banks are few and rocky shores abundant. For eons, the ingenious birds have managed to overcome geography by nesting in the mudslide banks of beavers. In this case, they expanded their repertoire to include landfills and sandpits.

ॐ

Dr. Jeffrey Kelly, of the University of Oklahoma, updated Mic's entry in "Birds of the World" in 2009, still the latest version.

"The birds are hard to catch, and they are smart," Jeff said when I called. Knowing he had lived in Missoula as a research associate, I asked him what he thought of Rattlesnake Creek as nesting habitat. "Hmm . . . that would be challenging." He noted the rocky and unsuitable banks that line much of my local stream but did not dissuade me from the search. Kingfishers are known to dig nest tunnels within the soils of the roots of toppled big trees, something I would see years later while paddleboarding on the Deschutes River in Oregon.

I quizzed him for tips on finding active nest holes. "Always look for the double groove on the bottom part of the entry hole marking the entry and exit of shuffling bird feet."

Like Mic, Jeff had spent hours, days, and months in the field chasing kingfishers, beginning with his research for his 1996 PhD dissertation. For three Colorado summers, he'd tracked the wily birds to test a well-known hypothesis, of birds timing their nesting based on the availability of food. To find out, he trapped and banded belted kingfishers over three weeks when the parents carted fish to their young.

To intercept an incoming kingfisher, he set up a mist net in front of the burrow entry. Bird researchers choose mist nets because the fineness of the netting is difficult for a flying bird to discern. To capture an exiting bird, Jeff covered the hole with a landing net, similar to what an angler would use to scoop up a big fish on a line.

After comparing nesting kingfishers given supplemental fish (provided by Jeff) with those without extra food, he determined that another factor is key to timing—the arrival of females at nesting banks, where males guard territories replete with fish. Jeff did find that supplying extra fish resulted in heavier nestlings and a greater likelihood a pair would re-nest if the first attempt failed. Dangers to burrows include flooding and predators like snakes or minks slithering into holes.

Jeff's study would apply to Montana too, I thought, since male kingfishers also tough out winters by ice-free waters while females tend to head south for the winter.

❧

On the alert for kingfishers on Rattlesnake Creek, my running shoes squelched on a muddy and leafy trail through Greenough Park, a half mile downstream from home. Just as a song sparrow and dipper sang their a cappella of spring, I stopped in mid-step.

The chattering call of a kingfisher is like and unlike a scolding pine squirrel. The tune harmonizes with the higher-pitched melody of a rocky rivulet. If I could learn to roll my Rs, the vibration of air across the tip of the tongue would come close to mimicking the fastest lightest trills. When giving commentary on the stream below, the calls are softer twitterings, but when alarmed, a higher volume *KKKKK* commands attention. Even the name Rattlesnake Creek sounds kingfisherly. Some say the name stems not from the snake, but from the sound of tumbling waters over stone. I say the rattle honors a fine avian angler on a sinuous creek.

A male jetted after another male, blitzing the currents. Racing after the duo, I tore through a labyrinth of black cottonwoods, alders, and ponderosa pines, cut a bend, and scrambled down a willow-rooted bank to intercept the race. Nothing. Running upstream and then bushwhacking to the creekside, I saw them carom by. Gone in two seconds.

With a quarry to hunt, my senses sharpened. Scribbled observations began to fill pocket notebooks.

Across the planet, a growing league of citizen scientists contributes eyes-on-the-ground data in a race against time as species blink out and ecosystems unravel from human-caused global warming and habitat destruction. The more who enlist, the better chance we have of taking meaningful actions to protect biodiversity.

Time is short to reweave our fraying tapestry of life. North America's bird population has dwindled by 2.9 billion birds since 1970, with losses in every ecosystem. While an estimated population of 1.7 million breeding belted kingfishers might sound like these birds have escaped this devastating trend, more than a million fewer birds now trace our waterways than in 1970. The North American Breeding Bird Survey shows a cumulative decline of 53 percent between 1966 and 2014. Belted kingfishers living inland from coastlines depend on fresh water, which is our lifeline, too. Our watery planet is 97 percent salty and only 3 percent fresh. We cannot afford to be cavalier.

The cause of this decline joins a list of unanswered questions. Secretly, I wanted to find something new about the belted kingfisher. After all, how many other people were out there questing after this bird? There could be a reason. Flying away in a disapproval of notes hardly seems welcoming.

෨

Every time I headed to the creek, I listened for kingfishers and began to pick up nuances. For advice on vocalization, I called biologist Jim Davis, who had studied their language in the 1980s. He suggested I listen to the pulses of sound, from single to doublets and triplets. In kingfishers, the vibrations are fine-tuned, falling under five categories: rattle, scream, harsh, warble, and mew. The rattle is the familiar kingfisher cry, with a slow pulse rate interval and lower volume that could mean "hey, you've come a little too close." Another version might be "I see you" or "I'm not sure what's going on." The highest pulse rates come from a "scream call," reserved for threats and confrontations. The "scream" is a long or short volley of loud notes.

A "harsh" call has longer intervals between the pulses of notes. This is a call to listen for early in the breeding season, often from the male before nest building. He may combine the harsh call with a scream. The "warble" is a quiet, low-intensity sound a female might give to a male when she's ready to mate, or when parents feed their nestlings. A "mew" is reserved for courtship, after mating, or in full on courtship aerial chase, according to observations from Mic Hamas in 1975.

Jim's research of five nests on two streams in Ohio suggested king-fishers recognize each other by call. Watch a burrow nest, and you will hear the mate outside rattling upon arrival, he told me. Deep within, the mate comprehends who is there. To quantify his observations, he played calls outside the burrow, while recording the heartbeats of a kingfisher incubating eggs.

First, Jim and a helper selected an active burrow. They measured the length and dug a back door from the top of the bank down into the nest-ing chamber. Then, they captured a bird by plugging the front hole to prevent escape. Next, they opened the back door to grasp the kingfisher, mark the bird, and place a stethoscope and tape-recording contraption below the eggs.

He chose three recordings—the rattle of the mate, the cry of an intruding kingfisher, and the ululating notes of a northern flicker. The heart rate fluctuated only with the sound of the unfamiliar kingfisher. If I were in the position of a bird trapped in the burrow and handled by the researchers, wouldn't that feel intrusive? Still, I longed to be one of those privileged scientists.

An Alaskan biologist set me straight, sharing his experience netting, banding, and taking blood samples from kingfishers as part of a mercury study conducted from 1997 to 2003 in Maine. The study showed varying levels of mercury in blood and feathers depending on where the birds fished, with reservoirs as the source of highest levels. I kept his email as a reminder of the cost of up-close experience:

> One bird immediately scissored my index finger with its bill, extracting a significant blood sample. Quite a tool, that bill—sharp as a razor, and lightly serrated in some fashion so that the wound would not stop bleeding or "seal off" even after a couple of hours wrapped.

Still, a sharp slice might be worth it if part of conservation research. The practice of catch and release was not applied in 1953, when H. C. White shot kingfishers to evaluate their stomach contents. The impetus came from fishermen who suspected the birds of plundering "their" fish. To White's credit, he preferred analyzing fish bones in kingfisher pellets, the regurgitated indigestible parts of their prey.

Reading White's published paper on kingfishers in Canada's maritime provinces, I was struck by a black-and-white photo of the scientist holding a kingfisher he had hand-reared. Tall and heron-like, with a beak of a nose, White looked down at the bird with a tender smile. I'm reminded not to be quick to judge our early biologists.

ଓ

When it came to enlightened perspectives, Dr. Dan Albano embodied them. His poetic depictions reflected his hard-won affinity for the birds he'd witnessed for five years on the Hudson River north of Albany, New York, which led to a doctoral dissertation in 2000. His adviser was the esteemed Dr. Donald Kroodsma, known beyond the scientific circles for *The Singing Life of Birds*. In the book, he wrote of recording a northern mockingbird mimicking a belted kingfisher's rattle five times within a half hour of a stunning 465 songs. He also posed a question: "Why does the mockingbird mock?" Another enigma.

My call with Dan began with a basic question, "What makes belted kingfishers special?"

"They have so much charisma and attitude," he said. "They dive for fish, which is miraculous itself. They dig burrows for breeding in summer and roosting in winter. They are so aggressive, and their voice is loud and amazing. I love watching their crests rising up and down, and the way those beautiful white breast feathers never look dirty in a nest. They have those funny feet too, and they are powerful flyers."

Spend time with kingfishers and marvels multiply, he said, like fishing for the exact right size of prey for nestlings at each stage of growth. In the first week, the parents deliver tasty fingerlings less than two inches long and, by the month's end, are feeding five- to six-inch-long fish to juveniles about to test their wings.

Dan downplayed his dissertation on behavioral ecology, calling it "long-winded and old fashioned." I asked him for a copy at once. His studies of wintering male kingfishers showed their commonsense approach to frigid nights. They dove into their holes to sleep in thermoregulated nest burrows. Dan also observed parental care and noted that males and females shared many responsibilities almost equally, from incubating eggs to feeding and raising chicks.

Egalitarian parenting had puzzling implications for the red belt mystery, which intrigued him as well. The most well-studied bird exhibiting this rare color reversal (from the norm of the brighter male and duller-hued female) is a shorebird called a phalarope. The resplendent female phalarope has little to do with nesting beyond egg-laying, leaving the camouflaged male to shelter the eggs and young on an exposed ground nest. Why, then, is a belted kingfisher female more glitzy than a male? There must be another reason beyond nesting roles. Dan urged me to continue the detective work.

The red belt conundrum appealed in the way of the halcyon myth. Both have to do with one of life's profound mysteries, the role of love between two beings, which cannot be neatly categorized. For Halcyon and Ceyx, their union led to transformation into kingfishers, yet the Greek gods also assured they would nest and raise a family.

ॐ

Why not use "love" when it comes to courtship, mating, and rearing young? The early naturalists may have erred in their anthropomorphism, but they also offered astute details from field observations. Reading A. C. Bent's 1940 compendium of naturalist accounts, I chuckled as I read the observation of Miss Frances Densmore of Red Wing, Minnesota, submitted (by a man) in 1928. A pair of kingfishers dug a hole "taking turn and turnabout, except when she thought he hadn't stayed in long enough and sent him back."

We can't know what a kingfisher female thinks, yet Miss Frances describes a classic scene as if the bird were to say, "Honey, just where do you think you're going? We're not done yet!"

By the mid-twentieth century, scientific publishers had abandoned the personal account and set a standard of manuscripts written in the passive voice, without the word I, so we'd have no idea, say, whether Miss Frances appeared on the scene. "The pair was found."

The "I" has returned to science. What's often missing is the poetry, like naturalist Henry R. Carey's 1909 observation of a kingfisher chase scene: "Two birds swirl by like two blue flashes of light, to disappear in an instant of time on perfectly controlled wings."

஧

In my "instant of time," I attuned to the kingfishers on the singing Rattlesnake Creek, which shifts melodies by the season. Each fall, bull trout nose upstream from the Clark Fork River to spawn in the clear, cold creek bottom. Each winter, Bohemian waxwings flock here like smoke signals from Canada to feast on mountain ash berries. Each spring, caddisfly and mayfly hatch from the waters as warblers wing their way from south to north.

To visualize the watershed, cup two hands together. Rattlesnake Creek flows down the center, twisting, ebbing in summer, and rising with the spring floods. Your fingertips form the headwaters in the high peaks of the Rattlesnake Wilderness. The creek births in springs and seeps fed by rivulets and waterfalls that tingle down your fingers. The stream in the middle gathers strength with every incoming tributary and winds across your palms to join the Clark Fork River at your wrists. The voyage on the landscape is twenty-six miles from headwaters to confluence.

Each morning, I woke to the distant hush of creek when sunlight limned the North Hills to the west, fanning embers into flame. To the east, Mount Jumbo loomed like the namesake elephant. Gazing north, the peaks of the Rattlesnake Wilderness castled the sky. Proximity to wildness began outside my door, starting with native plantings of red osier dogwood brushing against the window and harboring songbirds.

Wildness extended to the spirit of the Missoula community when voters passed an open space bond in 1995, assuring the Mount Jumbo elk herd could migrate to a winter range never blocked by subdivisions. The same funds would conserve a homestead and gnarled apple orchard resting in a wind-protected pocket of the North Hills, and an ancient pathway to the buffalo plains created by the Salish people, who crossed the Mount Jumbo saddle to skirt the Hellgate Canyon of the Clark Fork River, where the Blackfeet set ambushes.

Cup your hands. Cherish the place you love.

For millennia, the Missoula Valley has known the footsteps of the Salish, who call themselves the Séliš (pronounced SEH-leesh). Their place names came from either creation stories or traditional ways of sustenance, particularly the once-abundant bull trout. Not so long ago, the sizzling fragrance of fresh trout cooking on a fire permeated their camps as they dried and stored fish for the winter ahead.

Rattlesnake Creek is Nɫʔay Sewɫkʷs, which translates as Small Bull Trout's Waters, and Mount Jumbo is Nmq̓ʷe, Humped Mountain. The middle Clark Fork River has the particularly lovely name of Nmesulétkʷ, Shimmering Cold Waters.

The entire aboriginal territory of this easternmost tribe of the Salish language family (extending to the Pacific coast and mostly north of the Columbia River) encompassed both sides of the Continental Divide until the mid-1700s. Then, epidemics and Blackfeet armed with rifles led them to center their lives in the Bitterroot Valley and north to Missoula. They still hunted bison on the eastern plains into the 1800s.

A couple of years before the kingfisher quest, I'd had the honor of accompanying Salish elder Louis Adams on the banks of the Shimmering Cold Waters, Nmesulétkʷ. He stood as straight as a pine, his graying hair in two tight braids. A line of horizontal wrinkles across his forehead resembled the geologic layers on Esmoqʷ (It's a Mountain) or Mount Sentinel above us. He spoke with deliberate enunciations and kindness.

He told the story of his grandmother Louise Vanderberg, born near Rattlesnake Creek's confluence with the river, where his family had come to catch bull trout. The confluence name is Nɫʔaycčstm, meaning Place of Small Bull Trout. Salish speakers use the shortened form of this name—Nɫʔay—for the city of Missoula.

As a child, Louis joined his relatives digging for bitterroots a few miles west on land now covered by a Shopko and parking lot. Each spring, they gathered to pray, give thanks, and dig on the best grounds of all their territories, until development in the 1960s destroyed the abundant native prairies. Each summer, Louis' grandfather Victor and his companions rode on horseback into what is now the Bob Marshall Wilderness to hunt, fish, dig roots, and pick berries.

"No one was in a rush then, because everywhere was home," he said.

Listening to Louis intersperse English with Salish words, I noticed how the language was at once guttural and melodic in the dynamic way of a homeland shaped by fires, floods, and winds. I could hear Salish in the call of the belted kingfisher.

The Salish word for kingfisher is čális, pronounced "ts ah lease"—a watery three syllables. Tribal member and fluent speaker Aspen Decker shared the word with me, including a recording of the pronunciation. When I connected with her in 2021, she spoke only Salish to her young children as she pursued a graduate degree in linguistics—intent on sharing her people's language and traditions of harmonious relationships with lands and waters.

The story of the Salish people, like so many of the tribes, is one of resilience, revival, and pride in the face of terrible injustice and near genocide.

Signed under big pines next to the Nmesulétkʷ (Clark Fork River), the Hellgate Treaty of 1855 marked another tragic chapter in American history. Within fifteen years, the Flathead Reservation (thirty miles north of Missoula) would become the designated location for the Bitterroot Salish, Upper Pend d'Oreille, and Kootenai tribes.

As Louis Adams told me, his people never gave up their intimate connections to vast territories, and passed down their knowledge of the land, of plants, animals, fish, and spiritual traditions.

In 1972, archeologists unearthed a ceremonial burial of a Salish ancestor in the upper Rattlesnake Valley that carbon dating revealed to be more than five hundred years old (1460 AD). They found thirteen animal rib bones, one bird-bone whistle, one large chert flake, one small chert tool, and one drill with a broken tip. The University of Montana returned the human bones to the Salish and Kootenai tribes in 2003, but the other items had become separated and a few years later were repatriated to the tribe. "One bird bone whistle." Was this bird the spirit guide for the person buried with ceremony some thirty-two years before Columbus "discovered" America?

Soon after I began my search, I met with Louis to find out what he knew about the kingfisher. He told me his father often laughed at the bird's funny crest and cheery chitter, and always with respect, a way of being Louis shared:

> I was raised that we are equal to wildlife. We have legendary stories. When the Coyote was told by the Great One, before the people got here, that animals were the people—and the animals all talked— the Great One told the Coyote that when the world finally changes and there are people [humans] you won't be able to talk anymore. Then, we have to tell the guardian spirit to take care of us.

Louis turned to face me. "The animals have no voices, so they depend on us."

Their languages are as varied and interlaced as trees that perceive, converse, and aid one another through an underground fungal network. Louis is right. Wild animals, birds, and trees have no voice for speaking up in the human world. Our actions can be either destructive or life-giving.

When it came to the kingfisher, I had much to learn—if I could find a nesting pair.

∞

One day in April, when bicycling back from the post office, I pedaled the paved trail north and uphill from downtown through Greenough Park. Not surprisingly, I glimpsed my Henry-David-Thoreau-meets-Johnny-Appleseed friend.

John Pierce was pulling up hound's tongue, a noxious weed with lentil-sized seeds, which stick to you like Velcro. Tall, boyish, and ageless, his stride was so long I'd often found it easier to jog than to walk next to him. John's idea of a day off from his botanist job was to be in Greenough Park, restoring creekside native habitat. He might have a nesting tip. I braked and climbed down the bank to quiz him. "I hear them squawking by above the creek now and then, but I've never seen one come out of a hole," John said. He promised to take notice.

Later in the afternoon, I biked up the road north of my home past the Garden City Harvest farm fields, searching for burrow sites. Pedaling by sunlit grasslands over the brow of a hill, I paused near a little marsh. Two black-billed magpies repaired a basketball-sized messy stick nest secured within the spiny branches of a black hawthorn. An unimposing earthen bank shouldered up beyond straw-colored cattails swaying with red-winged blackbirds. Maybe? No. Too close to a house and vulnerable to predators, plus being a half mile from the creek.

Duncan Drive ends by a power station, a conglomeration of metal poles and structures on flat ground colliding with bunchgrass hillsides and the creek. The trailhead is at the end of the cul-de-sac. Gliding down the needle-lined trail across a footbridge to the east side of the creek, I pedaled upstream and north a half mile to stop above Mountain Water Dam, visible through ponderosas and cottonwoods.

When I first moved to Missoula from Oregon in late 1986, anyone could walk across the small dam. That changed after the fateful day of September 11, 2001. The unimposing dam, serving then as Missoula's backup water supply, was deemed a terrorism risk. A high chain-link fence topped with four strands of barbed wire surrounded a pond, a newer log home on its south shore, a scattering of faded ash-gray outbuildings, and the concrete dam. Security signs posted warnings of twenty-four-hour surveillance. Forbidding. But to a kingfisher? How perfect—a closed area. Several holes pockmarked an east-facing earthen bank across the creek. Hiding my bike behind a tree, I tiptoed to the imposing fence, but hesitated at the warning. I'd ask permission first.

Cycling with gusto downhill to home, I was breathless when I called the Mountain Water Company manager. No problem, he told me. He'd notify his maintenance people that a woman with binoculars was on a research project.

Like a hunter finding fresh elk tracks, I couldn't wait to return. Early the next morning, I followed a lesser-used trail a half mile upstream on the west side, ending at the dam. A red-breasted nuthatch called *yank Yank YANK*. The air smelled like pitch, earthy humus, and faint musk of a passing animal, perhaps a black bear. I'd seen a telltale sign—an overturned log torn apart to reveal tasty grubs.

Four signs glared from the chain link fence: NO UNAUTHORIZED PERSONNEL, Mountain Water Company; WARNING: Tampering with This Facility Is a Federal Offense; Interstate Alarm; SECURITY NOTICE, this property is protected by video surveillance; and NO TRESPASSING. Scrabbling up a nearby vertical bank of the creek, my foot slipped on powdery soil, and I skidded down. Grasping a root, I edged across the canted slope to a potential kingfisher nest hole, threaded with spiderwebs. Three more were just out of reach. Would those yawning openings invite kingfishers to freshen one up for spring? Or send a signal to dig a new one?

As if to cinch the answer, I heard the telltale rattles. Ponderosas leaned over snow-infused currents rollicking with promise. I jumped down and couldn't resist a spin, lifting my arms to the sky and to this bird.

CHAPTER 2

Courting Kingfishers

Saw and heard a kingfisher—do they not come with the smooth waters of
April?—hurrying over the meadow as if on urgent business.

—Henry David Thoreau, *Thoreau on Birds*, April 15, 1855

The kingfishers were courting. April 11 marked a breakthrough. At 9
a.m. sharp, I met Paul and Lisa Hendricks at the trailhead. Today, as
then, Paul has the precise mind of a scientist spiced with the romantic
flair of a nineteenth-century naturalist. Compact and trim, with a pleas-
ant round face and glasses, he carries a pocket notebook always at the
ready. Lisa is similarly hardy, yet softer, with her heart-shaped face, elfin
smile, and dark hair cropped short. She had taught fifth grade for many
years in Missoula, inspiring hundreds of kids to go outdoors and ask
questions about nature.

A few months earlier, I'd contacted Paul, then a zoologist for the
Montana Natural Heritage Program. Did he know of any kingfisher
nests in Montana recorded through the state database of species and
habitats? After a quick search, he was surprised to find only one nesting
note from a Glacier National Park Service biologist in 2008, on the
banks at the confluence of McDonald Creek with the Flathead River.

At a brisk clip, we hiked the half mile north along the main west-
side trail and turned down a private driveway to Mountain Water Dam.
Within seconds, the alluring rattle coasted toward us. The kingfisher
hurtled through the air on arced wings. He circled above us once and
whizzed away. We saw a single crisp blue band on a white chest, etched
on an incandescent sky.

Pointing out the holes on the opposite bank, Paul was about to
comment when again we heard the signature call. A different kingfisher
landed on a high dead branch of a ponderosa. "She's a female," whispered

Paul, noting the reddish belt. The male returned with another encircling flight. This time, the female chattered back, then launched from her perch to fly with him in a double helix of ascension.

Turning to Paul, I gave him an impulsive hug. Rattlesnake Creek. Place of the bull trout. Home stream. We'd found a pair of courting kingfishers, and only two and a half miles away from my house.

ಐ

Dan Albano twice observed high perimeter flights of a courting pair during his dissertation study. Considering he had watched paired kingfishers on overlapping territories for five years, our sighting rang with beginner's luck. Dan described one of those aerial paths as an inverted hairpin. The male and female flew close to the water and then rose in unison sixty feet up a cliff of air before swooping down.

Throughout the spring, Dan witnessed spats before kingfishers settled down as seasonal pairs. Where two territories overlapped, he could not tell whether the high-flying birds were proclaiming territories or attracting a mate.

One hundred and fifty-three years earlier, also on April 11, Henry David Thoreau wrote, "Saw a kingfisher on a tree over the water. Does not its arrival mark some new movement in its finny prey? He is the bright buoy that betrays it!" Traipsing after kingfishers reminded me of high school years in Thoreau's home community of Concord, Massachusetts. There, I explored the hardwood forest behind our colonial home on Revolutionary Ridge, close to the Louisa May Alcott's Orchard House and not far from the Emerson and Longfellow residences. One day, I splashed through a woodland bog to reach a floating island of sphagnum mosses interlaced with predacious pitcher plants and sundews. Dwarf tamarack trees grew from the earth, which shook and rolled beneath my rubber boots.

Surely, no one else had been there, except Henry David. I'd found one of his notations from February 1, 1858:

> When the surface of a swamp shakes for a rod around you, you may conclude that it is a network of roots two or three feet thick resting

on water or a very thin mud. The surface of that swamp, composed in great part of sphagnum, is really floating.

Years later, Gowing's Swamp would earn protection as a natural area, credited as the one bog in New England brought to light through literature, specifically Thoreau's journals. I credit my father for teaching me the art of the bushwhack early in life, which often led to off-trail wonders.

In fall of 1977, after one last summer job at home—planting, weeding, and harvesting bountiful produce grown on the fecund soils of an organic vegetable farm by the Concord River, I headed west to attend the University of Oregon. There, I would run cross-country and track until I left the team in favor of backpack trips, environmental activism, boy crushes, and a deep dive into the joy of hands-on fieldwork at the Oregon Institute of Marine Biology. I would go on to live in northeast Oregon with my conservationist boyfriend and lobby for the passage of the Oregon Wilderness Bill of 1984.

The westward journey was inevitable. Thoreau guided me to Gowing's Swamp, yet it was preservationist John Muir who epitomized the craggy western peaks that held me spellbound since Mount Rainier. The words below my yearbook photo with my short curly hair and earnest freckled face set me apart from most seniors with their cool quips. Instead, I quoted Muir:

Climb the mountains and get their good tidings. Nature's peace will flow into you as sunshine flows into trees. The winds will blow their own freshness into you, and the storms their energy, while the cares will drop away from you like the leaves of Autumn.

Muir and Thoreau's writings, my father's constancy of spirit, and now Paul and Lisa all accompanied me as naturalist mentors on the kingfisher quest. Like Thoreau, who "traveled a good deal in Concord," I was spending more time along the creek than ever before. The reward? I would follow a pair of kingfishers throughout their entire nesting season, or so I presumed.

ॐ

Easter interrupted a return to the nest bank with traditions of egg hunts across two backyards and baking my great-grandmother's Moravian coffee cake, which called for butter (the size-of-an-egg), copious quantities of brown sugar, and cinnamon topping dabbed with more butter, one of my father's favorites. Despite loyalty to the event, I chafed to be back with the courting birds. Not until the afternoon was I free to run to the burrow and pause there to stretch, listen, and watch. All was quiet.

When Dan Albano replied, he advised we "keep an eye out for pairs at the bank and territorial disputes—chasing and high-pitched rattling/screams."

Morning clouds swaddled the valley on Monday, April 13, 2009, the day my son Ian turned twelve. Parking at the trailhead, I scooped up binoculars, write-in-the-rain notebook, sharpened pencil, and umbrella. The frown of clouds sunk lower. The air thickened with an impending storm.

Luna trailed twenty yards behind. I'd found my loyal and sweet canine friend as an abandoned puppy digging up petunias outside a caretaker's trailer within Two Moon Park on the Yellowstone River in Billings—on the full moon. Luna was the obvious name. One friend dubbed her a "golden heeler." She had thick golden fur, alert raised ears, a spotted tongue, a long tail often curving above her back, an obsession for ball chasing, and in her prime could jump a six-foot fence.

We crossed the familiar footbridge where the creek ran full and glassy over rounded rocks in garden hues of basil, eggplant, pumpkin, and beet. Snowmelt from the peaks dictates the rhythm, volume, and clarity of the creek in spring runoff. On warm days, the increased water from thawing snow may overflow banks. By nightfall, cold temperatures forestall melting, and translucence returns. On this wilderness-spawned creek, the rocky banks are so woven with protective roots that it takes a mighty runoff for waters to turn brown and silty.

Brushing through thickets of red osier dogwood, birch, and alder quivering with black-capped chickadees, I looked across the creek to the promising bank below the ten-foot-high dam. Constructed in 1902, the dam would come down in 2020 to free the creek to run unimpeded from source to river. However, the loss of a century-old pond would have unintended consequences for kingfishers, swallows, and waterfowl and set me pondering. Could there have been a way to retain a pond in the planning? I'll hope for beavers to step in to build one.

In this first season of the watch, I would come to value the pooled water for kingfishers, and the fish ladder constructed in 2002, which offered bull trout passageway to spawning grounds upstream. Since that date, biologists had steadily counted higher numbers of juveniles. Bull trout are Montana natives that depend on cold, clear, and connected waterways. How many fingerlings have generations of belted kingfishers fed to their hungry chicks? To be a young trout of any kind is to learn fast to elude predators or be beaked by a kingfisher, heron, osprey, bald eagle, or snapped up by a bigger fish.

A kingfisher duet burst from the far side of the creek. Choosing a wine-barrel-width ponderosa to hide behind as the first raindrops fell, I hoped to escape the birds' exceptionally sharp eyes, a triumph of evolution. The birds have evolved to hover while keeping their heads rock steady to spot a fish ten or fifteen feet below. Red oil droplets in the retina reduce glare and refraction. Their eyes are packed with cones for sensational color viewing. On a practical level, sneaking up on a king-fisher takes stealth.

Concealed by the tree and separated from the creek by a copse of pine, willow, aspen, and shrubs twenty feet below, I struck gold. Two kingfishers flew in for a smooth landing on one of several wires link-ing a red-roofed shed to a pole. They chose a polite social distance of six feet apart and faced in opposite directions. The male gave a gentle warble. Could this be an avian version of the mythic Ceyx and Halcyon? I couldn't resist naming the birds right then. While Greek in origin, the names link to all myths of animal transformation—a common denomi-nator of ancient cultures.

Names aside, I vowed to observe as an open-minded naturalist. In my notebook, I penned the symbols for male and female. A male is a circle with an arrow pointing northeast, the identical symbol for the planet Mars. A female is a circle with a cross below it, the symbol for Venus. The steely blue-and-white male was Ceyx, the son of the morning star. The female was Halcyon, the radiant daughter of Aeolus the wind god. I noticed her belt not quite meeting in the middle, an identifying marker.

The newly dubbed Ceyx flew to the earthen bank, aimed for the roundest hole, landed, folded his wings, entered partway, backed out, and flapped to the wire. Halcyon followed suit. The invitation to nest required no translation. I'd read that, once committed, kingfishers would either dig a new burrow or tidy up an old one. They repeated the flight to the hole two more times, giving chiming rattling calls with every takeoff.

What Ceyx did next was not recorded in any of my preparatory readings. He flew to the bank and spread his wings wide on the sandy soil like a blessing—three times in a row. Halcyon watched. They sidled a bit closer on the wire. As the tenor of their chitter rose in pitch and volume, their stubby tails flicked in near synchrony. Was this the precursor to intimacy? I was reminded of the pair I first saw on the Yellowstone River in a rainstorm, as the scene became even more familiar with a barrage of stinging hail enunciating the drama.

Halcyon dove headfirst into one of the holes in the bank. Soil puffed. Backing out, she flurried up to the wire and repeated the foray three times, accompanied by the rapid notes of the unseen Ceyx. Was he assessing her quarrying skills?

Just then, a pickup truck roared down the driveway, pulling a trailer full of mowers and weed whips. The timing was awful. Two men got out, slammed doors, and opened the gate to the fenced enclosure around the pond. They were heading for the log house that the California owners of the private company visited on the rare occasion. Snugged close by was the original modest gray clapboard house, by the spillway and nearest to the nest bank.

Within minutes the mowers revved up. On cue, the kingfishers departed up creek in a noisy drenching of disapproval. Both dismayed and undeterred, I made plans to return first thing tomorrow and to pack an extra jacket.

Luna had stayed next to me without a sound, proving she could be the ideal naturalist dog. We retraced our steps with the cadence of kingfisher calls punctuating every sentence written on the currents.

℥

On the same day, twelve years earlier, I gave birth to Ian and nursed him for the first time. On this day, I watched two kingfishers in a prelude to mating, nesting, and raising a family. Yet, there was danger. Those lawnmowers, the kingfishers scything the air to escape. Would they return?

At home, I switched gears for birthday festivities and extra hugs for Ian, whose head reached my shoulder. It wouldn't be long before he'd exceed my five-foot, five-inch height. He'd grown slimmer and adept at dribbling soccer balls past opponents under the watchful eye of his father, who was Ian's coach, as well as his biggest fan and critic.

On smooth-sailing days with my then husband, our ride was as buoyant as the wedding tango we'd danced on rough floorboards. Our courtship, like the kingfishers, had begun in April. A month later, I'd flown to Alaska on a summer-long writing assignment. When I mentioned I missed the blooming lilacs in Missoula, a package arrived in Anchorage—a bouquet on dry ice. I'd said yes to a marriage proposal in August, an act of impetuosity that precluded knowing each other well. When Ian was born a year after our meeting, I was thirty-nine. I'd never thought I would be a mother. All had changed in a single year. All began with the ritual of courting we shared with so many species on earth.

ଚ୍ଚ

That evening, I reviewed what Mic Hamas had written in 1975. A pair tended to select their nest during courtship, as the male began to "slash and probe" the bank with his bill, and the female remained the watcher. Already, there seemed to be something different in Montana. Halcyon appeared an enthusiastic participant in the courtship ritual. She caressed the bank with spread wings as if to suggest, "try this spot."

Training a spotting scope on a choice hole across the creek below the dam the next morning, I wondered. Which hole, if any? I'd sketched the bank and mapped out six holes, with a particular round one standing out as prime candidate, a couple of feet down from the top and eight feet above the ground. My fingers ached with the chill of dawn.

A pair may dig multiple burrows in a single bank and then occupy one. That would make sense if the birds struck roots or rocks deep within the soil. A bounty of holes can reflect the industry of many seasons of digging. I wondered, might numerous entries baffle a predator? A marsh wren male may construct a dozen or more softball-sized woven and domed nests in the reeds. The array of nests might flummox predators or help him woo a mate, since females inspect the workmanship. Nests also serve as backups if one fails and as extra shelters for both fledglings and adults in winter. Sounds smart to me.

Song sparrow melody blossomed from dogwoods, like a prelude to the still slumbering wildflowers. Cold seeped in. Four white-tailed deer faded into the Douglas-firs above the pockmarked steep bank. A light-phase red-tailed hawk crossed a cerulean sky. Six tree swallows wheeled in. A mourning dove angled past, plump-bodied and tinted in dawn colors. The sound of the creek was a steady wind on a windless day of waiting.

ℬ

A month before my father died of colon cancer in 2002 at the age of seventy, I'd sent him a decorated cigar box filled with ribbon-tied paper scrolls. On each one, I'd penned a few lines, inspired by the nature he'd taught me to notice. I wrote as if the words might keep him breathing. By the time the scrolls arrived, he was too weary for reading. Instead, I spoke haikus over the phone—of new leaves unfurling to the susur-rations of warblers, of spicy pungency of firs, and clouds and sun in a flamenco of the moment.

"Hey, Dad," I whispered from the stream bank watch. "I'm freezing. I know. We're tough, aren't we? Remember that long Boston race by the Charles River in the icy rain when I couldn't feel my legs? We kept going. We didn't give in." Throughout my high school years, we often ran ten- or fifteen-mile-long runs in Concord, and competed in road races on weekends. My father took it to the next level, running the Boston Marathon in under three and a half hours—twice.

ℬ

Clutching my pencil with gloved partially numb fingers, I wrote in child-like lettering and invoked Thoreau, who would not let a little weather get in the way of note-taking. Thoreau's scrupulous journals from October 1837 to November 1861 would become an invaluable benchmark for the timing of blossom, bird arrivals, and wildlife movements in Concord.

In 2008, modern researchers compared the blooming dates he had recorded for more than five hundred species of wildflowers with those of today. They also unearthed complementary work by fellow resident

Alfred Hosmer, born in 1851. A photographer, naturalist, and early Thoreau promoter, Hosmer took copious notes on flowers and blooming times, from 1878 to 1903.

Reviewing forty-three common plants in Concord, Massachusetts, the scientists determined wildflowers now bloom ten days earlier, and that over the past 155 years the average temperature increased by an estimated 2.4 degrees Celsius. Twenty-seven percent of the species Thoreau and Hosmer recorded can no longer be found in Concord, and 37 percent of species once common are rare. As planet warming worsens, those changes must become even more severe.

Citizen phenologists (those who study plant and animal life related to seasons and climate) note flower bloom times to monitor the effects of climate change in hopes of taking informed actions to stave off the worst impacts for wildlife and insects that evolved with this predictable pattern of blossoming. Climate disruption gives more urgency to listening to the father of ecology Aldo Leopold's warning of 1938:

> Our tools are better than we are and grow better faster than we do. They suffice to crack the atom, to command the tides, but they do not suffice for the oldest task in human history, to live on a piece of land without spoiling it.

Stamping boots to warm numb toes, I was restless after an hour of waiting and noticed the gate was open to the impoundment. Why not go in? I walked past the SUV with California plates and knocked on the log house door. A tan, athletic, middle-aged woman opened the door as if she'd been waiting. "I own Mountain Water Company," she said, informing me that she would stay for three days. Her name was Nyra.

We talked about kingfishers. Nyra smiled. Promising. "I love birdwatching." Better. Nyra had even volunteered on a peregrine falcon reintroduction project once. Bonanza. And then she invited me to look around. I was in. Here, I could study the kingfisher holes from a new perspective and examine the creek racing below the cliff and separated from the soccer-field-sized reservoir. Although some water was diverted for the pond, the gates to the dam were often open, giving the bull trout easy passage, instead of requiring the fish ladder.

After a satisfying prowl, I waved goodbye to Nyra and resumed my watch beside the big pine. It was getting late in the morning. Perhaps the lawnmowers had driven the kingfishers away for good. Thoughts wandered to a writing assignment featuring University of Montana professor Doug Emlen, who studied beetles with ornate horns and antlers, the stuff of science fiction, and maybe relevant to kingfishers. Most everything felt related. Just as I'd lost mindfulness, the reverberating notes of incoming kingfishers had my full attention.

Halcyon and Ceyx alighted on the wire. Ceyx raised his notched crest, as if admiring her captivating belt. She glanced at Ceyx, took two flaps to nuzzle the earth, and then returned to the wire, giving him a honeyed lilt of syncopated song. He edged closer. She responded with a raising and lowering of her crest. Then, she flew away in a chaff of chatter. Ceyx shook his tail feathers and, with a peal of notes, lifted off in Halcyon's direction. I heard the echo of my longing. Gone. After a half hour more, I departed. Like the kingfishers who must fish to eat, I had to earn my keep.

Planted at my desk, I read about the horns on male beetles employed in stylized duels with competitors, all wooing females. Wrapping up a first draft, I turned to bird crests. Could their feather-raising be connected to winning over females?

Crest feathers are semiplumaceous (soft and bendable) and attached to a long rachis (stem), giving birds the ability to flash their headgear at will. Crests are uncommon in the greater family of kingfishers, and limited to the *Megaceryle* genus: the ringed, crested, giant, and belted. Why these related species dwell far apart (South America, Asia, Africa, and North America) would be a question to tackle later. Familiar crested birds include Steller's jays, blue jays, cardinals, flycatchers, waxwings, California quail, and pileated woodpeckers. Their headgear can be ostentatious or subtle, like the rare flash of a ruby-crowned kinglet's peak. For some birds, the jaunty caps are a seasonal affair. A double-crested cormorant male sprouts plumes on either side of his head to wow females in spring. Kingfisher crest-raising appeared to denote high alertness—whether courting or fishing.

I was a smidge jealous. On two perilous occasions, my long hair stood on end during a lightning storm, once on top of a peak and the other on a soccer field, when my son's hair also splayed out in all directions. The kids laughed and pointed at each other. The parents? Terrified. We recognized electricity and danger. The referee blew the whistle, and everyone ran to safety.

The next morning, I had a plan. I would zoom in on each raising and lowering of kingfisher crests, but Ceyx and Halcyon had other ideas. Over the next four days, a mink shimmied through jumbled dogwoods and willows. A bald eagle whumped to a landing on a pine branch, and a three-note spring song of a chickadee wended into all that was budding, greening, and renewing. Drawn by kingfishers that did not come, I was there for other splendors. In the late afternoon, while walking along Rattlesnake Creek closer to home, a male kingfisher sculled by in a distinct pattern of wingbeats—a flutter and five flaps.

The following day at predawn and bundled in a coat, hat, and mittens, I heard faint calls of kingfishers upstream from the pond. Paul joined me as six Canada geese skittered to a landing. We sat for two hours waiting, hearing only one more accelerando of notes from the same direction.

Quiet. Nothing. Puzzling. Rain fell in a steady beat. I walked to the ponderosa hiding place in the darkness of predawn the next morning. No luck.

It was time to check in with Dan Albano. I emailed him a photo of the holes in the bank, reporting on observations, the lawnmowers, the return of the birds, and their absence. After two more kingfisherless mornings, Dan wrote back on April 20:

> It's not unusual for a pair to initiate digging at a number of holes before settling on one, and it sounds as though they may have moved on from the hole you are watching. If you can get down to the entrance, you might want to gently place a small twig (inch or two long) at its mouth, and this will tell you if they are entering/exiting while you're gone. Probably the easiest/fastest way to see if they've got alternative sites going is to canoe or kayak down that stream.

Kayaking would be treacherous on this section, even if I had the skills. However, I was anxious to try the twig project and to expand the search, but there was another life to lead. A few days later, I was on a plane to the Yucatan Peninsula to meet my mother at a traditional Mayan resort, an excursion we'd taken annually since my father's death.

My parents' courtship began in a classic 1950s way—over chocolate sundaes. They rekindled their spark often, on the silky white beaches of the Yucatan, starting in the 1980s when Cancun was small and the coast unspoiled. Dad birded the mangrove forests and recorded species in notebooks. I was pleased to see kingfishers on his penciled pages.

South of the Mexico border, species diversify in the tropical climate. Migratory belted kingfishers join residents—the ringed, Amazon, green, and American pygmy kingfishers. One morning, lounging on the beach, a male belted kingfisher passed above me like a hand across my brow. Startled, I sprinted after the bird evanescing into the Caribbean Sea. A Caspian tern hovered above the tropical sea like a breezing white flag. I felt transported for a moment to Rattlesnake Creek, where perhaps a kingfisher hovered like held breath above the currents before a minnow's world became a tsunami.

Snorkeling close to shore, kicking my way after schools of luminous yellow and blue fish, I popped up next to a floating brown pelican and tumbled into his gaze. For a few seconds, we were no longer separate beings.

My mother and I never tired of the pelican squadrons riding the air currents above the waves. They reminded her of courtship days of the 1950s. Dad was the dashing jet pilot flying for the US Marine Corps, racing the clouds for a few war-free years. Under starry nights, he would switch off his radio to fly in silent meditation. He also penned daily love letters, which our mother kept in a box as her most precious possession.

I can understand why he would drive eight hours north from his post in Cherry Point, North Carolina, to see my mother, speeding in his 1953 Mercury Monterey Coupe he'd dubbed Bittersweet for its orange-gold hues. I glanced over at her, where she read a mystery novel under the shade of a palapa. Tessellations of wind rustled through the palm frond shelter. Every ocean wave was a flirtation.

My mom, who was Cate and not a Kate, had brown eyes that were large and round, like those of a nocturnal flying squirrel. At age seventy-six on that trip, she applied bright red lipstick every morning to her full lips that I wish I'd inherited. Her face, framed by her short, coffee-colored hair, reminded me of Lisa back at the kingfisher watch— heart-shaped. Growing up in an era when men believed it would be dangerous to women's health to engage in overhand throws in basketball, my petite mother would later demonstrate tennis and ping-pong prowess in our family competitions.

Tracing circles and spirals in the sand with one finger, I sketched the kingfisher's diving impact as circles emanating from the middle until all was halcyon repose. Drawing next the curves of the creek and the positioning of the holes on the steep bank, I knew where I'd gone wrong. I'd become so enamored and fixated on the one spot by Mountain Water Dam, I'd lost sight of the possibility a second nest bank could exist, well hidden within the stream's twists and turns upstream.

℘

From the Missoula airport, I called Paul and Lisa. While I'd idled, they'd been busy. Paul had even followed the twig advice and reported slipping and sliding on the loose soil. With characteristic thoroughness, he had not missed a single potential hole. The twigs remained untouched, except for one opening. Maybe they were still around? Yet, they had not seen one kingfisher and heard only a few vexing calls from farther up the creek.

Spring splashed with wildflower brightness, even among the last of the snow patches. Yellow bells drooped their heads, while glacier lilies appeared ready to lift off like sunny firecrackers. I got serious about the expanded search and bushwhacked upstream from the dam as close to the creek as possible. A half mile north, there it was—the equivalent of a kingfisher mansion. The arcing bank dotted with inviting potential nest holes rose above a wild stretch of Rattlesnake Creek. No wires, no buildings, and no dam. Of course, the birds had chosen this refuge, yet why was it so quiet?

On the last night of April, I woke from a dream of a sleeping baby on the banks of Rattlesnake Creek. A mountain lion edged closer, stealthy, intent, and long-tail twitching. Not sure what it all meant, I tiptoed to Ian's room and listened to his regular breathing.

In the morning, a snowstorm shook feather flakes on greening lawns. After walking Ian to his bus, I drove up the valley and hiked to a promontory overlooking the floodplain with the new nest bank a hundred yards away. Training the spotting scope on one hole after another, I struggled to clear the lenses as snow pelted down.

After two hours, I descended the deer trail to the stream's edge. Studying the spattering of many holes, I counted six possibilities. Like staring at doors in a game show, I was poised to pick one. The birds would direct me if I was there for the watch.

CHAPTER 3
Lost Burrow

> They chiseled the dirt out with their bills, and pushed it along with their
> tiny feet. As near as I could estimate, it took them a week and a half to finish
> the burrow. The hallway sloped slightly up, and ran back four feet, where it
> ended in a little dome-shaped room. From the door into the nest were two
> little tracks, worn by the feet of birds as they went in and out.
>
> —William Lovell Finley, *American Birds*

I'd become obsessed with holes, sketching mapping scribbling, and list-
ing the pros and cons. Which one might be the kingfisher burrow? My
notes looked like this:

Pro: Right size, location, three feet down from top of bank. Con:
Cobweb in opening, upper edges ragged.

As April folded into May, the kingfishers seemed bafflingly absent,
except for far-off rattles. I was coming to know this wide floodplain.
Ponderosa pines, Douglas-firs, larches, cottonwoods, alders, birches, and
willows form a luxuriant grove. Every root of every tree taps into water
from the wilding creek. The sandy cliff, eroded from layers of sand and
silt deposited during glacial times, ascends some forty feet high and is a
hundred feet long. A layer of cobblestone midway up the bank indicates
a time of higher velocity.

The mountains of the Rattlesnake watershed are composed of billion-year-old rocks of the Belt Supergroup, bent and broken along faults
and pushed up into mountains. Much more recently, in the past ten to
hundred thousand years, glaciers advanced and retreated in response to
cooling or warming climates. Ice and glacial debris may have regularly
blocked or shaped streams.

The most famous of ice age dams created Glacial Lake Missoula some fifteen thousand years ago, backing up the entire Clark Fork River and drowning the Missoula Valley. The ice dam failed, releasing a Noah's ark–worthy deluge of water, which raged west to the Pacific Ocean, six hundred miles away. The plug would break free, reform, and break again—causing multiple floods.

ℂ℃

The days without success stretched into the first week of May. Troubling. What if I'd missed the excavating altogether? What if every time I was at the upper bank, the kingfishers had fooled me to return to the lower bank?

Surely, I could find an active hole like the one so clearly described at the turn of the twentieth century by William Lovell Finley (1876–1953), Oregon's beloved wildlife photographer, biologist, and advocate for the protection of birds. One of my favorite photographs of kingfishers is his black-and-white image of fledglings he labeled, "Six of the frowsy headed Fishers in a pose."

"Six of the frowzy-headed Fishers in a pose," William L. Finley, Herman Bohlman. Photo appears in the 1908 *American Birds*, by William Lovell Finley. Courtesy of OSU Special Collections & Archives Research Center.

Reading Finley's folksy account of kingfishers along the riverbanks of Portland near his home, I circled his depiction of a young chick in a nest, cheered by his humor:

> A young kingfisher seems to grow like a potato in a cellar, all the growth going to the end nearer the light. He sits looking toward the door and, of course, his face naturally all goes to nose. Everything is forfeited to furnish him with a big head, a spear-pointed bill, and a pair of strong wings to give this arrow-shaped bird a good start when he dives for fish.

On the fourth of May, in a bone-chilling morning drizzle, I set up the spotting scope on the viewpoint above the hidden creek bend. For two hours, I shivered and often shook my feet and hands to regain feeling. All week long, the trees and plants soaked up the life-giving showers, squalls, and mists. Temperatures never rose above the low 40s. Dressed in fleece layers under my raincoat, I vowed not to miss a day or stay less than two hours.

I did something else with regularity. I ran after kingfishers along Rattlesnake Creek. Tapping into the cadence of my feet navigating roots and rocks, then quickening over needle-strewn smooth stretches, I was alert to the passage of every bird, every song, and ready to brake for my bird of desire. Sometimes I spread my arms wide as I tilted right and left as if skimming rapids. When a kingfisher graced a run, I'd stop midstride to note the flight pattern—head held high meant a strolling pace, while head in line with body signaled speed. I covered five, seven, ten, and up to eighteen miles at a time close to the creek and closer to my primal self, on the hunt with every synapse firing.

The running and the stillness began to merge. Sitting close to the earthen bank and with my back pressed against the fissured trunk of a creekside Douglas-fir, I fell under the hypnotic spell of birch branches trailing in the currents as if always on the run. Examining the holes with determination, one day I was convinced I had found an active hole, round and smooth-edged, with a flat rock at the entry. The next day I chose another.

An occasional lone kingfisher zippering the morning light above the creek offered a ray of possibility. Once, a pair of ospreys sewed their way north in single file—gargantuan ghost shapes. A male common merganser formed the bright coat of a day, with a loden-green head, cottony breast, and night wings. Mesmerized by waters swirling clear before the snows melted, I watched like never before. Currents carried a universe of droplets, each with its own origin, yet fused into a streaming galaxy of fresh water.

The creek danced a syncopated samba over protruding stones, smoothing sharp edges and tumbling a colorful mosaic of maroons, purples, sage and jade greens, ambers, and golds. The stones originate from mud and sand washed into an ancient shallow sea more than a billion years ago, piled up over the eons and gradually metamorphosed to rock as sediments were buried and exposed to the heat of the earth. This combination of overlying pressure and heat at depth caused the hardening, but not so much to eradicate the original features. Thus, we can still see billion-year-old ripples and mud cracks.

The colorful palette derives from small amounts of iron minerals: oxidized iron in the case of red and purple rocks, and unoxidized iron in green and gray rocks. These ancient stones are part of the Belt Supergroup underlying much of western Montana and northeastern Idaho.

There's more to the magic. Unseen stoneflies live beneath rocks and in the air pockets where they interlock. There, these aquatic larvae find anchorage in the swift currents. Net-spinning caddisfly larvae thread their gossamer silk strands between stones—catching plant detritus and even regulating the flow of a river. Mayfly nymphs filter feed or scrape nutrients from the rocks. All claim the word "fly" for what they will become through metamorphosis, growing wings to shimmer above the currents.

There, by the creek's edge, I was catching on. Transformation lay not in some mythic dreamland. It was here—from sand to stone, larva to winged adult, seed to plant, snow to water, and egg to chick. In the midst, I was far from immune. I might still wiggle toes and fingers the same as ever, but my senses had begun to morph from dull and rusty to alert and shiny.

As the creek skated over the stony bottom, the water words seemed to whisper . . . *We know . . . we know . . . we know . . . where . . . where . . . where čális.*

Could it be the water and the kingfisher speak each other's names? Practicing pronouncing the Salish word for kingfisher, I pressed my tongue to the back of my front teeth for the first syllable and then relaxed my lower jaw for the final two syllables, "ts ah lease."

As I listened, Rattlesnake Creek sang in murmurs, swishes and swirls, hushes, thumps, slurps, and the syncopations and rhythms of water splitting, dividing, funneling, spraying, frizzling, jigging, and showering over rocks. As air mixed with water spray, the refrains varied.

Scrunching numb toes inside my boots to warm them, I took a deep breath and applied a skill I'd learned of wide and close focus. Once, I inventoried a five-foot radius: Douglas-fir, water birch, red osier dogwood, wild rose, snowberry, dandelion, pine grass, arnica, Oregon grape, twisted stalk, wild geranium, yarrow, moss, fluorescent green lichen on top of a birch limb; frilly quarter-shaped lichen of white, green, and black on all sides of the birch; orange and green lichen as flat as paint also on the birch; a brown pancake kind of lichen on a broken birch limb; beetle holes in a decaying log; thick humus of soil at my feet of leaves, needles, twigs, and cones; a dandelion leaf I picked to taste the tangy greenness; and palm-sized stones of salmon pink.

Somewhere, the wings of a kingfisher feathered above the currents. Somewhere, a protective parent warmed eggs deep within a burrow. What nourishes Rattlesnake Creek? Leaves and needles falling into waters leach organic molecules. Packed together against logs and rocks, they offer slimy surfaces for fungi, bacteria, insect larvae, and crustaceans to feast on, a banquet for insects that feed the fish that feed the kingfishers.

𝕏

Each day mattered. What was I missing? On May 7, my soul sister Sandra Murphy arrived for a week from her home, which was then in Flagstaff, Arizona. My friend is gentle yet strong, and with sky blue eyes, shoulder-length auburn hair, a lean frame, freckles everywhere, and long skilled

fingers. She has woven intricate pine needle baskets and often carves
wooden spoons from tree branches. We could be actual sisters, despite my
brown eyes, shorter stature, and decidedly unskilled hands. It must be the
freckles.

Taking the animal trail upstream, we hugged the edge of the rising
creek as rains fell and dippers dipped. Every day, we spent hours by the
burrow bank. In drowsy warm afternoons, we wrote in our journals.
Admittedly, what we weren't doing was separating to seek the missing
birds.

Sandra and I found each other in graduate school in Missoula in the
fall of 1987. From our first boogie out on a dance floor, we knew a lasting
rhythm. We met at a seedy bar, but soon discovered our twin passion
for what lies outside. For her thesis in environmental studies, Sandra
wrote a book, *Graced by Pines*, an eloquent tribute to ponderosas. Her
sunny calm soothed my growing disquiet. Maybe the kingfisher pair
had eloped far upstream, those triplets of song bewitching the wildest
of Rattlesnake Creek's inhabitants—the black bears, mountain goats,
elk, wolves, and mountain lions. Or would their ringing laughter be
quelled regardless of where they are? This was the time for incubation
and hiding.

Scents of wild onion buffed the air. Furled maple leaves dusted the
sky. A wild turkey promenaded past us, his hot pink wattle flashing like
an orchid in the jungle depths. The first mosquito of the season bit Sandra's forehead. Not total bliss.

After Sandra returned to Flagstaff with not even one view of a kingfisher, I was discouraged. Alone at dawn, a dipper flew by with a *chip chip*,
as if to say, "chin up!" I came to full senses when a ruffed grouse rumbled
the still air, warning off any other males. He strutted on a decaying log,
where I'd startled him before. Puffing his feathers and rising to his fullest
height, he rotated his wings forward and backward in a blur of fifty beats
in ten seconds. The pacing reminded me of playing an African drum,
warming up with a deliberate slow beat and then speeding up until your
hands are galloping.

Musing on kingfishers, I listed the reasons to care about these exas-
perating, elusive, and downright frustrating birds. Time to give them
some credit.

They're funny with those crazy, comical rock star crests. Their fishing prowess is breathtaking. When it comes to diving, they would be top Olympic contenders. Not every dive is perfect, yet a lifetime of repetition hones skills to rival or exceed those of a professional athlete. Their smooth entries into water appear effortless. Their chittering call awakens. They have a loyalty to their nesting home. They've mastered the art of solitude, except when pairing up in breeding season. Clearly, they are nonconformists who shun stick nests for hidden recesses within the earth. And that enigmatic red belt, outshining the male's blues, grays, and white feathers? I was drawn to the idea of a hidden female power yet to be uncovered.

I remained steadfast by the streamside. Raven wings touched the smoky wisps of clouds in a pale blue sky. Tree swallows orbited the creek, home after a winter in South America. What was I missing in the wispy light of dawn? I started setting my alarm for 4:30 a.m. to hike down to the bank with my headlamp.

May 13 offered another glimmer. There, in the predawn dimness, a kingfisher fleeced by with the stealth of an owl. Resisting the desire to pirouette around a pine, I waited for a return that did not happen. The next day at 5:45 a.m., with a blanket wrapped around me in the 45-degree chill, a familiar dipper hurled by in a grayness matching the somber sky. The creek was a milkshake of waves. An osprey stormed upstream on wings like snow, and then downstream a half hour later. Again! A male kingfisher clipped by on quickening wings, turning his head in flight with a slight rattle. I noted the time: 7:01.

Elation. Befuddlement. The birds must have a nest that I had yet to find, but what was I missing? I'd scoured every hole, and none seemed quite right.

From what I'd read and consultations with Dan Albano, the early morning silent flights indicated the kingfishers were incubating eggs. One bird would spend the night deep in the burrow, and in the morning, the mate would take his or her place. Both the male and female birds have a brood patch, featherless skin filled with blood vessels near the surface to warm the eggs. Likely, I was witnessing the dawn exchange. Was the male departing from a hidden burrow below or above me?

It was time to enlist help. Paul was game for a dawn watch before work when he could, within a busy field season. At six the next morning, he took up a station at the lower end of the bank. I guarded the upper end. The knee-high grasses and shrubs dripped from the night's drenching. I'd worn old green rain pants that were not keeping me dry. Noting the surroundings took my mind off the misery. Coppery ponderosa needles herringboned the forest floor. Horsetail grew knee-high. Officially known as *Equisetum*, the bamboo-like stalk has an ancient lineage dating to the dinosaur era.

The snowberry, gooseberry, and currant bushes softened with new yellow-green leaves. A lone Rocky Mountain juniper slouched over the water. Behind an ample Douglas-fir, the ruffed grouse was again drumming, a muffled thumping like shaking out a quilt. Across the creek, a larch sprouted tender, yellow-green needles.

Rattlesnake Creek remained the continuum, like blood rushing through arteries. An hour passed. It was 7 a.m. and time to check in with Paul. I walked well away from the creek to avoid detection and found him with a coffee cup in hand, looking pleased.

"Did you see her just now? She flew downstream from where you were and rattled." I shook my head. Timing is everything. As we conversed in lowered voices, the kingfisher flew past us. There must be a hole. In case we were wrong, I took one last look at the lower burrow bank. Like Paul, I struggled to find footholds in the sandy soil. My flashlight beamed on spiderwebs crisscrossing the holes. Crumbled edges. Abandoned. Cross this bank off the list.

In the next few days, the temperatures rose as the volume of the rushing creek swelled to a Beethoven-worthy crescendo.

More early mornings. What passed by unseen? A crafty kingfisher? Meanwhile, a slow cavalcade of birds arrived from the south to court, mate, and nest.

Northern rough-winged swallows looped about the holes on volitant wings that bore them for thousands of miles on their migration north from South America. Often, a pair inspected a potential dwelling. As the day warmed, the birds appeared like strobes of light before swinging in unison up and over the treetops.

Rough-winged swallows do not dig their own holes, and benefit from the industry of kingfishers. Dan once found a pair that covered kingfisher eggs with nesting materials. The birds abandoned the nest, dug a new burrow, and laid five more eggs.

A full sixteen days after my last sighting, a kingfisher flapped north at 6 a.m. on the twenty-ninth of May. No rattle. Silent flight. Slim wingtips brushed a cresting wave. One glance away, and I would have missed the vision. How often had I looked the wrong direction or down at my journal?

I kept searching beyond the creek bank for the elusive hole. I made worried calculations. If the birds incubated eggs for twenty to twenty-three days, I had a window of forty to forty-six days for the nesting season. If the birds laid eggs at the end of April, I still had a chance.

&

On the fourth of June, I worked my way north from the dam, vowing not to miss a single spot along the creek, even if I needed to wade. Native bees thrummed and flashed into thickets, leaving an impression of iridescence, stripes, and glass wings. My entomologist friend Byron Weber would have been pleased.

"The way of the naturalist is slow," he reminded me the day I spent investigating insects in his yard as research for a children's book on bugs. He taught me the special way of wide and close focus. Approach a bush buzzing with insects and take everything in. Then zero in on one leaf.

I practiced the art of tossing the day's to-do lists in the June breeze. The birds might come in stillness. Before my saunter upstream, I sat for an hour on a ponderosa pine stump above the pond by the dam. Clouds passed over the sun. I pulled my jacket closer and listened to the pounding of a pileated woodpecker. The mighty excavator spiraled his way up a dead pine, intent on finding insects in the heartwood. His stiff tail and zygodactyl feet, with two toes forward and two toes facing back, gave him a solid hold on the side of the tree. The swept-back scarlet crest, chisel bill, striking black and white colors, and sheer size, almost as big as a crow, make North America's biggest woodpecker a charismatic superstar. After a few minutes, he oscillated away in flight with a soft clucking call.

A sleek doe and buck with budding antlers waltzed by, their reddish summer coats afire. I turtled my way north upstream. By 11:30 a.m., I'd made it as far as an overhanging rock cliff with a round mossy dipper nest on the underside and the creek below. A tiger swallowtail butterfly swayed like a yellow and black leaf twirling in a spiderweb. A Hammond's flycatcher nipped the winds with a three-note song of precision. Everything was courting, nesting, mating, hatching, growing, metamorphosing, blooming, and singing. Somewhere, the kingfishers were right in the midst of it all.

ॐ

With warblers, vireos, and flycatchers converging in song, I could almost hear my father's gentle baritone telling me how to identify the red-eyed vireo by that pure whistle of a slurred question, "Where are you?"

My father could identify a litany of songbirds by ear. When he would hear the euphonious chords of a hermit thrush, his expression was as rapt as if Placido Domingo's flawless tenor rang through a forest. He'd fallen for birds in 1944 at age twelve, lying for weeks on a daybed in his Moorestown, New Jersey, backyard as he recuperated from an illness. On one snowbush, dozens of species of warblers gleaned the leaves for insects, something that would be rare to see today.

Soon, he joined his older brother Bob on outings with the high school's birding club. The two boys often accompanied their uncle, George Hallett, to Pennsylvania's Hawk Mountain to watch currents of eagles, hawks, and falcons plying the line of Appalachian Mountains south in fall migration. I remember my Great-uncle George as a vegetarian who ate more eggs in a day than I'd ever seen. He was a renowned civic leader and birder of New York City, honored with the designation of the four-acre Hallett Nature Sanctuary in Central Park. A passion for birds runs deep in my Richie and Hallett roots.

Looking back on birding and hiking trips together, I recalled a day that may have foreshadowed this halcyon calling. In 1986, I joined Dad to backpack the Appalachian Trail's hundred-mile wilderness from

Monson to Mount Katahdin, Maine. For the final decade of his career, he served as the AT project manager (a position he created) for the National Park Service, overseeing major land acquisitions to protect the 2,190-mile-long corridor. He also backpacked the entire AT in sections. This was his final leg and the wildest.

One morning outside our shelter, two belted kingfishers arrowed low toward us and then swirled away as the sun parted the dawn mist over West Chairback Pond. Like halcyon, the beauty was fleeting—and yet the memory? Indelible.

Out seeking kingfishers, I often felt my father's protective spirit by Rattlesnake Creek. While aching for his physical presence, I could almost conjure him beside me with his thick sandy eyebrows and ponderous brow below his receding hairline and the laser vision of his golden-brown pilot eyes. He would always be perpetually fit, wiry, and marathon-ready. My mother, too, sensed his presence among certain birds. Over the phone that coupled her home in coastal North Carolina to mine in Missoula, we shared inexplicable visitations, like the red-shouldered hawk often accompanying her solo walks.

ᚯ

Continuing my slow-steps and closing in on the lower end of that oh-so-perfect burrow bank absent of kingfishers, I saw where I'd gone wrong. I'd never ventured onto a small island just downstream from the steep creek bank. By not crossing the irrigation ditch separating the island from the shore, I'd missed one essential stretch, even if this island was a mere twenty-five yards long and ten yards wide.

Crawling through rosebushes, mock orange, and willows, I found a downed log over the five-foot-wide flowing ditch. Crossing to the upper edge of the island, I took a sharp breath. The earthen bank I'd watched for so long did not end above the island but extended a little farther. Like the final arc of a rainbow hiding out of view, I'd missed the anchoring point.

I'd barely settled in to search for a hole when it happened at 12:26 p.m. Midday.

June 4.

A female kingfisher docked on an immense boulder protruding from the far side of the creek. She bore a silvery minnow held lengthwise within her beak. Rattling once, she cranked upward and into the perfect nest hole, the one I'd missed all along. The round hole showed the telltale two furrow marks at the base and rested about two feet down from the top of the bank and four feet up from the canorous creek.

Halcyon backed out of the burrow empty-billed. Her white chest and russet belt and sash sparkled. She hovered, streaked down to the water, deep enough to wet her crest, and muscled up with another fish in her black beak. Landing on the boulder as if to catch her breath, she chattered, launched into flight to the hole entry, pressed her wings closed as if in prayer, and tucked inside with food for the chicks.

A halcyon bird. A halcyon day.

CHAPTER 4

Nest Watch

> Ceyx grips a four-inch fish lengthwise in his bill. His rattle is muted against the rushing of the creek, which carries snows and springs of headwaters, songs of birds, and the fish that kingfishers so deftly pluck from the currents. He looks toward the blind. I freeze. Satisfied, he lifts off the boulder and flies with a few strong swift wingbeats up to the hole, folds his wings, dips in, backs out, pivots, and flaps upstream.
>
> —Marina's journal, 5:53 a.m., June 17, 2009

The first night after the jubilant June discovery, I dreamed of Ceyx, the male kingfisher. His vibrating call shook the cobwebs of sleep. The watch began. At last, I would be one with the nesting kingfishers. Or not. Halcyon and Ceyx were "skitty" birds, as my scientist advisers had warned. To be smitten by hatchlings would not mean letting down their guard, but the opposite. Doesn't all wariness heighten with the responsibility of a young family to guard?

Each day, I wore muted forest colors to be as concealed as the "green man," the archetypal figure who found his pagan way into Christian medieval sculptures. My camouflage efforts fell short. The birds soon caught on. Tactics had to change. I ordered a turkey hunting blind from the Cabela's catalog. The picture and description appeared to fit the need: a teepee-like tent with green and brown leaf patterns, roomy enough for two lawn chairs, in case Lisa or Paul joined me, and sturdy enough to be left in place for a month or so.

On June 5, the day after the Eureka moment, I returned without a kingfisher in view. Screened by alder branches, I dangled bare toes above the currents and fluttered fingers over the keys of my laptop balanced on my knees. I vowed not to miss a beat. Soon, I was typing fast without looking down:

2:18 P.M.   Arrival
2:19   A kingfisher thrums out of the hole—*kkkkkkkk!* Male or
            female?
2:20   Three plump dippers flap upstream.
2:22   Halcyon lands on the boulder, rattles, stares my direction,
            and flies off.
2:24   Returns. FISH (I will put fish deliveries in capital letters).

I catch a silvery glint in her bill. She spritzes to the hole. Her flight away
is as rapid as creek flow.

2:25   Swallowtail butterfly suspends above the currents on sun
            chip wings.
2:31   A chittering Halcyon steers by the hole.
2:32   FISH. Chattering, she squeezes in the hole and stays.
2:37   Ceyx touches down on a high branch of a Douglas-fir.
            He's wet, with his crest partially flattened, and seems
            leaner than his mate.

Ceyx cantered away in flight, as I typed: "Did I mention that I'm
happy? I'm so happy. I've found my Ceyx and Halcyon, and they have a
family." After weeks of glimpses, I was breathless with the pace of fishing
and feeding. In the interludes, I thought of Halcyon within the hole,
brooding her young.

Kingfishers are born featherless—in scientific terms, "altricial."
Feathers along the humeral tract (where the wings attach to the body)
emerge at about six days. By sixteen days, most have sprouted. The nestlings begin to explore beyond the comfy alcove into the tunnel. The flight
and tail feathers remain sheathed until the last ten days before fledging.

Could as many as seven chicks slumber within? I'd brought along
Dan Albano's dissertation to review. Only after a significant lull of at
least fifteen minutes did I dare turn the pages. Risky. If not watching the
hole every second, I might miss a kingfisher's arrival in the rare instance
of a sneaky approach without a rattle.

Dan noted that the parents alternated brooding and feeding for the
first four to five days. One of the pair would make two to four trips

with fish, and then stay in, relieving the mate of nest duty. From what I observed, they left the nestlings alone for brief periods, which could indicate six or seven days after hatching. Fragile and safe in an earthen womb, the chicks knew only the dark, the pink skins of their siblings, and the feather coverlet of their parents.

Parenthood can give you a protective fierceness, balanced by hours of rocking and nursing. Now, in an observer role, letting go of presumptions was essential. Whenever a kingfisher sleeted into view with a fish, I was on high alert. Questions eddied. Staring into that unreadable hole, I could only guess the length of the tunnel. Some record-breaking shafts extend as far as nine or ten feet, but three to five feet is more common.

Halcyon and Ceyx had scraped and smoothed every inch of the burrow. With each arrival and departure, the furrows at the entry deepened like ruts in a muddy road. Studying the hole with the two tracks, I noticed the similarity to a keyhole. If only one could simply place the correct key and turn the latch. The door would open. I could step in.

Like waterfowl and many songbirds, kingfisher mothers lay their eggs at about one per day, until they have a full clutch, and only then do they begin incubating. Waiting to warm the eggs at the same time ensures the chicks will emerge together, an event called synchronous hatching.

First, the featherless chick must chip a hole in the shell to break free. With head tucked down by the breast and the beak at an awkward angle poking from beneath a wing, the wee bird thrusts and pokes with an essential tool—an egg tooth at the tip of the upper mandible. A few days later, this chunk of hardened calcium falls off.

Dan wrote, "As the chick begins to rap on this blunt end of the shell with its egg tooth, the sound is audible to the human ear from as far as a half meter." He suggested the chicks might coordinate hatching by hearing the rapping sounds. To visit multiple nests, he'd built back doors to the burrows, carefully shoveling down from above after measuring the tunnel length. While he risked disturbing the incubating adults, his methods yielded thought-provoking results.

Males were more apt to stay put with their eggs, while females would "scamper" away down the tunnel when he opened the intrusive door. Is the male more committed? Are females less maternal? I pondered a potential clue to the puzzle of a colorful belt.

For the chicks to hatch, the pair would trade places to keep their eggs at a constant warm temperature for seven hundred hours, or thirty days. Only one parent would hear the rapping of a new life.

ॐ

On the near side of the stream, a dipper snorkeled for insects and then air-skipped away with a string of *peep . . . peep . . . peep* calls. The dippers had raised their young in the mossy basketball-shaped nest glued beneath an overhanging rock, located two creek bends below me. Only the female incubated her clutch of four or five eggs. Their chicks also hatched synchronously and without feathers.

By 3 p.m., it was time to pack up to be home when Ian stepped off the school bus. I had my own chick to raise, one whose fledging would take eighteen years.

ℂℂ

A kingfisher screamed. The high-pitched concussive sound came from the closest tree and only three feet overhead. Shaking. Every fiber vibrated. Another sensation? Fear. Irrational, yet powerful, as if the bird were the size of a pterodactyl and could skewer me.

The scream happened on the second afternoon of the watch, after I'd decided to hide slightly upstream from the island. There, I could see the hole and give the birds more space. I'd noted first one and then a second kingfisher bolting by. Ceyx landed on the boulder with a fingerling trout. Instead of feeding the nestlings, he flew across the creek to land on a fir tree branch, cantilevered above the rolling waves. He glared at my hiding place in the alders and gave a brief rattle. Then, he flapped past me away from the burrow. I took a deep breath, afraid to exhale. But then, he backtracked and aimed for the hole—trout delivered! The wash of relief proved short-lived.

That's when Ceyx swerved toward me, knifing the air. He cut his flight short, jamming his landing close by. The jolting shriek was unmistakable: "Get out!"

With ears ringing, I scuttled away among the budding wild rose, tender birch leaves, white clusters of mountain ash flowers, and a lake of arnica flowers radiating yellow light under the rain-laden sky. Until the camouflaged tent arrived, I'd have to be ultra-careful. The next day on the island, I struggled to see through tangled alder branches swaying in the wind.

"Please," I begged to the trees, "Hide me well."

Ceyx skimmed by the hole without entering. Seconds later, Halcyon flicked by, uttering a higher-decibel phrase edging toward a caterwaul.

ℂℂ

Despite my growing concern, I'd made plans to show the nest to ornithologist friends Sue Reel and Dick Hutto and their two bird-centric sons, who were teenagers at the time. Whenever I had difficult questions on birds, I turned to their expertise. As a longtime professor and researcher at the University of Montana, Dick founded and then directed the Avian Science Center and once hosted the nationally televised PBS series *Birdwatch*. His research over the past thirty-five years has particular significance when it comes to the hottest topic in western forests—wildfire. His work shows that birds like the black-backed woodpecker are nearly restricted in their distribution to severely burned mixed-conifer forests, suggesting high-intensity wildfires are naturally occurring and special sources of biodiversity.

Sue and I look uncannily alike. Whenever someone called me Sue, I was flattered. We were both slim, small-boned, of medium height, and so it went on, with our brown eyes, oval faces, slightly sharp noses, and a tendency toward a smile over a frown. Our work was similar, too, with a shared emphasis on interpreting the ways, wonders, and conservation significance of birds and wildlife for the public. We'd met in graduate school when she was earning her master's degree in wildlife biology.

From our observation point north of the island and well beyond the place of the scream, we were rewarded within minutes. Halcyon raced by the burrow once, twice, three times. Dick pointed out how she turned her head to stare at us. Definitely jumpy. She slowed to balance on a fir limb above the hole with a fish held lengthwise in her bill. Then, with a quick ratcheting up of notes, she lifted off. Six times she flew by and never once dove into the nest. We had to leave. On our way out, Sue turned to me.

"Did you notice you could barely see the fish in her bill? She held it the long way, rather than crosswise, so her beak looked thicker."

"I did. So all we need to know is the length of the kingfisher bill to know the size of the fish."

"Right, and that could give us a clue to the age of the chicks in the burrow."

A belted kingfisher's beak is about two and a half inches long. The young rainbow, cutthroat, or bull trout were a tad bigger. Dan had told me an effective way to estimate the age of chicks is by fish size. In the first week, the parents bring in fish so dainty they are hard to see, held lengthwise in their beaks. As the chicks grow and can swallow bigger prey, the kingfishers carry the fish crosswise. A parent always turns a fish to feed chicks their meal headfirst, assuring the sharp spines or fins are facing away and down for easy swallowing.

Sue agreed the chicks were about a week old. Doing the math, if they had hatched on or soon after May 29 and the period from hatching to fledging was twenty-seven to twenty-nine days, I still had much of the rest of June for a daily watch.

I imagined a nod of approval from the naturalist women who preceded me by more than a century. Clambering up high stream banks in sturdy yet cumbersome skirts and boots, they showed remarkable enterprise. Back in 1905, the thirty-eight-year-old Irene Wheelock found a kingfisher nest and took a hands-on approach to publish her observations, which were met with the ire of a male-dominated ornithology establishment.

Like modern biologists I had interviewed, she, too, had measured the tunnel and dug down from the top of the bank to the nest chamber:

As soon as feeding was completed and the adult out of sight, we opened the nest at the false back, took out the young, then one day old, and examined the crops. They contained a dark gray, oily mass, nearly fluid and vile-smelling, but with no bones or scales in it.

Her conclusion? The parents regurgitated fish in the first few days until the young could swallow a minnow-sized meal. Kingfishers, like most fish-eating birds, do not have a crop (a muscular pouch near the throat or gullet for storing food). But they do have gizzards, which are part of the digestive system and lined with thin muscles. It was Wheelock's claim of regurgitation that would set off a kerfuffle in the bird world.

Born in Michigan in 1867, Irene Wheelock spent much of her life with birds and wrote a 1902 book, *The Nestlings of Forests and Marsh*. Two years later, her second book hit the shelves, *Birds of California*, a 578-page narrative on three hundred species she studied over eight years. She also brushed shoulders with the likes of John Muir, whose property at Muir Station was home to a great blue heron rookery. "The noise of the young birds at feeding time can be heard half a mile away," she commented.

Irene's controversial suggestions of adult birds regurgitating fish for their chicks irritated the famed zoologist Joseph Grinnell, who would later serve as editor of *The Condor*, the esteemed publication of the Cooper Ornithological Club from 1906 to 1939. He reviewed her book in the magazine with a telling exclamation point: "An occasional resort to the gun would have resulted in a less sweeping generalization in regard to 'regurgitation' than is hurled at the reader in the preface!"

Today, the "Birds of the World" species account credits Irene for what we know of the first four days of a belted kingfisher's life:

> For 3–4 d[ays] after hatching, adult returns to nest with no visible food in the bill, but esophagus is visibly swollen. An oily bolus of several partially digested fishes is regurgitated and apportioned among nestlings (Wheelock 1905). After 5 d[ays], nestlings consume whole fishes, but only one fish is delivered to the burrow during each feeding trip.

Despite Grinnell's grumble at this upstart woman in a man's world, Irene Wheelock acknowledged him, and Muir too, in her book. She reserved her highest praise in the preface for the birds: "To live among these fascinating feathered folk and not long to know them, one must have eyes that see not and ears deaf to Nature's music."

❦

Rain clobbered the skylight above the bed. I thought of Halcyon and Ceyx and their young, forming one warming bundle of feathers deep within the burrow. The next morning, I flipped a few pancakes for Ian, waved him off, and jumped into action.

I had a practical transformation ahead—to become so invisible in the much-anticipated blind I could be one with the trees. I'd identified a tent-sized clearing under the alders and dogwoods with a diagonal view of the nest and centered on the landing boulder. The bison-sized rock was chiseled on top, smoothed by currents on the sides, and splotched in somber lichen, which turned vivid lime green when wet.

I knew the blind should be placed farther back than twenty-five feet from the water. However, I counted on the screening trees and the creek separating the tent from the burrow to give the birds a sense of security. Despite intentions to avoid disturbance in the pre-blind-arrival days, I made more mistakes. On the evening of June 8, I couldn't resist the look my dog gave me as I headed out the door. Arriving at 7:45 p.m., Luna was restless and wanted to drink from the creek. Guiding her back and putting my arm around her, I pressed my nose into her honey-colored fur.

Soon, Ceyx landed on the boulder and looked straight through our leafy hideaway. He fled in a crescendo of contempt. Had he seen Luna? I gripped her collar. She gave me a reproachful look. Five minutes later, Ceyx was back, his calls as crackling as a campfire. Then, he sizzled north like a flaming torch. Two minutes passed. Ceyx docked on the rock, compressing a bluish fish the long way in his bill, so the unlucky trout's head dangled off the tip. He jerked his head to the right and left. Edgy. At last, he scrolled up from the boulder to feed the young.

Walking the trail homeward at 9 p.m. in the protracted daylight of a Montana summer, I paused mid-step to avoid a rubber boa, a docile snake shaped like a stick with smooth ends, an adaptation to fool predators. I picked up the boa with one hand placed below the head and the other in the middle. When threatened, this snake will wind up into a tight ball with tail exposed to look like the head. Better to be chomped on the tail and live. Kneeling to release the boa to the safety of the forest well away from the trail, I felt the clammy scales of his upper brown body and yellow underbelly slide through my hands like a day's glide away into night.

ℂ

When would the blind arrive? Impatience. After three days of thunderstorms, I tried another hiding spot a few yards above the ditch that separated the creek from the island. The hole was not visible, but I could see the "perch root," another favorite landing spot. The Douglas-fir root exposed from the earth by bank erosion formed a two-foot-high letter J.

Ceyx was fishing like a skillful chopstick user, capturing two the same size in a half hour. Each time, he paused on the root before levitating to the nest. I'd escaped his notice. Recording the times and intervals of fish transports, I sought clues to how many chicks waited to be fed, while never tiring of describing the mesmerizing birds. Blue and white feathers glistened. Wings iced the frothing rollers. When Ceyx flew into the sun, the rays of light fractured his tail feathers.

Alexander Skutch, a famed naturalist of Costa Rica, observed Amazon kingfishers nesting on his farm from 1943 to 1946, which would lead to his writing "Life History of the Amazon Kingfisher" published in *The Condor* a decade later. He wrote this poetic description: "So rapidly do its wings beat while it poises in mid-air, that, to one standing directly in front or behind, its body seems to be suspended between two misty spheres."

He also gave this observation on hole-watching, which resonated whenever I grew weary:

> The great difficulty was to keep my attention so firmly fixed on a hole where for long hours nothing happened—a sort of yogic exercise in the contemplations of nothingness—that I did not miss the sudden, unannounced exit of a kingfisher.

On June 10, the UPS driver walked up the sidewalk with a backpack-sized box. Five minutes later, I was driving to the far trailhead and the shortest route to the nest downstream. The lightweight, saucer-shaped blind came in a case with straps for easy carrying on my back. Grasping a folded camp chair, with binoculars swinging around my neck and notebook crammed in a long-sleeve shirt pocket, I paused to regain my balance on the log bridging the ditch. All was quiet on the island at 1:30, although a siesta was nonexistent for kingfisher parents feeding their young.

As soon as I unzipped the case, the blind snapped open as if alive—a tent in a single shake. I secured my hiding place with stakes and pull-out cords tied to branches. The muted browns, greens, and blacks forming leaf and floral patterns melded into the surroundings. Perfect. The blind featured a back door with a zipper and screen windows forming half-circles on three sides. The windows had zip-up flaps on the interior. The trick, I'd heard from photographers, was to keep the back door closed, so the birds could not see a human profile.

I set up the chair, stepped in, zipped the door, and kept the flaps on the window open, hoping the camo-print on the screens would be enough to hide me. The setup took fifteen minutes, fortunately coinciding with kingfisher absence.

The "blind" watch began. Within five minutes of settling into the camp chair, I heard a rapid soft chitter. Halcyon dropped anchor on the boulder with a plump, dark-colored trout the size of an anchovy and compressed lengthwise in her bill. Within my hiding place, I could zero in on the upper blue band, the lower auburn belt, and the way her blue feathers shone on a day of clouds and sun. White speckles sprayed over blue wings, and the white barring on her flirty tail shimmied with each flick. Like a ballet dancer, she flew in a relevé of grace and muscle. I counted three flaps to the hole, where she tucked inside for two minutes before the élancé of a leap skyward.

The world had changed, from within the blind. On the one hand, it felt confining. On the other, I was like Harry Potter wearing his cloak of invisibility. Brits have a different term for "blinds." They call them "hides." I could see the advantage of both names. I wanted the birds to be "blind" to my presence as I hid like a child in a game of hide-and-seek.

A robin cantillated into song worthy of a sea shanty, just five feet away in an alder. A yellow warbler brushed against the tent fabric and landed within hand's reach. Showy as a dandelion, her voice was honey pouring from a jar. A black-capped chickadee jigged among branches. The world had come closer in five minutes.

Bang! A dipper clanged into the front screen. I ducked as if someone had thrown a dirt clod. The groggy bird staggered to his feet and lurched into the air. The dipper's world had changed, too. A few minutes after the crash, Ceyx touched down with a tumbling of clickety-clackety notes and a fish. There on the boulder, he turned his head toward me. I met his sharp, beady forward-facing eyes right when I lifted my binoculars.

Darn. With all three window flaps down, looking through the camo-tinted screens, I was too visible after all. Any movement would be noticed. Sure enough, Ceyx huffed upstream. I heard jangled notes a few minutes later from downstream. But he returned to dash into the hole, evaporating into the darkness for the span of one breath. He backed out sans fish, turned, and parlayed away.

It's hard to say which parent was more dedicated so far. Dan had noted males edging out females in numbers of fish deliveries. Would that be true here? My intent was to identify gender and listen to their language.

No rattle was alike, in the way of Rattlesnake Creek, haven of kingfishers. Tunes varied on any given day, and by season. At the blind, curtains of water brushed over boulders like the sound of a receding ocean wave across the sand. Churning mini-whirlpools emitted occasional slurps.

Staying within tight confines would take practice. Longing to jump from the blind and thrust both hands in the frigid water, I planted my feet instead. This first afternoon, I stayed within for three hours and recorded four fish feedings: Halcyon at 1:48, Ceyx at 2:20 and 2:32, and Halcyon at 4 p.m.: a fifty-fifty shared effort.

ℰℭ

The spotting scope on the tripod fit well by the chair and promised to magnify more than the birds. I had zipped the screen flaps up higher for better screening. At 9 a.m. the next day, sun brightened the nest entry. The creek had receded with the ebb of spring floods and mild weather. Two-foot-high waves sprayed festive jets in a funnel of whitewater alongside the boulder.

A faint rattle up the creek. Then nothing. Forty-five minutes later, Halcyon's *kkkkkk . . . kkkkkkk* ushered her in. Poised on the boulder with her beak pinched down on a fish, she was the circus actor about to perform an acrobatic feat. Or so I thought. As I moved to look through the scope, she turned to face me. Suspicious. Halcyon fled. How would a kingfisher ever be "blind" to my presence? Six minutes later, she flew in with the same fish, silvery in the light and four inches long, double the size of what I'd witnessed a week ago. The trout head draped off the end of her beak.

Even inching my head to the right to look through the scope proved too much motion. She fretted away in silence. Why was she so leery? I would not move a muscle. Two minutes later, she returned, glowering at the blind. When she spurted up to the hole, I sighed in relief and confusion.

Stymied. What could I adjust? Then I saw the problem. Sunlight entered the blind through the downstream screen and revealed my silhouette, even with partially closed side windows. Fixed, but the interior had turned cave-like. Ten minutes later, Ceyx rattled and darted into the hole with a fish. He then zinged upstream, a master of efficiency. To so quickly beak over his fish, he must have met the chick near the entry.

During the ensuing lull, I reread Dan's dissertation on feeding and fish size. By the third week, the parents bring fish of about three and a half inches in length. The growth rate is highest during the first ten days after hatching. In sixteen days, the nestlings are almost fully feathered and as big as the adults.

୨୦

My journal entries proliferated with fish deliveries and scrawled notes on the passage of dippers, swallowtail butterflies, and rough-winged swallows. Often, I added my unchecked elation. How was it possible for the parents to depart from a sandy, dusty hole without one speck of dirt and feathers all in place? If I'd trundled into an earthen tunnel, I'd come out smudged and rumpled.

Enamored with so many views of their blue feathers morphing in sunlight, I researched the whys. Scientists had long theorized birds look blue in the same way as the sky. When the sun's white light enters the atmosphere, red and yellow wavelengths pass through, but the shorter blue wavelengths bounce off particles and scatter.

Richard Prum, an ornithologist at Yale, challenged this premise after an intensive study of blue feathers. In 1998, he and his colleagues published their research. Within each feather are molecules made of stringy keratin. Those protein molecules separate from water, like oil from vinegar. When a cell dies, the water evaporates and is replaced by air. The keratin then looks like loose spaghetti. The feather structure is ready for the blue phenomenon. When white light passes through a feather, the keratin patterns that are unique to different shades of blue feathers cause the red and yellow wavelengths to cancel out and the blue wavelengths of light to strengthen and intensify each other, and then reflect to the observer.

So, yes, the blue does come from light striking the feathers, but it's the shapes and sizes of the air pockets among the keratin that creates the arrays of blueness.

Light matters. Feathers matter. Sun always illuminates.

This watching was about stepping into the light, experiencing each fractal and unexpected beam.

༄

Every day the birds took notice. The slightest movement from within caused a head swivel in my direction. The rattling notes were a torrent of disapproval. Sometimes I succeeded in stillness. Like a sapling tree, I had much to experience. Often, I felt both astonished and gifted by the salvos of fish feedings, accompanied by so many chatters and rattles.

Lisa and Paul soon joined me, and Lisa often covered the watch when I could not be there. Whereas once two hours had seemed like a long stint, soon four hours was easy. Paul added a laminated sign. "University research project. Please do not disturb blind. Thanks."

I'd grown reluctant to attend to the other world beyond the blind, the creek, and the birds. My field journals brimmed with questions about life within the burrow. The rapidity and number of fish suggested a full brood of perhaps seven, but could there be fewer? It was all so new.

How did Halcyon and Ceyx determine who hadn't eaten yet? Dan Albano had the same question and found one answer from studies of common kingfishers in Europe. The chicks line up in the tunnel in a strict rotation. Once fed, a nestling shuffles to the back so the next one in line can open his or her beak wide for a meal.

I breathed kingfishers. When not there, I tracked them in my mind, conjuring crest feathers rippling in the wind as a parent perched on a limb and scanned for motion in the eddy below. Not any fish would do. What human angler could so precisely pluck the fish of a specific size from within a swimming school?

༄

If I were a biologist sticking to protocol, I would have selected certain times to collect data on morning, midday, and evening. Ideally, I would have been there from sunrise to sunset, like a fire lookout in a tower scanning for the first wisps of smoke.

The researchers I'd interviewed followed a rigorous schedule to test their hypotheses in the field. My observations were less consistent, yet what I recorded had merit. What was the question I was trying to answer? While tempted to settle on one query, other entrancing possibilities arose in addition to the mystery of the female's colorful belt.

Where did the kingfishers like to fish on the creek? What kind of fish were they catching, and when? Were they angling for other prey, and visiting ponds or ditches? How did the chicks spend their days in the dark? Next spring awaited with the promise of filling in the blanks of mating, excavation, and incubation I'd missed during the month of the missing burrow.

The jumble of questions reminded me of eleven-year-old Sam Beaver, the main character of E. B. White's classic, *The Trumpet of the Swan*. When I was about that age, I read of the boy with raven hair sneaking up on the swans, walking with one foot straight in front of the other, and never snapping a twig on the ground. I even changed my gait to be like him. I remain a bit pigeon-toed.

Sam kept a diary by his bed, and before going to sleep, he wrote what he'd seen and thought about and often sketched a picture. He ended with a question to ponder, like, "How does a bird know how to make a nest?" In this time of kingfishers, I was finding my inner Sam.

When I left for a family and friends camping trip to Yellowstone National Park from June 13 through 16, I fretted over what I might miss. Every day counted at the nest watch. Upon return, there was the coveted email from Paul:

Lisa and I visited the blind on Saturday for 2 hours (10:20 to 12:20). The female appeared on the boulder with a head-length fish at 10:28. She didn't like what she saw in the blind, left, and then returned to the boulder with the fish at 10:35, still didn't like what she saw and departed. Then, at 10:42, a kingfisher (I didn't see which sex, but probably the female) flew directly to the burrow with a fish and

went in for 15 sec., then departed. And that was the last kingfisher
activity we saw during our watch.

Paul went on to reflect, as he often did: "It's possible that by that time
of day the young have so many fish in their stomach that they need time
to digest it all before having space to take in more."

Hiking to the blind on June 17, I recalled a string of images from
Yellowstone. A black bear waddled up a hillside in the burned forest of
the Blacktail Plateau. At Tower Junction, two grizzly bear cubs trailed
behind their immense mother as she walloped a log with her paws, sending the chips scattering, and clawed out grubs. Later, a brindled black
wolf swam the Lamar River as we listened to the primeval bugles of
sandhill cranes and the stomps, exhales, and grunts of bison.

Snapping back to attention, I focused on this enclave of wildness I'd
come to know. I valued the richness of Rattlesnake Creek within a context of a wilder west of our past. After Yellowstone, I could better picture
this valley long before Europeans arrived, when the Salish camped to
fish in season and grizzlies trundled up and down the creek corridor.

Missoula's proximate wildness still exceeds most medium-sized
western cities. Wolves howl. Grizzlies are padding south into the Rattlesnake Wilderness from the Mission Mountains that tower above the
Flathead Valley. My nook of kingfishers on one bend of stream shines
like a crystal bead in a necklace within the Northern Continental Divide
Ecosystem, extending from Missoula into Canada and covering sixteen
thousand square miles—including Glacier National Park.

The forested path on the way had changed in three days with intriguing new blooms. Readying to cross the ditch to the island, I gasped
at a bodacious clump of mountain lady's slippers—a type of orchid.
The name for the genus *Cypripedium* derives from the Greek "Cypris,"
an early term for Aphrodite and from *pediolon* for sandal (the slipper
formed from the orchid's modified lip).

Three stoneflies had entered the blind. I picked one up to place on
my arm, the better to admire the long wings like stained glass etched in
brown. The creekside stones bore the shed skins of the nymphs with their
two long tails. If people could hear in the register of an adult stonefly,

they would note the drumming of a male as he taps his abdomen against a hard surface—and if he's lucky, a female would drum back.

What I did hear that morning were kingfisher calls like skipping stones skittering across the creek to the far side. Even so, two hours passed before Halcyon descended to the boulder with a stupendous fish held sideways, as if she'd sprouted a handlebar mustache. Her eager tail flipped up and down. Although edgy, she looked in a direction other than the blind. I bathed in the view of the classy queen holding court. In my journal, I wrote, "I'm ecstatic. Just when I'm feeling restless in the blind, she transforms this place, a bringer of life, yet in her bill, she clasps a very dead fish."

Returning at 3:30, I wondered if this would be a languorous or a romping afternoon. Five minutes later, as a dusky flycatcher hid in an alder a few feet from me, Ceyx landed on the boulder with a burst of *kkkk kkkkkk!* Without thinking, I turned my head. He flew away in a frenzy, but not before I could see his slicked-down crest from his recent dive and a fish clenched in his beak. Two minutes later, blue and white wings strobed by, flashing. Another minute passed. He landed, whistled up to the hole, dropped off the fish, and spurted off. Three minutes later, he returned with one more. A romp indeed.

Lisa took the evening watch and sent a note:

It was a peaceful evening by the creek. I got there at 6:08 p.m. The male showed up with a fish at 6:28 p.m. and landed on the boulder. He rattled, looked around briefly, and then delivered the fish and flapped upstream. The rest of my time was spent imagining kingfisher calls and thinking for sure I could hear chainsaws cutting down the forest. Neither turned out to be true. I left at 7:55 p.m.

ॐ

Willing kingfishers to come my way, I often heard sounds that my mind invented. "Shhhhhh. Isn't that a rattle?"

With each passing day, the longed-for fledging edged ever closer. Lisa had become equally obsessed. We exchanged notes in the blind, placing them in my trusty old copy of *Golden Guide to Birds of North America,* featuring kingfishers on the inside cover.

> Hi Lisa, the kingfishers got going an hour later. I arrived at 4:45 a.m. The female fed two fish in 17 minutes, arriving first at 6:56. The second time, I got caught! She rattled, flew downstream, and then entered the hole from upstream. At 7:18, the male delivered a fish. Left at 7:45 a.m. (June 18).

> Hi . . . Three deliveries. Male at 6 a.m., female 6:10; male at 7:05— Big Fish! Do you wonder if the adults know that a big fish should last them for a while? 8:05 leaving. (June 19).

Grasping a travel mug of coffee in one hand and over my right shoulder slinging a canvas bag heavy with my laptop, notebook, pens, and water bottle, I jumped the ditch. It was all too wonderful to leap out of bed at 5:20 a.m. and drive four miles up the road and hike to the blind, a half hour from bed to another home on a halcyon arc of stream where all that mattered was to witness.

Leaves glowed after the rain showers. Swainson's thrush song steamed skyward like a whistling tea kettle. This animal trail had become so known I could close my eyes and sense where the path angled downstream and then forked to the left and toward the waiting blind. Ponderosas, cottonwoods, and Douglas-firs crested high as ship masts above roller waves of mock orange, chokecherry, serviceberry, dogwood, and alder. A male western tanager streaked by in a flash of fruity colors—tangerine, lemon, and blackberry.

I often chewed on new questions, like, "Are these birds smart?"

Even after I'd spent a week in the blind situated twenty yards from the burrow, they still treated any motion at all from inside as a threat. With the camouflage flaps raised partway, I dared not move when the male or female commanded the boulder.

Kingfishers may be what scientists call "evolutionary smart." They don't habituate to us like a chickadee plucking a sunflower seed from between our thumb and forefinger. Instead, they are always on alert, especially with chicks in a burrow. A mink could slink up from the creek bank, a bull snake could slide into the nest, or a goshawk could even grab an adult from the boulder.

That could explain why the kingfishers stared, chittered, and surveyed for danger. I appreciated their watchfulness, which improved my stillness skills. Other birds (far less perturbed) came closer. A certain Swainson's thrush would land at arm's length from the blind. How could this subdued, brown, robin-sized bird with a white eye-ring open his beak and pour forth a glory of chorded notes? My father had an affinity for thrushes and opera. However, if he had to choose a favorite, he would have picked the ethereal song of the thrush.

An insect wriggled across the laptop keyboard like an animated long grain of rice. Bees, wasps, and flies hustled in and out whenever I opened the screens. Always, the creek resounded with gusts, sighs, and breezes. Like a mayfly rising and falling in the air currents above the waters, my brain fluttered with perplexities. How big were the chicks? When would they shuffle down the tunnel to peek into the sky? How would I make sure not to miss fledging? I'd circled June 27.

Eight days to go—maybe. Three minutes after settling into the blind at 5:50 a.m., Ceyx crystallized on the boulder. The creek roiled. His beak moved, but all sound belonged to the Rattlesnake. The snows were melting, and the pell-mell race of water overtook the songs of birds and of predators hunting prey. Ceyx turned toward me. I froze in the act of reaching for a granola bar with what I thought was the slowness of a sloth. Phew! He gave me a pass. When entering the hole, he pressed his wings tight, vanished, remerged, backed out, pivoted, and lifted away. I never tired of the dance move.

The fishing must have been fabulous in the high waters, which remained clear even in snowmelt. When Halcyon jigged in at 6:12, her crest wasn't even wet, as if she had scissored a flying fish. She wasted no time. After three seconds on the boulder, she flew to the hole. Ceyx returned at 6:26, gripping a fat fish. His calls seemed to urge, "Come closer!" The tactic worked, as if the chicks were almost at the entry. He bowed and departed. No time to waste with chit-chat.

The kingfishers quieted for an hour and a half. I never stopped looking at the hole. Blinking my weary eyes, I turned my attention to a historical account I'd brought with me.

In 1938, a naturalist named Henry Mousley observed a burrow in a pastoral scene where young boys tussling in the creek proved a nuisance to the kingfishers. One day, three cows ambled to the edge of the bank right above the nest. When the kingfisher parents returned, the pair "made the grove ring with their united rattlings." He wrote,

> First one and then the other would fly directly almost to the mouth of the hole, but instead of entering it, would rise up suddenly and fly over almost touching the backs of the three standing cows in an endeavor to frighten them away, whilst rattling all the time to show their displeasure at this intrusion of their home ground.

As a recipient of kingfisher "displeasure," I could imagine the scene. Deer often passed above the burrow, but what if a black bear plopped down for a rest? That would be a far greater possibility, where there were no cattle or children running wild.

ℰ

When Ian was seven, he met the bright-eyed and daring Clara, who would become an outdoor friend leading the way. Clara's mother and I cheered their continuing scrambles into thickets, building forts, climbing trees, and dunking in the creek. We welcomed their scratched, hungry, and grinning returns to the kitchen. Alone, Ian's tendency leaned toward reading.

Not long after I moved to Missoula from Oregon in 1986 to attend graduate school in journalism, I stumbled upon the urban wilds of Greenough Park. I'd often bring my notebook to jot ideas for the weekly column I wrote for *The Kaimin* (University of Montana's student newspaper). One day, as I scanned Rattlesnake Creek for a dipper, a boy of about ten came up to me and said, "Are you looking at that big bird up there?" He pointed to the perched osprey twenty feet above me. I had my theme, of missing the obvious and learning to see anew through a child's eyes.

A few months later, I'd joined a crusade to save the beavers that Mountain Water Company had proposed to trap in an ill-advised attempt to rid Rattlesnake Creek of giardia, a water-borne parasite, which entered Missoula's water supply in 1983. Until then, the creek served the city with "pure" drinking water. The company then tapped the valley's aquifer, with the creek as a backup supply. Although beavers can spread giardia, so do many other animals, including pets, livestock, and people.

We called ourselves CASTOR, Citizens Against Senseless Trapping Of Rodents (*Castor canadensis* is the scientific name for beaver). I wrote a column chastising Mountain Water Company and lauding the beaver as a keystone species. Without the keystone, the ecology collapses. Someone cut out the column and posted a laminated copy on a prominent sign within Greenough Park. I was pleased. The head of Mountain Water Company was not. We did win the fight, and beavers continue to dam various arms of the creek, creating pools that serve as nurseries for young trout, the prey of kingfishers.

I've known and defended this creek over the years; at last, I was becoming an inhabitant. My idea of community was shifting. My home creek had become a sentient being, the holder of all stories, sustaining life and carrying memories toward a confluence.

ॐ

The night's rain lacquered the forest. It was 5:50 a.m. on June 20, a week before the potential fledging day. For almost two hours, I waited for a kingfisher's arrival. A day earlier, Lisa had counted three feedings in the early morning. I could not discern a pattern of heightened feeding times. When least expecting the birds to show up—say, in the heat of the day—one or both would arrive with fish. Whenever a kingfisher cascaded in, all musing ceased.

At 7:20 a.m., I wrote, "Fish delivery! She flies in from upstream—*k_k_k_k_k_k_k_k!*"

The fledging day was close at hand. We did not want to miss the show.

CHAPTER 5
Fledging

> It's a different kind of world to grow up in when you're out in the forest with the little chipmunks and the great owls. All these things are around you as presences, representing forces and powers and magical possibilities of life that are not yours and yet are all part of life, and that opens it out to you. Then you find it echoing in yourself, because you are nature.
>
> —Joseph Campbell, *The Power of Myth*

Summer solstice. June twenty-first. Would the miraculous event come on the longest day, even if drizzly and dreary? As mythic birds of the winter solstice, the young kingfishers must surely feel an irresistible draw toward the light sifting into their darkness.

In one hour and ten minutes, I'd clocked new speed and size records of four feedings, with each trout close to five inches long. First Halcyon, then Ceyx, then Halcyon, and then Ceyx. For once, the diligent parents did not care about slight motions within the blind.

All was quiet for an hour, except for a hummingbird whirring above the waters. On the inside of the tent screen crawled a paperclip-sized aphid assassin with sea-green wings and golden eyes. To be fair, most species of adult green lacewings tend to be nectar eaters, but the young larvae with grabbing mandibles? Fierce devourers.

The round dark hole reminded me of *sipapu*, a Tewa word for the place of emergence from a prior world. In Hopi, the word is *sipapuni*. The fully feathered young kingfishers would soon appear at the hole entry, one at a time. This was their *sipapu*. Ahead lay the immensity of a fluid creek, rooted trees, and boundless sky.

⁗

At age eighteen, I graduated from Concord-Carlisle High School half-way through my senior year to explore the west for the next several months. My father encouraged the adventure. He, too, missed the big wild country. First, I flew to Seattle and hopped on a Greyhound bus to visit colleges in Washington, Oregon, and California, and then wound all the way to New Mexico.

On the long bus ride, I read James Michener's saga of a novel *Centennial*, passaging through the time of dinosaurs, early inhabitants, Arapahos, mountain men, and cowboys until stumbling off the bus at Farmington, only to find my trusty frame blue Kelty backpack was no longer in the luggage. The pack found its way back to me a week later, dustier and torn.

For three months, I volunteered at what is now the Chaco Culture National Historical Park, the site of the most elaborate and confounding of all ancient Pueblo civilizations. Prairie falcons carved the infinite sky above Fajada Butte. Canyon wren song trickled down the arid mesas that bore the spirits of the long dead. From 850 to 1250 AD, many people converged in this land of little rain for ceremonies, traditions, and knowledge sharing, according to their Puebloan descendants. Within great houses like Pueblo Bonita are kivas of all sizes. Each ceremonial round room features a small *sipapu* in the center, by a larger sunken round firepit.

I spent weeks submerged in the mysteries of ancient people, and one unforgettable day among the Hopi as a guest of park superintendent Walter Herriman and his wife Eleanor. Over the years, the Herrimans often traveled to a sky-filled mesa as honorary members of a Hopi family. I can almost taste the blue corn tortillas ground, shaped, and baked in their adobe oven. Then, we had stepped into the plaza and a timeless ritual of costumed, painted men and women dancing the seasons and stories of their people, who had emerged from darkness to the First World, the Second World, the Third World, and into this Fourth World.

Within this hole I was watching, the chicks were cocooned, except for a pinpoint of light. Even the soil seemed alive. The young kingfishers edged ever closer to the *sipapu*.

ಜಿ

On the afternoon of June 23, the calm felt deceptive, as if the curtain were about to rise. Sunlight flirted over the columnar Douglas-firs above the burrow bank. A spider wove a web of perfection. Rough-winged swallows wrote invisible program notes on the sky.

I waited for an hour until a rattling volley jolted my reveries. Two breaths later, Halcyon alighted on the boulder, chittered, and snared me with her incriminating look. My presence was still a threat. Halcyon tweaked her tail once and then twice, keeping a firm grasp on a prized trout. She perched parallel to me with her feathery crest flung back, as if buffeted by wind. Turning toward the burrow, she escalated to the entry. I pictured the juvenile with beak open wide and inching toward the light.

A stocky dipper ruffled by on sturdy wings; castanets of calls receded in the wake of passing. Eight minutes passed. Halcyon was back, parking on the boulder with her next slippery fish before the quick transfer. The creek had slowed in the summer lassitude, even as I grew energized by the coming event. Whitewater nudged and nipped the landing boulder that knew the toes of kingfishers, the tickle of wingtips, and reverberations of rattles deep within glacial knowing.

A few years earlier, I'd learned of living rocks in the company of Wilbert Fish, a Blackfeet ethnobotanist and herbalist. I remember a certain twinkle in his wide eyes beneath glasses as he told me the medicinal qualities of sagebrush and smaller plants nestled among the bunchgrasses. I was gathering information for writing a nature trail brochure for the First Peoples Buffalo Jump State Park, near Great Falls, Montana.

We hiked up the switchbacks under a scorching sun and passed more than one rattlesnake seeking shade. Here, his ancestors and other tribes had driven herds over the buffalo jump that in Blackfeet is Pis'kun, kettle of blood. Above us, a golden eagle saddled the wind. Wilbert, who wore his black hair in braids, pointed to a round bear-sized rock and recounted the story of the boulder chasing Napi to regain the buffalo robe that the trickster had first given and then stolen.

After gazing so long at the kingfisher boulder, I could imagine the similar-sized rock rolling across the creek toward me, an admonishment of all my spying on Halcyon and Ceyx.

ℰℐ

Rattlesnake Creek chorused in ever-changing verses and singers, from the bass notes of rocks tumbling on rocks to the bubbling tenor of flung droplets arcing into the air. In one soporific lull, I mulled over a scintilla of an early morning dream; the kingfisher chicks had at last fledged, and they were as big as pelicans.

The sun was no longer on the blind. Chill advanced with the shade. To warm up, I jumped the ditch and entered a sunny glade in the pines. Stretching with arms high to the sky, I imagined exchanging the burrow darkness for the fiesta of Rattlesnake Creek.

ℰℐ

Clouds smoldered below Stuart Peak, a beacon of the Rattlesnake Wilderness and visible from my house. Heading to the blind in early morning with renewed hopes of fledging, I thought how my relationship with the open peak had become intimate since the prior November 24, the day before I turned fifty, and the day Ian and I hiked to the summit bearing my father's ashes.

Ian was five when my dad died, yet he has inherited his grandfather's endurance. On that grueling round-trip trek of eighteen miles that started in the bitter cold and ended in chill and darkness, I witnessed his cheerful resolve. When at last we came within a quarter mile of the top, the snow deepened. With each step, I broke through the crust up to my thighs. Ian, who was light as a weasel, scampered along the surface. I faltered, and it was Ian who encouraged me to keep going. The high-elevation whitebark pine forest fell away below us. The sun shone in a blue sky of a shortening day. There on the windswept Stuart Peak, a flock of redpolls flew past us like a living wind.

It was time. I took off the pack and lifted out the packet of ashes. Ian and I stepped closer to the dizzying drop-off to the north. The breeze whispered. We took turns reaching in the sandwich bag for a handful of ashes. With each toss, we offered a remembrance.

"Here's to Dad soaring like a red-tailed hawk." I flung a half of a fist-ful to the north, and the ashes feathered into a blue void above a string of alpine lakes.

"Here's to all the stories you told me about Granddad, especially the one about the bees," said Ian as he pulled back his arm and threw. Watch-ing Ian with so much love, I remembered a scene a few days before Dad died. To find relief from pain, he lay on his back on the living room rug with his knees up and feet down. Ian, who was then in kindergarten, dropped down next to him, mimicking the exact pose. It was then Dad told him the story, one that I had never heard before.

As a little boy with shoulder-length blond curls, he had toddled outside into a bright yellow swarm of beautiful things dancing in the air. He entered the humming cloud with arms wide as if to gather up the dazzling rays of sunlight. Instead, he felt throbbing pain and fled back inside, where his mother tended each bee sting, as I tried to do for Ian whenever my son encountered the injustices of life.

And so it went. Before each throw a tribute to a memory, a lesson, a funny expression like, "Here's to 'it's just around the next bend!'" That one Ian knew well, as I continued my father's tradition of cajoling him up switchback trails, although, on this day, my son never needed urging or bribing with promises of broken-off squares of Kendal Mint Cake. I asked Ian whether he would like the honor of sending the final remnant of his grandfather into the wilderness.

"Let's put the rest right here on the top, Mom, so that we can come back and visit, and I'll bring my kids, and they'll bring their kids," he said.

We sprinkled ashes on the brow of Stuart Peak and set a part of my father's spirit loose into the high western mountains he loved to climb.

Whenever I touch the waters of Rattlesnake Creek, I know a few of those nurturing ashes filtered into headwaters to become part of the web of life that nets aquatic insects, young trout, and kingfisher chicks.

ဆ

From within the blind, I tapped the news of a yellow-rumped warbler's two-part ascending trill. An hour passed before Halcyon showed up with the lunkiest fish of the season. Her call was a thrilling triplet phrase of *chkchk! . . . CHKCHK! . . . chkchk!* She repeated the rising and falling phrase three times. Her fish was dark and shiny with speckles, maybe six inches long.

A friend once asked me, how does a kingfisher call with a fish in her bill? Whereas we need exhaled breath for our vocal chords to vibrate, birds do not. The secret lies in the syrinx (a word of Greek origin, for the pipes of Pan), located at the base of the lower trachea, which divides into two bronchi, the tubes connecting the right and left lungs. Only birds possess this resonating chamber. Just as a violinist or guitarist presses fingers on strings harder or softer to change pitch, so can a bird apply specialized muscles to the membranes.

The syrinx in birds varies in complexity. For example, parrots can mimic human speech and songbirds can sing melodious riffs. A kingfisher's syrinx may not rival that of songbirds, yet what other bird can so closely evoke the music of the stream?

On cue, Halcyon gave a lilting series of single notes with a fish in her bill before she scaled the vertical air, her flight a cadenza. Six minutes later, at 7:01 a.m., Ceyx landed with calls like a percussionist playing kettle drums ever faster. He gripped a fish about five and a half inches long, his biggest yet. Facing away, he opened his wings to show the twilight sky of his back and wings—stars on dusky blue feathers. Winging up to the hole, he entered farther in than Halcyon, until the tip of his perky tail was just visible. After the customary bow, back up, and turn sans fish, he flew upstream.

The parents were on top of their game. With each larger fish they delivered, their young edged closer to impending flight.

⁐

This was not the time to be cavalier, yet on June 25 I was late. After helping pack for Ian's soccer tournament in Seattle, I arrived breathless at the blind at 10:05 a.m. It didn't help to be limping with a sharp knee pain after a recent twenty-mile trail run, yet another injury thwarting my desire to trace the creekside trajectories of kingfishers—a counterpoint to hours of staying put. I'd also hoped to chalk enough miles to run a marathon in honor of my father. Was I taking on too much? And at what cost?

The day before, Lisa observed Halcyon entering the burrow with a fish and staying for a full thirty seconds, disproving my assumption of a new phase of quick drop-offs. Inside, were the lusty juveniles busy in a fish tug-of-war?

Opening a side window flap a few inches more, I flushed a kingfisher in a tree only a few feet above the blind. Battle cry. Heart pound. The parents were guarding the burrow with extra acuity. Lisa, too, had upset one on her arrival yesterday.

Ceyx fizzed by like a blue-and-white sparkler. For the first time in my observations, he emitted a sharp ringing phrase as he passed by the hole. Twelve minutes later, I wrote in all caps, "WOW! FIRST NESTLING HEAD APPEARS AT ENTRY OF THE BURROW HOLE!!"

The first chick of my longing appeared in a hesitant foray, blinking in sunshine. The sprightly crest was navy blue. The black eyes gleamed. The angling bill probed the earth for a few seconds before backing out of view.

Three minutes later, Halcyon swooshed by. Five minutes passed. Ceyx seared past the entry. His catenation of notes gave a clear message: "We're not coming in to feed you. Come. Come out."

A chick peered out for a full two minutes, drinking in the planet before retreating. After all was quiet for a good ten minutes, I took a chance to duck out for a needed break. Ceyx was poised on a low branch only five feet from me. His scalding calls matched the scorching flight away. Counting on a hiatus after the transgression, I opened Dan's dissertation to the fledging section. He described a male tempting the nestlings by bringing a fish, perching within view, and rattling.

Ten more minutes. Then, a chick glanced up, down, side to side, and withdrew. A half hour later, a sibling leaned out of the hole so far that I could see the buffed bronze colors in the slaty-blue band below the white neck feathers. That poplin of blues and coppers is the telling detail of juvenile plumage for males and females alike.

Ceyx again whooshed by without pause. The youngster popped inside the tunnel and reappeared, only to be confronted by a rough-winged swallow inches away. Retreat. Lisa joined me at 1 p.m., and I gave her a run-down of chick sightings. Not once had I seen either parent feed a fish to their hungry offspring.

Sudden winds pummeled the blind. Clouds billowed. Then, a curious juvenile poked out a midnight-blue crested head and tilted a bill upward as if to examine the sky. Lisa's eyes were wide—and her smile? How could I describe—like halcyon, an indelible moment of pure joy.

Another nestling took a turn, opening and closing a bill. We could hear the soft series of notes. Three minutes later, Ceyx landed on the boulder with a fish of light and dark grays. The head-first position indicated he would offer the fish, but no. He called. The chick chittered. Ceyx stroked up to the burrow and veered off. The juvenile watched his departing flight with what we had to believe was dismay.

A few minutes later, a soggy-crested Ceyx flew back, clenching a fish with a white underbelly and reddish-yellow spines. He chattered three times to the chick at the entry. Again, he flew up from the rock and skimmed past the burrow. The chick gave a plaintive *kkkkkk . . . kkkkk!* An encouraging reply drifted down from upstream. For the next hour, we noted the flyby of Ceyx every few minutes and the duet with the juvenile. Halcyon was nowhere in sight.

At 2:16 p.m., Ceyx hastened into the burrow with a fish. Three seconds later, he flew off with the fish. A chick at the entry opened an empty beak. Confused? A minute later, Ceyx was on the boulder with the same trout—rattling, rattling, and rattling. Lisa and I sat next to each other, unmoving, transfixed.

My notes were multiple bullets. Like sportscasters in lowered voices, we called the play-by-play of Ceyx teasing the youngsters with fish. His flights past the burrow were speedy, his calls insistent, and the fledging seemed imminent.

I wrote seventeen entries from 2:23 to 3:04 p.m. and logged five straight hours at the blind. Lisa's presence stoked the fires of a dramatic afternoon, and her eyes danced with creek shine. The laptop battery had run out of power. I switched to a notebook. A chick took a bold stride forward to lean halfway out, pulled back, tilted forward, and backpedaled.

After I left to greet Ian at home, Paul joined Lisa, and the action slowed as the light waned.

એ

Why would Ceyx take on the role of luring the young kingfishers to first flight? Only yesterday Halcyon bore the trophy fish to the burrow. So far, anecdotal findings supported Dan Albano's, of the male assuming greater responsibility in the final days. Both birds had dug the burrow, incubated, and fed the young. However, Halcyon laid the eggs, one a day until time to brood. Maybe this was simply the moment for Ceyx to step up.

If nature is more about fitness than fairness, is there some advantage to the male who defends this territory to assure his progeny thrives? Is there a stronger attachment to place than for the female who migrates in winter and returns to seek a mate with a premier fishing spot and burrow bank? Questions punctuated a day of exclamation marks.

ॐ

The dawn walk toward the burrow on June 26 resonated with the chorale of warblers, flycatchers, buntings, vireos, and thrushes; I heard the kingfisher soloist as I edged into the blind.

Halcyon was back. At 5:55 a.m., she flew to the boulder with a thrumming of insistent notes. She clamped a littler fish in her bill than I'd seen the whole week. A chick leaned so far out I could see the tiny feet pressed on the entry furrows. Halcyon sped toward the hole with the fish, jinked away, and returned to the rock. The exchange continued as yesterday, except Ceyx joined her. Once he flew so close to Halcyon that if she'd flung out a wing an inch farther, they would have brushed by like lovers touching hands.

Then, I listened to something I'd never heard, a three-part harmony of Ceyx, Halcyon, and a chick. After Ceyx flew away, she continued her coaxing calls. After ten minutes of crisscrossing flight, Halcyon dropped off a fish.

Seven minutes after Halcyon's conclusion-defying arrival, Ceyx graced the boulder with a warbling phrase. He pumped his head up and down, shaking the sardine-sized trout in his bill. When his mate whooshed by, even her call flickered at a higher velocity. Ceyx called for three minutes. No chick appeared at the entry.

Finally, he flew up to the burrow. "Fish delivery. 6:05 a.m.," I noted. My fingers were white with morning chill. The saga unfolded as both parents continued to fly by with chicks begging. Once, I almost leaped up after a skirl of a bagpipe-worthy screech. How was I spotted?

In this past week, the birds had ignored the blind, unless they spied one of us coming or going. All had changed in the pre-fledging time of danger. Their long-protected chicks now would be exposed. Through the magnification of the spotting scope, I noticed subtle differences. One chick's blackish bill was lighter, another's coppery-blue upper band seemed brighter. I drank in every detail, like the flash of a nictitating membrane over an eye. When a beak opened and closed, the rhythm was like the rolling waves of the creek below.

There was one problem. I had an appointment I could not cancel. I would miss two hours. Lisa would watch. Preoccupied, all I wanted to do was race back. When I slid back into the blind undetected, she told me the big news: a chick had fledged at 10:26 a.m., only ten minutes after I had left. I was crestfallen. Now I know the meaning of that word, like a slicked-down kingfisher crest that was once perky. Lisa told me how it happened—the juvenile calling and then flailing forward on spread wings to glide across the lustered creek to the waiting parent in a tree. Together, they flew downstream to fade into the woven basketry of pliant willow and fluid cascade.

I did not budge for two hours until, at 2:45 p.m., a nestling's head popped out like a jack-in-the-box with wee feet set in the twin furrow grooves. Relief.

Later that evening, Lisa joined me in my long blind stint with a gift of crickets in a sandwich bag for Ian's pet gecko named Bluefire. She also uncorked a bottle of wine. The fledging party commenced. A little tipsy and mesmerized, we watched same chick, imagining the pattering forward from dark to light and the retreat to dark, only to gain courage once again. Over wine, we had become chatty. Lisa confided she was ordering the same blind.

"Where will you put it?"

"In the schoolyard. It's for me. So I can hide from the kids."

Laughing, we packed up in the twilight and crossed the ditch without mishap. When the evening song of the Swainson's thrush coiled above the cottonwoods, the lullaby soothed the remaining chick or chicks to sleep—maybe for the last time in this burrow.

ꝏ

It was Saturday morning, June 27, at 5:38 a.m. of the predicted day. The dawn was bracing and cloudless. I'd heard a kingfisher calling as I entered the blind. Seven minutes later, Ceyx landed on the boulder with a silvery trout twice the length of his bill. He gave a prolonged stuttering sequence of notes. The coaxing session continued for several minutes with flybys and landings.

Lisa arrived two hours later. We admired a spider with an oversized abdomen on a mass of white silk that she had spun on the screen window. After seventeen days, the blind had become habitat.

Halcyon landed on a boulder with a fish surpassing the male's five-incher. Her no-nonsense, multisyllabic phrase reminded me of a track coach announcing a tough workout. But the message was not for the chicks. She stared at the blind as if to pierce the nylon fabric. Lisa stayed for an hour. I kept watch for five more. Hours passed with intermittent warbler song, rough-winged swallow arcs, hummingbird hum, creek yawn, and not a flash of a kingfisher sighting.

Somehow, maybe on a brief break, I'd missed the final fledging.

Mid-afternoon. A rough-winged swallow landed on the lip of the burrow. After eight hours mostly in the blind, I stepped into the sunshine. A pair of flycatchers quipped from an overhead limb, their two-notes forming my question: "What now?"

Taking off my shoes and socks and wiggling toes in the creek, I reread Dan's email of June 18, which I had printed out and carried with me for this past week:

When the nestlings do start tumbling out, it can happen all at once, in an hour, while other times it can take over a day or two—one or more might be too chicken and stay at the entrance. When that happens, the parents feed and herd fledglings in the trees and then go back to the nest trying to lure out the stragglers. After they're all out, they will stick together in a loose band, most likely wherever the parents do their fishing. Then, kind of like Brownian motion, they just slowly drift apart and away over the next weeks.

Somewhere, young kingfishers on beginner wings careened through the pine-scented air above Rattlesnake Creek. Somewhere, Ceyx and perhaps Halcyon flew near them. They would still feed their young and teach them skills, but not for long.

How much is life like Brownian motion, a physics term for the erratic and random movement of particles as they collide with molecules in a fluid? By circling this one tight place on the planet, I'd experienced wonders by being open to all that is random and erratic. Everywhere I sensed the presence of kingfishers—napping, perching, fishing, flying, hovering, and autographing Rattlesnake Creek.

❧

Before the day's end, Lisa and I decided to ford the fast-flowing creek and press our hands on the entry, the *sipapu* of kingfishers.

Pulling on snug river sandals, we attempted to cross upstream of the island in smoother waters above the little rapid that runs down past the burrow. We each held a beaver-stripped cottonwood branch staff for balance. Lisa led the way into the icy water. The current tugged hard. I admired Lisa's steadiness as the water deepened to her waist. Lifting each foot with the slowness of a heron, I flailed for balance. If I fell, I'd be bashed and bruised before I could paw to shore. Just then, Ceyx flew downstream, close by our heads and with a chuckle as if to say—"You're no threat to me anymore, and you don't belong in the water."

Message received. Signaling to Lisa, I retreated. She waved and kept going. Tenacity. As my white feet tingled in the welcoming sun, Lisa pressed through clusters of willows, dogwoods, and alders to the hole a few feet above her. She put one foot on the sliding soil and found purchase, stepping up until she was beaming her flashlight into the nest hole. Crossing back to my side without incident, she told me that the tunnel took a right turn, as if the birds had dug around a root.

Back at home, I sent the day's report to Dan, who responded five minutes later: "sounds like you were very diligent, but maybe just got a bad break—most likely the last nestling popped out before 5:30 a.m." Early morning is not typical for fledging, and Dan wondered whether the chick had built up courage during the night: "You may not have seen much anyway, with just the one, because it probably just swooped down over the water and landed clumsily on the other side. Then it probably made a lot of noise, and when a parent showed up, both flew away."

He wasn't surprised that the parents continued to fly back and forth past the burrow, suggesting they would want to make sure all the chicks had fledged, and also out of habit, a reflection of the "rote/mechanical avian mind." Maybe we all have something of that rote mind when it comes to parental worry and double-checking where a child might be. Dan then advised I search a neighboring pond or backwater for fledglings "waiting around dopily and staring at things, with sporadic fits of activity and noise whenever a parent comes around with a fish."

The kingfishers had left. Lisa was the only one among us to see one fledge. The other juveniles took their first flights when we weren't looking. The good news? We knew where to find them.

ஐ

The next morning, I intended to head straight to the pond at Mountain Water Dam, returning to the courtship scene of April. Instead, like the kingfisher pair, I was drawn back to the fledging hole. I let the Brownian motion ping me in that direction when I left the house at dawn. Luna was with me. We sat outside the blind on the stream edge in the sunshine and I stroked her thick fur.

Euphoria had swept through me on April 11 with courting aerial kingfishers high above the pines, and on June 4 as Halcyon flew into the lost burrow, and once more when I saw the first chick, blinking in the kaleidoscope of creek, stone, forest, and sky—all new, and all for the first time.

Frustration and humility had marked May, the month of seeking and not finding the nest. Yet, my vigils were far from fruitless. When my best friend Sandra had joined me by the creek, I still fretted, yet rejoiced, too, in the ways our hushed exclamations amplified the small wonders of the neighborhood, from the vine maple leaves feather dusting the sky to the wind-up toy commotions of a pine squirrel.

After finding the nest hole on that breakthrough day of June 4, I found happiness accentuated, refined, and honed by the counterpoint of kingfishers coming and going. Watching their fierce, unstoppable devotion to their chicks deepened my connection to the birds as a mother of the son I loved.

Washed in feelings, I hugged Luna and then stood up. On cue, she stretched her front and back legs. We meandered downstream to where the young kingfishers were likely assembling. Even as I felt anticipation, I was not rushing. Why would I? This was all home.

CHAPTER 6

Art of Flying and Fishing

> If you watch carefully when a kingfisher is hovering, you'll see the head remains stationary in the air, holding a fixed position over the water, while the wings flap, the tail adjusts, and the body shifts around, doing the work of flying. It's important to hold the head steady so that the eyes can remain fixed on a potential target below, but the sense and the control involved in this are truly remarkable. The bird has to have an exquisitely delicate sense of body position so that it can adjust wings and tail to compensate for air movements.
>
> —David Allen Sibley, *What It's Like to Be a Bird*

A kingfisher fledgling pecked at the bark of a ponderosa branch only fifteen feet above me. A second youngster bumped to a landing on the same limb, greeting his sibling with carefree chitter. The two males shook their wings, exposing reddish feathers down the sides of their bellies, colors they would lose as adults. Their single breast bands below white neck rings glowed like burning coals, bronzy plumage also marking them as juveniles.

After a chat, they zigzagged off to the far side of the pond and skidded with jarring bounces on a concrete ledge that divided the small reservoir from the main creek channel. An incoming triplet of single syllables cleaved the sultry air. Halcyon hovered above the unruffled pond, dove, plucked a trout from the surface, and flapped back up to the ledge where her two offspring waited. She walloped the fish on the concrete and turned the four-inch trout from crosswise to lengthwise. One of the young kingfishers opened his bill wide and gulped down the meal. The other looked on. Halcyon had twice defied expectations—showing up for the fledging finale and now feeding her young at the pond behind Mountain Water Dam.

Soon after cheering for the two juvenile males, I was thrilled to see their sister, replete with the telling coppery blue upper band and a carnelian red belt sweeping across her white belly—unlike her mother's unclasped one.

Only a few days after leaving the nest hole, the juveniles had entered a critical phase of flight training. Hollow bones and feathered wings were the given essentials, but the nuances of flying kingfisher-style would take practice. Before striking the pond's surface, Halcyon had first hovered with her head rock steady and then morphed into a streamlined rocket, entering the water at a steep angle, with only a breath of resistance, to outwit a nimble fish.

Even horizontal flight varies in complexity depending on the intent. I'd noted a familiar pattern of several rapid beats and then a glide with wings half-closed, followed by more downstrokes. I'd also seen kingfishers lower their heads to become aerodynamic and accelerate with muscular flaps. Add slaloming around trees and reversing course with precision, and the fledglings had much to learn.

Every kind of bird perfects a flight style adapted for occupation. You can tell much by wing shape. A bald eagle passively soars on plank-like wings with long primary feathers, which extend into the air, creating slots to capture vertical warm rising air and help the massive bird float across the sky. A gull actively soars on long narrow wings that serve for gliding and fast flying with the aid of air currents.

High-speed wings are always slender. Think swifts, falcons, terns, and sandpipers. A rounded wing shape plunks the kingfisher within a pack of nonspecialists. Other birds in this category include blackbirds, sparrows, robins, and ravens (exceptional stunt flyers).

&

When I interviewed avian flight specialist Dr. Bret Tobalske of University of Montana, I found another belted kingfisher fan.

"Nothing about their flight anatomy emerges as particularly unusual, and yet they behave in a particularly unusual way," he said. Bret had that look of a scientist who might study grizzly bears, with his black beard and burly physique. Instead, he'd found a niche as a hummingbird expert

and continues to direct the university's field research station at Fort Missoula and oversee a state-of-the-art bird flight laboratory.

Kingfishers "hold the corner on the market" for rounded-wing birds when it comes to multiple styles, he said, from chattering flight to hovering, quick turns, plunging dives, and liftoffs. Competing every day in the air, kingfishers sprint, plummet, climb, hover, perform courtship flights, and skim so low that each downstroke of the wing appears to chalk the water. The typical "strolling" is the flap and glide that's fuel-efficient.

What Bret told me about chattering flight surprised me. He was referring to a modified version of flap and glide, with the glide replaced by slow, shallow wingbeats. Another bird known for this flight adaptation is the black-billed magpie. Bret explained that the "chattering" term comes from the era of propeller planes in wartime. To maximize their range, the pilots would accelerate and rapidly climb, reduce thrust, and slowly descend without turning off the propeller (blades shaped like wings designed to produce thrust—lift in a forward direction). In this way, pilots could fly farther on the same amount of fuel than if they had kept the propeller power constant.

I could see applicability. Take gliding with an acceleration. As a long-distance runner prone to injuries, I knew that the repetition of one foot after another for miles accentuated any imbalances. Throw in quick steps and a shift of pace, and I might feel some extra running power. Leaning slightly forward on downhills, I could let gravity take over and fly a little faster without effort.

In this search for the halcyon bird, I'd begun noticing bird flight anew; even the kingfisher tango was more than a quick-quick . . . slow. Navigating the skies, all birds stay aloft on wings that serve as airfoils. The curved shape accelerates the air over the upper surfaces of the wing, which causes lower air pressure above the wing and higher air pressure below the wing. Voila! Lift happens.

In kingfishers, with each downstroke the feathers press together to form an airfoil to push the bird forward. On the upstroke, they separate for air to pass between them. The fan-blade shape of the wing generates weight support and thrust. Another force comes into play for landing. Drag is essential for slowing down. Both the structure and alignment of flight feathers are keys to deceleration. Spreading feathers wide for more air to slot through slows a bird. Drag cannot exceed lift, or a bird would fall like a stone.

Within the basics of belted kingfisher flight come multiple variations, including intermittently folding wings in a bounding flight, like woodpeckers. Other times? They enjoy the glide. When it comes to liftoff, Bret had more praise for the kingfisher. Typically, a bird shoves off from a branch with toes and legs for initial power, and then the wings paddle down hard. Think of that boost when swimming laps by pushing off the pool edge with both feet.

After a kingfisher dives, she smacks her wings on the soft surface of water (hence the splash) to launch upward. To gain gravity-defying vertical lift takes mighty chest muscles, more than most other birds. So many times, I'd watched the act of spearing the water and ascension. Now I knew this was no effortless bounce. With that superpower, nothing could upset my day.

Bret wasn't done with accolades, especially when it came to hovering, a favorite subject for a researcher of hummingbirds, the only true hoverers. Helicoptering in place without the aid of wind, hummers' minuscule wings revolve in a blur of figure eights. Mobile shoulder joints allow their wings to twist and generate lift on forward and backward strokes.

In contrast, a kingfisher hovers by flying into the wind at a speed equal to that of the wind. Flapping fast with the body rocking and rolling takes superb neural control of neck muscles to absorb the motion and keep the head fixed in place. With eyes fixed on the prey below, the hover becomes a fermata—in music, the pause that is prelude to drama.

৪১

Like kids in a gym class performing drills, the fledglings repeated many takeoffs and landing that ranged from clumsy to cool. Over the next few days at the pond, I was relieved every time I counted all three juveniles. Why weren't there six or seven as I'd anticipated? It seemed like such a small brood for all the activity over the past month at the burrow.

Reporting to Dan on the brood of three, he speculated the parents may have each taken half the family at fledging, or that three chicks of a bigger brood had survived, an unlikely scenario. The other possibility? Halcyon had laid three eggs, also highly unusual. "Let me know if you see the female again," he said. "I always had the suspicion that they tended to stop parenting before the male, but it's hard to say."

Ceyx stepped up as the lone parent offering some vestige of food and safekeeping for his offspring mastering the art of flying and fishing. I'd seen Halcyon only once.

The more I learned about flight, the more I wished I could ask my father, with his experience as a US Navy jet pilot and then a Marine Corps captain in the mid-1950s. As a pilot of the Grumman F9F Panther (the first jet of the Blue Angels) and then the Grumman F-9 Cougar, my father had the "right stuff," keeping his nerve in tight formations and executing touch-and-go landing on aircraft carriers in the Atlantic.

ॐ

On the third day out of the nest, a juvenile male flopped headfirst off
the low ledge three times into the pond. Even without catching fish,
his maneuver showed ability, especially powering up off the water. His
female sibling observed, as if to gain a few tips, but when next I saw her
land, she toppled face-first on the ledge.

When I arrived on the first of July, in early afternoon, the gates were
open to the compound. Three men in orange work shirts lounged at the
pond's edge on lunch break. I got off my bike, took a deep breath, and
walked right in to announce, "I'm here to watch the kingfishers." The
workers' boss, Jack, balding and jovial, said he'd known about me ever
since I called Mountain Water Company in the spring.

"Sure wish I'd brought my BB gun," he said in that joking Montana
guy kind of way.

I smiled back and shrugged as I turned away.

"Hey, I'd really like to see those kingfishers. Think you'd come on in
and show me one?"

While the other men munched sandwiches, we walked to the junc-
ture of the pond, the creek, and the dam. As I set up the spotting scope,
all three young kingfishers whizzed past us over the dam and downstream. They formed a resplendent trio of blue with white baubles on
their wings and that dash of reddish feathery bling. One landed in a
leaning fir tree with improving accuracy. I focused the scope on the juvenile female, who was looking a tad disheveled.

I nodded to Jack. He squinted through the scope for a long time.
When at last he turned to me again, there were no more comments
about BB guns. The crew was there to close the fish ladder and open
the dam's gates so the stream could rush unconfined, he said. The pond
would have enough water to stay full.

Within a half hour, Jack and the crew left. Solitude prevailed. Five
days after fledging day, the young kingfishers began to show skittish-
ness. No longer could I swagger right up to them. Like their parents,
they knew to give a racketing flourish and fling away. Their flying, diving,
and even perching mostly progressed, too. I cheered when one juvenile
balanced and swayed on a supple bending willow limb at the base of

the sedimentary cliff. The longer I studied the rock face, the more the furrows and clefts took shape as noses, lips, mustaches, bird beaks, and even a pirate with an eye patch.

Under a periwinkle sky of mid-afternoon, wearing a tee-shirt and shorts, I watched a spotted sandpiper fly on skinny wings as if to snip the air. Rough-winged swallows skimmed the pond surface, scooping up insects. A swallowtail butterfly flitted in midair like an errant yellow leaf. A dipper dipped, dipped, and dipped. A red-breasted nuthatch called a nasal *yank*, and a song sparrow offered his version of the mnemonic, *maids-maids-maids-put-on-your-tea-kettle-ettle ettle*. A western wood peewee sang a keening high-to-low phrase of *Peeeeeeer*. Bees chirred. Coiling ripples marked fish rising.

From the cliffside, a kingfisher's call whipped the languorous air. Ceyx smoked down from a ledge to land on a spindly cottonwood branch at the upstream edge of the pond. The waiting fledgling turned his head to keep him in view. I compared parent and offspring, the same size and yet so different. Besides the youngster's shorter bill, darker blue head, and bronze flecks on a slaty blue neck ring, there was a certain insouciance.

Ceyx was focused. And junior? Even with all his flight advances, he reminded me of one of those stuffed animals that you squeeze to make a squeaky call. Dopey? A little. The brave young male emitted a buoyant rattle cry and belly-flopped into the pond. I felt a surge of pride. He flapped up unsteadily, leveled out to fly over to my side of the pond, and stuck the landing like a gymnast. Bravo.

Ceyx remained motionless, tilting his beak downward. A finger-nail-sized feather dangled from the tip of his bill, perhaps from the last time he fed one of the fledglings. I'd offer a napkin if I could.

A floating common merganser shook her chestnut crested head, accentuated by her formidable scarlet fishing bill. A kingfisher dives from above to fish, while a merganser swims underwater, kicking her webbed feet set far back on her body. She snatches prey in her serrated beak. As the merganser preened her feathers, Ceyx stayed in full-on fishing mode, never flinching.

Another fledgling plopped down on the ledge not far from Ceyx. This spunky male dove and nabbed a floating object, flapped back to the shelf, and swallowed. Was that edible? He then dropped down headfirst to scissor what looked like the scale of a pinecone. He beat the object on the ledge with his bill and then shook his head hard. He rearranged the thing as if to swallow and might have done so. That did not look like food.

Meanwhile, I'd missed Ceyx catch a slippery fish; his jingling calls seemed to beckon the two male fledglings. Their wings fluttered, beaks gaped, and tails bobbed. No luck. Ceyx bolted off with the youngsters in pursuit. I lost them in the greenery.

Ceyx came back to the ledge, this time trailed by the female juvenile. After a bouncy landing, she nudged over toward Ceyx, ready to be fed, but he strummed away to the upper end of the pond. When next in view, the fish was gone. Did Ceyx eat the meal?

Parenting is such a balance of yielding to pleading and exercising tough love. I thought of Ian's toddler years and the occasional tantrum when protesting a destination hike with its tedium of one foot after another.

❧

Every young kingfisher must become an expert angler with scant help from their parents. That's why I'm suspicious of popular accounts of kingfisher adults teaching their young angling skills by dropping a stunned or dead fish into the water. This "fact" comes from an unsubstantiated 1922 report by Floyd Bralliar (author of *Knowing Birds through Stories*).

The juveniles I watched practiced a demanding plunge, which could be straight or a spiral into the water like a screw turning into wood. Throughout nature, the logarithmic spiral repeats, from the flight path of a moth to a bighorn sheep ram's curl. Spirals range from a hurricane gyre to a skin pore, which is corkscrew-shaped for sweat to stream out. Turn on the faucet and the water twists. A sunflower's whorl of seeds is no accident.

The logarithm illustrates the elegance of mathematics: called the Fibonacci sequence, the numbers begin 0, 1, 1, 2, 3, 5, 8, 13, 21, 34, and so on; each number is the sum of the two numbers that precede it. The expanding spiral represented in this sequence is considered a fundamental pattern of the universe. You have only to look up into a dark night sky at the spiral arms of the Milky Way.

When John James Audubon wrote of the kingfisher who "dashes spirally headlong into the water, seizes a fish, and alights on the nearest tree or stump, where it swallows its prey in a moment," I was impressed he could see the spiral at such high speed. Then again, he was a practiced observer.

Why choose spiral over straight? The answer lies in the height of the dive and a way of seeing that is far different from humans. In kingfishers and other predatory birds, the retinas (the light-sensitive layer of tissue at the back of the eye containing rods and cones) have more cones than ours. The rods improve vision in low light, while cones function best in bright light. The kingfisher's eye has about two to five times more cones per square millimeter than the human eye.

Within a kingfisher's eye are two foveae, distinct areas in the retina with a high concentration of photoreceptors that optimize vision. We have one fovea that forms a central pit for sharp views. A kingfisher's deep fovea for focusing is a convex pit packed with cones positioned close to the beak. The second shallow fovea for stereo view appears as a dimple in the retina closer to the head.

A researcher named V. A. Tucker linked the remarkable foveae to the Fibonacci-based spiral in falcons, hawks, and eagles. His findings also shed more light on the kingfisher spiral. He found that when raptors looked at prey closer than eight meters away, they locked their gaze front-on. As the distance increased, the hawks turned their heads more and more to the side. A spiral allows a kingfisher to fly toward their prey with their heads facing forward, keeping the fish at the optimal 45-degree angle for the deep fovea and remaining aerodynamic.

A kingfisher entering the water must compensate for refraction as light bends in the new medium. The bird retains the fleeting image of an escaping fish in the shallow fovea that specializes in stereo view while still employing the high-focus deep fovea. This is not something any bird with two foveae can do. The kingfisher lens forms an unusual oval shape that allows the stereoscopic fovea to rest in the eye's periphery, and switch between focus points.

Kingfishers have another advantage for stalking fish. The high proportion of red oil droplets in their eyes reduce glare by acting as chromatic filters, cutting out the blue light that scatters up from open waters and helping them discern fish. Some birds can perceive near-ultraviolet light, as well. A kestrel hunts mice by following the ultraviolet urine trails. A kingfisher may see some fish trails in ultraviolet.

According to naturalist Lawrence Kilham, the white spots between the eyes and bill aid in fishing, too. He raised three juvenile kingfishers after machinery destroyed their burrow in a road cut. Through his observations, he became convinced the white spots serve as a sighting device to locate fish. In addition to the white eye spots, double foveae, and red eye droplets, the kingfisher dive alone has become a source of inspiration for sustainable design in the field of biomimicry, nature-inspired innovations.

The spiral is elegant, but it was the noiseless entry into water that inspired a Japanese engineer (also a birder) in the 1990s to solve a design problem with the Shinkansen bullet train, famous for attaining speeds of 200 mph. When the train entered a tunnel, a pressure wave at the bullet-shaped front of the train caused a sonic boom upon exit. Today, the front of the train mimics a kingfisher's wedge-shaped head and beak, ideal for crossing a threshold between two mediums. As the redesigned train rushes into a tunnel, the air flows around the beak shape and assures a quiet departure.

ॐ

One day at the pond, I examined Ceyx preening his plumage with keen attention, noting how he turned his head to touch his beak to the base of a bird's uropygial (oil) gland. He coated a lifted underwing with the rejuvenating liquid, smeared a bit on an orangish foot, and scratched his head.

Pulling fingers through my wind-blown hair, I noted how Ceyx combed each feather with a fierce bill that's not always a weapon. Instead of tugging through tangles to leave hair smooth and straight, he was aligning feathers so the structures in the barbs could interlock. In the process, he removed any dirt, debris, and parasites as he added oil to prevent feathers from drying out and becoming brittle. The natural chemicals also deterred feather mites, lice, and the growth of fungi or bacteria. The oil likely contributes to waterproofing, while the feather structure with linked barbs prevents water from soaking through to the skin.

Birds can have up to twenty-five thousand feathers. The kingfisher likely falls more in the range of a songbird, at closer to two thousand feathers. That's still an impressive number to preen and to grow. As new pinfeathers emerge, a bird must bite and scratch to remove each feather sheath. Molting and regrowing feathers is part of life, and without that process, the feathers would become old, bedraggled, and useless. Kingfishers replace individual feathers or groups in a partial molt to avoid being flightless, like ducks that lose all their feathers in late summer.

ॐ

The pond watch continued. A juvenile tagged along after a sibling all the way to the other side of the pond. One was the female, her belt as spicy as cayenne pepper. Violet-green swallows tucked over the pond. A pine siskin's *ziiiiippp ziiiiippp* gave voice to the Douglas-firs. Then, all fell quiet.

From the somnolence came the unexpected. I sat up from a brief doze to trace the source of the incoming rattle. A young male flew up from the flowing creek with a fish! Holding the two-inch minnow in his bill like a pro, he slammed his prey on the concrete ledge, gave him a neat toss to flip him from tail first to headfirst, and swallowed. I clapped my fingertips in a whispered applause.

Heading home after a sumptuous day, I reflected on how much lay ahead for the three youngsters. I worried. Danger took the shape of skilled forest hunters with bright red eyes, known to dive on belted kingfishers and pierce them with their talons. I had yet to see a Cooper's hawk chase a kingfisher, but I read a startling account by Pennsylvania ornithologist Mike Lanzone. The drama took place at a fish-laden lake where several kingfishers converged outside of breeding season.

To elude a Cooper's hawk accelerating from behind, one kingfisher dove into the water. The raptor raked the surface and flew off empty-taloned. A few minutes later, a second Cooper's grabbed a kingfisher from the air but let go. Lanzone summed it up: "All in all, I saw six different kingfishers being chased over open water. As far as the score went—Belted Kingfishers 6, Cooper's Hawks Ø."

Even more threatening is the northern goshawk, a ghostlike gray raptor hitched to a life in multilayered forests with centuries-old trees. The larger goshawks and smaller Cooper's hawks are members of the bird-eating genus *Accipiter*, which includes the sharp-shinned hawk. Accipiters fly with rapid wingbeats on short, rounded wings. Their long tails act as rudders for agile twists to capture birds in flight. Once, I saw a perched Cooper's hawk grasp a limp northern flicker, almost the same size. Another time, I heard a crash only a few feet from where I weeded my native plant garden as a Cooper's ricocheted off a small fence, regained balance, and flapped off with a hapless junco held within curved talons.

To escape predators, kingfishers apply all their guile, even an escape into the water. They may trace the stream or ascend so high they seem to evaporate in the clouds. When a belted kingfisher flies overhead, the underwings flash a blur of white feathers. Looking down on the same bird, the feathers are the colors of a blue-black cloud.

The apparent explanation for white below and dark on top would be a double feather set. That's true for the coverts that fringe the leading edge of the wing, but not for primary and secondary feathers. The primaries are the largest flight feathers and farthest from the body, while the secondaries are closest. The illusion lies in the design. The central shaft divides each feather into a narrower edge and wider edge to cut through the air with the least resistance. In kingfishers, the thinner side of a single feather vane is primarily blue-black, whereas the wider and outer side is predominantly white. The feathers stack up and slide across each other like a folding fan. From below, we see more white, and from above, more black.

Many birds share this folding fan feather trick. Countershading is an evolutionary strategy that softens a defined shadow, because birds soak up bright light from overhead and reflect dimmer light beneath them. Seen from above, dark feathers tend to blend with the earth or water, and, looking up from below, white feathers melt into the sky.

☙

After two weeks, the halcyon birds left the pond, and the lower few miles of Rattlesnake Creek often rang with kingfishers. One day, I surprised a juvenile fishing a side channel of Greenough Park, where Rocky Mountain maples, alder, and cottonwood shaded pooling waters. From his perch on a cottonwood limb fifteen feet above me, he dropped like a paper airplane in a nosedive. Missed. I watched three more blunders in quick succession before he flew away in silence above a sea of wild rose and snowberry. Were they mistakes, or was each one an improvement on the last? Precision takes practice.

ॐ

It was time to return to the place of beginning for the three young birds, when they knew only earthen darkness and were unaware of the greater purpose of feathers, wings, and piercing bills.

Lisa and Paul were up for the task on a sleeveless-shirt day in August. Armed with a shovel and measuring tape, we crossed the swift yet shallower creek. First, we calculated the hole's distance from the top of the bank down, at two and a half feet. Next, Paul extended the tape measure into the hole and tunnel to record four and a half feet of hard-won slightly ascending excavation.

Kneeling on the top of the bank, we stretched the tape to the length of the tunnel, and then dug out a square flap of grassy earth that we would tamp down afterward. Taking turns shoveling in the reddish soil with few rocks, we broke through the roof close to the depth we'd measured. The burrow's stench was rank from uric acid. The chicks had ejected their excrement on the back wall and then pecked a bit of soil to cover it up. Fastidious.

Like people, kingfishers have stomach acids to aid digestion. However, the chicks hatch with an extra dose of acid to digest fish bones and scales. Before fledging, their chemistry changes. Acid levels diminish, and they cast pellets like adults.

The odor was so terrible that I pulled out a bag from my pocket and gathered some of the excrement-laden soil to take home in an overzealous act of writer research.

ℰℭ

In early September, I walked alone to the nest bank with a question. After so many hours living the whirl, lulls, and adrenaline of the nesting season, how would I perceive this place? Wading into the knee-deep stream that still knocked me off balance, I placed one sandaled foot after another on the slippery, smooth, frying-pan-sized rocks.

Climbing up on the commodious boulder tucked close to the nest bank, I sat with knees pulled up to my chin, bathing in the solitude. With nothing comparable up or downstream, this landing pad for kingfishers qualified as a glacial erratic, the term for a massive boulder carried far on a river of ice when glaciers carved valleys like this one.

Resting on the stream-carved boulder, I fingered the sandpapery lichen of pencil gray quarter-sized splotches. Sunshine cast a net of molten silver on the rapids. The perch boulder absorbed the day's warmth. The creek rushed with the sound of a thousand hushed voices. So many times, when writing in the blind, I had tried to articulate the shifting cadences.

Each time a kingfisher landed on this boulder, I'd hoped to escape those penetrating black eyes, even as my brown eyes drank in the vision of an alert bird in crisp patterns of blues and whites with slicked-back crest and a minnow gripped in a fierce bill.

The summer before, I'd had the privilege of teaching an outdoor bird class to children with vision impairment. I brought bird study skins, feathers, skeletons, and audiotapes of calls to a summer camp like no other I'd known. On the shores of Flathead Lake, we flapped arms, stalked like herons, hooted like owls, and whistled like loons. The kids drew the birds they could not see, and I was humbled. When night fell, there were no lights to guide us to cabins in the darkness. I stumbled without a flashlight. They did not.

While at the camp, I met Dan Burke, who had gradually lost most of his sight from a disease called retinitis pigmentosa. Dan was then working at University of Montana as the assistant director of disability services. Dapper in his trimmed salt and pepper beard, with the lofty brow of a thinker and a keenness for nature, he tapped his way with a white cane. When the subject of kingfishers came up, Dan shared this poem written by a friend:

KINGFISHER

Two old friends and a young boy's restless energy
beside a pond in brilliant October sunshine.

Still air cleaved by the chattering flight of a kingfisher;
blue blur against cloudless Montana sky.

It finds its perch on a highway of perfect vision,
and I know you cannot see it.

What does it look like?
you ask your son,
who has tracked every dodge and weave.

Does it have a crest?
What color is it?

He is becoming your sight,
as I have been,
and for a moment something tightens in my chest.

I remember other times, other October days
a thousand moments of shadow and light
and I wonder what you've lost.

Then Sean replies,
and I hear him learn the form of a kingfisher
by describing it.

It's all so perfect and eloquent
that tightness fades and memory shifts
to vivid moments, endless changing scenes

I've learned to see,
and he'll learn to see
through the lenses of your blindness.

For Dan, my friend (by Eric Wahler)

Through hungry eyes, I'd hunted for the kingfisher of jaunty crest, of strong bill, and shiny eye. In the many hours of solo observation, I'd whispered to my father, either asking for his help or describing birds, as if my words could reach an unknown sanctum. For Dad, Dan, and the children at the camp, I had a promise to keep.

I would do more than observe within a life-giving creek sustaining kingfisher, dipper, swallow, thrush, warbler, flycatcher, tanager, eagle, osprey, deer, bear, squirrel, chipmunk, mink, coyote, wolf, moose, elk, and all the multitudes of diversity. I would transcribe for others in the way of my favorite woman conservation champion Rachel Carson, who wrote, in *The Sense of Wonder,*

> For most of us, knowledge of our world comes largely through sight, yet we look about with such unseeing eyes that we are partially blind. One way to open your eyes to unnoticed beauty is to ask yourself, "What if I had never seen this before? What if I knew I would never see it again?"

Sliding off the boulder and into the nippy waters, I crossed to shore and hiked the hill to the main trail, where cyclists pedaled, people walked dogs, and runners leaped over roots.

Somewhere along this creek, the young kingfishers employed their innate qualities of superior eyesight, muscular and rounded wings, and bill and body shape ideal for a stealth dive. On their own, they roamed the dimensions of sky, water, and earth.

CHAPTER 7
Winter Story

Finally War Eagle laid the pipe away and said: "Ho! Little Buffalo Calf, throw a big stick on the fire and I will tell you why the Kingfisher wears a war-bonnet."

—Frank Linderman, *Indian Why Stories*

My fingers traced the faint lettering etched on the squared-off boulder set back from Rattlesnake Creek. As the powdery snow fell away, the words stood out: "In attending to this wilderness . . . I knew myself to have been instructed for life . . . Henry Bugbee."

The creek murmured below a shield of ice. The kingfishers had left. Ponderosas high above me twinkled with silvery rime on their long needles. I often wandered the sanctuary, a five-minute walk downstream from my door. Often, I paused by the quote that resonated even more after the first season of kingfishers. Follow the bird. Listen to the messenger. This was the season of reflection and storytelling.

For years, Henry had hiked almost daily up Mount Jumbo's canted flanks on the east side of the Rattlesnake Valley. Later, he switched to Waterworks Hill on the west side, ascending the more forgiving, yet challenging, trail up the North Hills ridge.

Every walk was a meditation and every step a grounded connection, while Henry examined the realms of the mind. I missed meeting him striding up the ridgeline with his trekking poles, his silvery-white hair blowing in the wind. Never did I feel intimidated by his prodigious knowledge. He was an eloquent wilderness advocate and philosophy professor at the University of Montana, retiring in 1978.

On a visit to see me, my brother David once disappeared for hours on what he thought would be a brief run on the North Hills. When he returned, breathless and animated, he recounted meeting a man of great brilliance on the crest of Waterworks Hill. There, where ravens converge on gusty days, they discussed Homer's *Odyssey* and time slipped away.

Henry reveled in chance encounters with kindred thinkers. He was also instrumental in saving what would become the Bugbee Nature Preserve. When developers bought the land to build houses in the late 1960s, Henry borrowed money to save the remnant eight acres, but loan payments proved difficult over the next few years. That's when his son Bruce Bugbee, then a graduate student, facilitated what would be his first of many conservation land deals. The Nature Conservancy partnered with a local land trust that resulted in Missoula County purchasing the land for a nature preserve in 1975. Henry accepted only enough money to pay off his loan and donated the rest; the creekside property had doubled in value by then. His condition? The preserve should be protected forever in a natural state and named for his father Henry Greenwood Bugbee, who he credited for leading him to the mountainous west and fostering his passion for fly-fishing.

The preserve is a sliver of cottonwood, ponderosa, mock orange, wild rose, dogwood, alder, and a lattice of creek-bottom plants upstream from Greenough Park. Hemmed in by houses, the sheltered nook is hardly wild in that grand way of Montana wilderness with the capital W, like the Selway-Bitterroot, Bob Marshall, Scapegoat, and Rattlesnake Wilderness. Yet here, I've seen a belted kingfisher glissading the pillowed air above the creek. In thickets, white-tailed deer bed down at night, as do black bears and the passing fox. Here, too, the trees harbor nesting black-headed grosbeaks, yellow warblers, lazuli buntings, and hairy woodpeckers.

Proximity to houses is perilous, because of outdoor cats that wreak havoc on songbirds. I hope the cats prowling the preserve grow ever fewer, just as the tansy ragwort is receding thanks to volunteers who have pulled two full acres of this invading weed and planted some two hundred native riparian plants as of 2021.

Hope lives in the promise of restoration. Hope lives in the local children who run barefoot in summer on deer paths, skip rocks, and wade in the creek.

When Ian was four, he'd often announce, "I'm going on an adventure" and hurtle off-trail within this preserve. After I taught him my Mount Rainier childhood game of "never touch the ground," Ian scurried across

logs with squirrel-like balance. All went well—except for that time he jumped into a patch of stinging nettles.

Within this pocket park, I began my initiation to Rattlesnake Creek's seasonal ebb and flow back in the early 1990s, when I lived in a modest rental by the preserve's edge. One day, feverish from the flu and half-dozing, my back resting against a gray fissured trunk of a creekside cottonwood, I blinked awake to the sound of a kingfisher. Soon after, I wrote a poem inspired by that moment and ending this way: "When I hear the kingfisher that cannot fly without echoing the sound of water crossing stone."

છ

Like the best of teachers, the kingfisher instructs in ways so radiant that I forget the rigor. Henry was that kind of professor. When I touched the carved letters like braille, I tapped into his nature-centered philosophy. Soon after he died in 1999, his wife Sally Moore asked me to help her choose a discreet memorial, a boulder with room for an inscription so muted that it would take a sharp eye to notice. Placing the chosen stone in the preserve with a view of Rattlesnake Creek, Mount Jumbo, and the North Hills would connect three of Henry's cherished places.

Sally chose the quote from *The Inward Morning, A Philosophical Exploration in Journal Form* that Henry penned in the 1950s when he was a professor at Harvard University. In his book, he explained walking as a prelude to writing:

> I weighed everything by the measure of the silent presence of things, clarified in the racing clouds, clarified by the cry of hawks, solidified in the presence of rocks, spelled syllable by syllable by waters of manifold voice, and consolidated in the act of taking steps, each step a meditation steeped in reality.

"Solidified in the presence of rocks" felt like an encouraging nod from Henry, as Sally and I hunted for the ideal boulder within the preserve. Coming up short, we headed out to the southwest side of town to a business that sells local rocks for landscaping. On a hot summer afternoon, we wandered among jumbled monoliths pried from the hills, valleys, creeks, and prairies in a widening circle around Missoula.

Poking among granite, quartz, limestone, and various geologic chunks in this strange shopping lot, my thoughts drifted to high school meanders in the Sleepy Hollow Cemetery of Concord. There, a five-foot rose quartz boulder bears a mounted bronze plaque that reads, "Ralph Waldo Emerson, Born in Boston, May 25, 1803, Died in Concord, April 27, 1882, 'The passive master lent his hand, To the vast Soul which o'er him planned.'"

Also in the cemetery is Henry David Thoreau's headstone, a low-slung gray marble marker bearing one word, HENRY. We were not looking for a tombstone; the memorial would mark a spiritual placing of Henry Bugbee. The two Henrys shared much in common as fellow philosophers who found nature's wisdom and simplicity in walking meditations.

Would the spirit of Henry Bugbee accept this boulder and inscription? Yes, he would, because Sally guided the act of remembrance. Their love for each other, found later in life, was romantic to witness as they strolled hand in hand. We knew when we had found the right stone, a granite monolith with faint ripple lines and yellow-green lichen.

"Attend." The word stands out on days when snow and ice trap the ever-persistent creek, and on others when frigid winds send errant leaves scampering among creaking cottonwood limbs. In my winter meditations ambling the Bugbee Preserve, I tasted snow imbued with the resin of pine needles. Within a season of short days, long nights, fog, ice storms, snow, or slush, the skeletal cottonwoods exposed all that had been hidden, like a hornet nest of gray paper swirled into a dome and hanging from a branch.

When cold fog pressed down on the valley, every pine needle glittered with ice like the tinsel Dad had taught my brothers and me to hang strand by strand on our Christmas tree. At the holiday's end, we removed each one, wrapping up the foil strings for next year. My father, too, shared much in common with the Henrys, including an ethic of reusing, consuming less, and appreciating the exquisite filigree of ice on a tree bough or along a stream's edge.

ॐ

Even when I did not see or hear kingfishers, I knew their wings had imprinted on each turn of the creek. Halcyon likely had escaped the winter on some southern river, while Ceyx remained untethered from his nest territory. The fledglings? Like their parents, they, too, would seek ice-free waters and, if they survived the perils of the first year, would return to find a mate. Perhaps they might come home to Rattlesnake Creek or wander off to another stretch of river or tributary.

I was pretty confident that Ceyx was the kingfisher I'd spotted on a high wire above the Clark Fork River downtown. I did wonder, though. How could he have become such a suave, natty bird who seemed to have forgotten the meaning of the word skittish in the environs of crows, pigeons, and house sparrows? He appeared so serene as cars rattled across Higgins Street Bridge. I came to see him often, surprised by his predictability along the winter-gripped river. If not on the high wire, he tended to be poised on a cottonwood limb, or patrolling his territory from Madison Street Bridge by the University of Montana to the Orange Street Bridge, a mile downriver.

One late afternoon, he scrunched down so that he resembled a baseball impossibly balanced on the wire. Then he grew slimmer and alert, snapping his tail and staring down at ice slabs coasting by. In the dimming light, his colors were fleecy gray without a speck of the typical blue. His crest flurried into a tattered peak. Where I found him was predictable only in the context of a dynamic river. With below-freezing temperatures, the ice expanded from the shore. The wire offered access to the river's center. I often saw him dive headfirst at an angle to snatch an escaping trout from black waters.

As I studied Ceyx on his wire perch one morning, I had that tingling feeling of not being alone. I turned to see an unshaven, middle-aged man in a torn jacket standing a few feet away.

"A kingfisher!" I said and pointed where my bird had landed on a hefty cottonwood branch.

"Yes, a kingfisher!" He nodded and we stood in slack-jawed appreciation of the bird with ragged crest, bulky head cocked forward and bill pointed downward.

"I see him here a lot," he added, gesturing to the riverfront by the Holiday Inn. "And I see those black ducks with the white patches on their face—those divers out in the middle there."

"Sounds like goldeneyes," I said. His smile widened on his weather-rough face. And so we watched, linked by the kingfisher that he saw far more often than I did as I made my tame forays from a heated home.

Most passersby ignored me in my regular vigil. A few would stop mid-step along the paved river trail and look curious. Then, they hurried on to their indoor destination, not like the man who lived all but forgotten by the riverbank. This kingfisher didn't stand out like a bald eagle swooping down to nab a duck on the ice, or a great blue heron high-stepping the shallows with long-legged precision, or the mergansers and goldeneyes rafting the waves. He appeared as wraithlike as the man I met, invisible until you took time to notice and then engage.

Once in the bird's thrall, I knew him to be a teacher of boldness. I never tired of his fast fall to beak the water. That said, when a gang of crows invaded his favorite cottonwood tree, he was nowhere to be seen. Intimidated? Or maybe the branches bent with too many scuffs and guffaws. I wondered whether my fellow kingfisher watcher also must evade his version of crows.

Ceyx often balanced for long periods on his perch in silent contemplation, another unusual behavior compared to the agitated and often garrulous behaviors of summer. When he did flap low to the river, his rattling notes were the concatenations of ice, water, fish, and survival.

He did not divide urban from wild. By the Clark Fork's edge were red osier dogwoods and willows among boulders blighted by a broken whiskey bottle, a wadded shirt, or a plastic cup. Yet beavers gnawed the trees. The wild nudged into the city. The city nudged into the wild. I'd always cheer for the wild to win, yet had to admit that if this wintering kingfisher could vote, he'd endorse the presence of wires over the river that gave him the ideal view of the fish below.

ℒ

The first snowfall of November marks the time for storytelling, or Sqʷlllú Spąni? in Salish. Only in this slowing-down time do children listen to tales of values, morals, and origins told with gestures and inflections. Winter was the right time to search for kingfisher stories, beginning with the Salish.

Ellen Bigsam (1860–1964) told a coyote and kingfisher story in the 1950s to George Weisel (a University of Montana zoology professor). She was a Salish leader and a knowledge-keeper of animals and plants. Her son interpreted Ellen's words that appear in Weisel's book, *Ten Animal Myths of the Flathead Indians* (there, he wrote her name as Big Sam).

Before Ellen Bigsam began, she warned that if winter tales were spoken after the snow melted, a snake would wrap around the leg of the storyteller on a walk. With that in mind, I'd advise silent reading of the following story if not in season:

Coyote was working in a sawmill one winter when he decided to visit Kingfisher. It was nearly dinnertime, but Coyote could see no food around Kingfisher's place. Kingfisher noticed Coyote's concern and told him not to worry. He cut some willow switches, climbed on a tree limb over the partially frozen stream, and dived in. To Coyote's amazement, he came out of the water with a fine trout. Kingfisher successfully repeated this performance until he had a large enough mess of fish strung on the switches for dinner.

A few weeks after this incident, Kingfisher came to see Coyote at the sawmill. Coyote had no food for his guest, but this did not upset him as he thought he would go out to the stream and catch some fish like Kingfisher had done. He perched himself in a tree over several holes in the ice that had been cut to draw water from, and plunged down. He hit the ice and broke his head. It was several days before Coyote could return to work.

I could relate to Coyote's desire, even as a message resonated: Know your place in the animal world. Respect the skills each being brings and put your talents to use in ways that provide for others.

Some stories offer a moral and others an entertaining and sometimes even racy "why." The Klallam of coastal British Columbia are part of the Salishan people whose territory once spread across the Pacific Northwest, divided into coastal and interior groups, including the Salish of Montana. Amy Allen of Jamestown, Washington, told a story, in 1953, that offers one startling possibility for why the female is more colorful than the male. Her explanation for "how it was that Kingfisher got red patches underneath her wings" could be a cautionary message of infidelity or simply what you might expect if you pair two incompatible birds together.

The Klallam story also uses the word "man" instead of bird, which reflects a worldview of all beings as people, a far cry from the Christian motif of humans holding dominion over animals.

The plot chronicles the crafty Kingfisher who fools her husband Great Blue Heron by pretending to be sick, but instead was cheating on him while he was off looking for food to bring to her. She even blew on the fire so her face would whiten with ashes and look pale. But Heron got suspicious, caught her in the act the next time, and stabbed her with his long sharp bill.

"When you see the Kingfisher flying, you see that red under her wings. And it's the same today," concluded the storyteller.

The point for me? Lighten up. Allow kingfishers to play the role of a villain now and then.

⅋

Old Man (or Napi) stories of the Blackfeet Nation honor Old Man's role as creator and offer morals through his many pranks. "Why the Kingfisher Always Wears a War-Bonnet" appears within Frank Bird Linderman's 1915 book, *Indian Why Stories: Sparks from War Eagle's Lodge-Fire*, a lively collection of tales told to him by elders of the Blackfeet, Cree, and Chippewa people, who trusted him as an ally and advocate. Linderman created a fictional storyteller, War Eagle (based on a close Chippewa friend and medicine man), who regaled his grandchildren with stories of the animal people on October nights after the first frost on the Upper Missouri River in Montana.

I've retained Linderman's rendition of Old Man as *Old*-Man and capitalizations of the Wolf, Otter, and Kingfisher wherever I've summarized the longer story. War Eagle began with a hook to capture the attention of his curious young listeners gathered around his lodge fire:

> You have often seen Kingfisher at his fishing along the rivers, I know; and you have heard him laugh in his queer way, for he laughs a good deal when he flies. That same laugh nearly cost him his life.

According to the story, the fateful event took place on a bitter snowy day when *Old*-Man and the Wolf hunted. They were hungry and had traveled far looking for meat. *Old*-Man grumbled at their plight. At day's end, they came to a river where four fat otters played. When the Wolf told *Old*-Man he would catch an otter to eat, *Old*-Man warned him not to head out on the treacherous ice, but the Wolf did not listen. He skidded after the otters.

Nearer and nearer ran the Wolf. In fact, he was just about to seize
an Otter, when SPLASH—into an air-hole all the Otters went.
Ho! The Wolf was going so fast he couldn't stop, and SWOW!
into the airhole he went like a badger after mice, and the current
carried him under the ice.

Old-Man cried and wailed as he ran down the riverbank hoping Wolf
would emerge where the waters flowed out from under the ice. Instead,
he found Kingfisher balanced on a birch limb, laughing at him. That
made Old-Man angry. He threw his war-club. Kingfisher ducked and
the club grazed his head feathers, so they stood up straight. War Eagle
ended with Old-Man saying,

> I'll teach you to laugh at me when I'm sad. Your feathers are standing
> up on the top of your head now, and they will stay that way, too.
> As long as you live, you must wear a head-dress, to pay for your
> laughing, and all your children must do the same.

In another story of the Blackfeet, called "The Bears" (recorded by
George Bird Grinnell), Kingfisher helped Old Man. The story began
with Chief Wolf granting Old Man's request of turning him into a wolf,
but with fur on only his head, arms, and legs. One morning, Old Man
told his companion wolf of a bad dream and warned him not to chase an
animal that jumped a stream. Soon after, the wolf bolted after a moose.
When the moose then splashed through shallow water to an island, the
wolf hesitated, but thought it was a small stream and his quarry was
tired, so he kept going.
    When the wolf did not return, Old Man asked all the birds whether
they had seen him. Kingfisher saw Chief Bear and his two brothers killing the wolf, eating the meat, and throwing the fat in the water, which
Kingfisher then dove down to catch. He told Old Man and advised him
to seek the island bears when they came out to play each morning. Old
Man would eventually fool the bears and kill them; their death led to
sharing their fat with all the animals that needed it, even bears. Kingfisher helped Old Man, and both participated in the cycle of death and
renewing life for others.

ॐ

Without the help of the kingfisher, the Arikara people of the Great Plains would not have found a better world. To journey westward from a hiding place underground (after the Creator sent floodwaters to eliminate giants), three birds helped them overcome obstacles to reach a better place—a kingfisher, an owl, and a loon. Coming to a chasm, Kingfisher reshaped the earth and laid down an enormous beak that served as a bridge. With a great flapping of wings, Owl cleared a thorny forest, and fast-flying Loon parted a lake. The people could choose whether to continue or turn into the bird that helped them. A kingfisher? I'd be tempted.

My friend David Liberty, who lives by the Columbia River in Hood River, wrote to me that the kingfisher is special to his Umatilla people:

> The Kingfisher was sure to impress a tribe of fishermen. It was that skill or "power" to catch fish that the locals wanted. A good fisherman was highly regarded. If one could "capture" the power of a Kingfisher it would increase your chance for success. The spirit of the bird from which you got the feathers is honored in hopes of gaining its assistance.

An actual kingfisher skin protected the wearer of an elaborate warbonnet made by the Cheyenne warrior White Bull, also recorded by George Bird Grinnell (1849–1938), who lived with the Great Plains tribe beginning in 1890, a bond lasting more than forty years. His Cheyenne name was *wikis*, or "bird," not for Grinnell's middle name but, coincidentally, for his seasonal bird-like migrations to visit and camp among their lodges.

The warbonnet appeared to White Bull in a vision when observing a thunderstorm. Later, he would re-create the design according to Thunder's instructions. In the front, he placed a buffalo horn over the browband that rests just above a warrior's forehead. Behind the horn and on top of the bonnet, he tied the skin of a kingfisher. On the front right, he laced the skin of a hawk. Two tails of eagle feathers were placed on either side—the right tail painted red and the left white. At the back was a barn swallow skin, and where the eagle feathers were red, he secured a bat. Every animal added protection. When the enemy shot at the horseback rider wearing the bonnet, the person eluded him like a swallow flying close to the ground. The bat, as a night flier, could not be caught.

Grinnell gave special attention to the most prominent bird:

> The kingfisher which is tied to the head behind the horn was worn for the purpose of closing up holes which might be made in the body by bullets, because when the kingfisher dives into water, the water at once closes over it.

Further, when White Bull presented the warbonnet to the warrior Roman Nose, he told him, "If you get into any fight, try to imitate the call of the bird you wear on your head—the kingfisher."

Following these and more instructions, Roman Nose wore the warbonnet into many battles, including one in 1865 where he "rode back and forth within twenty-five or thirty yards of lines of white troops, all of whom shot at him without effect." When Roman Nose died in a later fight, the belief was that he had accidentally violated one of the laws of the warbonnet.

ॐ

The kingfisher is the helper again in Grinnell's recounting of the Cheyenne version of the Northern Cheyenne and Sioux victory defending their last traditional hunting grounds in 1876. (Today you can visit the Rosebud Battlefield State Park in the prairies of eastern Montana, forty-five minutes north of Sheridan, Wyoming.)

The Cheyenne called their victory against soldiers, Where the Girl Saved Her Brother, dedicated to the lone woman warrior among the ninety-nine Cheyenne and an unknown number of Sioux. Buffalo Calf Road Woman had charged downhill toward the soldiers to rescue her brother Chief Comes in Sight, whose horse had been shot beneath him. He jumped on her mount, and they galloped to safety.

One of the bravest old-time warriors, Spotted Wolf, did not fight against the soldiers led by General Crook, but instead prepared his son White Shield (then named Young Black Bird) for battle. He gifted him with the power of the kingfisher, his longtime teacher.

Spotted Wolf painted a kingfisher facing forward on the shoulders and hips of the horse, applying blue dye from clay that his son brought him from a nearby spring. "Now," he said, "your horse will not get out of wind."

Just before the battle, Spotted Wolf held up his kingfisher (a stuffed skin) to his son and said, "This is the song sung to me when the spirits took pity on me. If the kingfisher dives into the water for a fish, he never misses his prey. Today I wish you to do the same thing. You shall count the first coup in this fight."

Spotted Wolf tied the kingfisher on the scalp lock he had placed on the horse's lower jaw. In the bill were some kingfisher feathers dyed red to represent the flash of a gun. He hung a whistle made from an eagle wing bone around his son's neck, telling him, "When you come within the sight of the enemy and are going to charge, put the whistle in your mouth and whistle. That is what the kingfisher does when he catches the fish. You shall catch one of the enemy."

Similarly, blowing the eagle whistle to mimic a kingfisher would protect his son from bullets when threatened. I can envision the bold young warrior painted in yellow and galloping on a horse emblazoned with a kingfisher, blowing his eagle whistle, *KKKKKK!*

Eight days later, the Lakota Sioux, Northern Cheyenne, and Arapaho would defeat Colonel George Custer and the 7th Cavalry at Little Bighorn (forty-eight miles northwest of Rosebud Battlefield), a place of personal significance for my family.

ॐ

Past and present blurred among the bunchgrass ridges and ravines in our 1969 adventure that spoke to my father's way of travel, preferring the backroads and seeking beauty spots. On that hot summer day, he drove the white Chevy 2 station wagon on an unmarked dirt road into what is today the Little Bighorn Battlefield National Monument. Turning a corner, all five of us gasped. Thousands of American Indians on horseback rallied on one hillside, and a sea of mounted US Cavalry in blue assembled on the opposite slope. We'd driven straight into the filming of the charge scene within the iconic movie, *Little Big Man*.

The horrified film crew waved us down, but did not send us away. My mother almost swooned upon meeting Dustin Hoffman, who puttered up to us on a motorbike. My brothers and I climbed up on Appaloosa horses to sit behind actors who smoked cigarettes on breaks.

ജ

In questing after the halcyon bird, I was chasing two worldviews and their intersections. Contemplating Henry Bugbee's quote on the boulder, I knew the answers swirled in the free-flow of wild waters. The kingfisher was my bridge across the chasm.

In the story of White Bull's warbonnet, the kingfisher is protector, helper, healer, and messenger. White Shield, too, plunged into a battle, guarded by the bird that dives and never misses a fish.

In the Greek myth of Halcyon and Ceyx, the Gods change lovers into kingfishers, and in the Arikara origin story, the people can choose to turn into their animal helpers. Could animal transformation be the bridge linking the two worlds?

Winter solstice. I imagined two kingfishers in flight. With each flap, they wove the torn fabric of the sky, repairing, restoring, and painting their favorite shades of blue. For seven days and seven nights before and after the solstice, I celebrated kingfishers as bringers of halcyon days, even in the roughest, coldest, and darkest of times.

Solstice originates from the Latin *sol* (sun) and *sistere* (to stand still). In that time, I felt the inhale of collective breath and the steamy exhale from the wild community of Rattlesnake Creek. The kingfisher was my moon in the sky on the longest night, lighting the path like a great beak across a canyon. All I had to do was cross.

Second Year

Ringed kingfishers

CHAPTER 8
Red Belt Mystery

Our New World kingfishers range in size from the tiny but elegant least green (pygmy) *Chloroceryle aenea*, only five inches long, to the imposing ringed kingfisher, fifteen inches in length. . . . The sexes are unlike in plumage; and in all but one of the American species the more colorful male has a greater area of chestnut or rufous on his under parts than the female, who may be quite lacking in this color. In the migratory belted kingfisher, strangely enough, the female alone wears chestnut on her breast. The mark of sex has been reversed!

—Alexander F. Skutch, "Kingfishers, Sovereigns of the Watercourses," *Nature Magazine*

A stiff headwind bore down on us. Within minutes, one canoe tipped over after hitting a submerged rock, spilling two people into the river. Soon after, a peregrine tore through the clear sky to rake a blackbird from the middle of a flock. The falcon flapped to the Mexico side of the Lower Rio Grande with the drooping prey grasped in sharp talons. A belted kingfisher flew ahead with a familiar rattle. Seconds later, a green kingfisher skimmed across the river like an emerald flash to flounce down near a male with a fiery chest, the brighter of the two.

Rounding an island to peruse the tranquil backwaters, we saw him. Perched on the limb of a sugar hackberry tree high above the river, a ringed kingfisher examined the moss-green waters—a shaggy-headed philosopher musing on the currents. He was enormous, like a belted kingfisher on steroids, with coppery red feathers attiring his entire belly.

Without warning, he pitched forward, folding his great wings before striking the water with his beak and then launching upward with a splash to land in another tree. No fish. I listened to my first ringed kingfisher call, a hollow, rib-knocking *Kuh-Kuh-Kuh-Kuh!*

Did my father guide me to this hard-to-find bird? I raised a paddle to him. One year ago, on his eighth of March birthday, a belted kingfisher had whorled in like an omen of all that would follow in the first nesting season. Thanks to Dad's belief that his children should master wilderness skills, I'd become an adept paddler after two summers at a Maine canoeing camp in my early teens. Graduating from the bow to the stern, I mastered the jay-stroke to steer through the whitewater of the Machias and St. Johns Rivers. Navigational skills later would prove essential for the kingfisher journey and my personal life, especially when I felt mired in whirlpools.

Reunited in some intangible way within this canoe, I imagined my dad and me admiring the imposing stature of our first ringed kingfisher (*Megaceryle torquata*). This largest of all kingfishers of the Americas is crow-sized, with a sword of a three-inch-long beak.

Only a month before my father's death, I'd walked barefoot with him on a barrier island beach near my parents' North Carolina home. Strolling along after a November storm, we picked up whelk shells and created a dream list of birding trips—one was to the Lower Rio Grande. I thought he would have more time.

On this five-mile stretch of braided river curving through thorn forests below Falcon Dam, all three kingfisher species had graced my father's birthday. Our guides were volunteers for the Friends of the Wildlife Corridor, each one dedicated to protecting the last vestiges of habitat. Even in 2010, the border wall threat loomed and would only become a starker reality of riparian habitat destruction that even bird wings cannot surmount.

The far southern border of the United States is a convergence of climate, with eleven ecosystems, plus a parade of rarities showing up, including a 2010 first sighting of an Amazon kingfisher (eighty-four miles north of Falcon Dam in Laredo, Texas). Birders still flock here for persistent wonders, including the prized trifecta of kingfishers.

&

"You were lucky to see one fishing; a ringed kingfisher will spend hours on one perch without moving," Dr. Tim Brush told me at sunset. We'd met at Edinburg Scenic Wetlands, a World Birding Center that's ten miles north of McAllen, Texas.

Roseate spoonbills, herons, cormorants, and egrets plumed the farthest edge of the pond in feathered finery of pinks, whites, blues, and blacks. A belted kingfisher chittered behind us. When a ringed kingfisher flew overhead, the golden light of day's end seemed to intensify on a tropical oasis. The mild-mannered ornithology professor remains an authority on the suite of tropical birds that nest on the Lower Rio Grande, including the ringed kingfisher, a resident only since about 1970, part of a trend of Mexico birds expanding ranges northward. On my morning paddle, I'd seen two of the softball-sized nest holes high on a steep earthen bank.

I'd come to quiz him on the red belt mystery. Had he noticed that the female ringed kingfisher also outshone her male counterpart if you compared the extent of reddish colors and intricacy of patterns? Could they be rule-breakers, too, when it comes to females flashier than males? Both male and female ringed kingfishers smolder with a Titian shade of lush chestnut. The male's entire belly is earthy red, while the female displays an upper bluish band highlighted in white, and then the lush chestnut color washes down her belly. Even half of her underwings are reddish, whereas the males are all white.

Tropical naturalist Alexander Skutch shared detailed observations of their nest-building behavior in a 1952 article for *Nature Magazine*:

> Once, in Guatemala, I watched a pair of big ringed kingfishers excavate their burrow in a low, sandy, riverside bank at the edge of a banana plantation. Male and females took turns, each working inside for about four or five minutes, while the mate rested close by, uttering from time to time a harsh *kleck*, which was answered by the other, hidden in the ground.

Familiar? Belted and ringed kingfisher mates show a similar shared devotion to excavating the nest hole. I pondered an ancient evolutionary divergence, when the ringed kingfisher pioneered the south and the belted kingfisher colonized the north. Could the belted female retain a reddish element that had benefited her life in the tropics? How does the color help her now? Why her and not the male, too? In shady habitats, red shows up as a display color. In more open environments, blue does. Given the ringed kingfisher's lush and often shadowy riverine homes, the reddish breast in both male and female fits that premise well.

Although the patient professor appreciated my enthusiasm, he was not willing to speculate. Tim reminded me that evolution is nuanced and complex. However, he was generous in sharing his firsthand knowledge of local kingfishers. "Belted kingfishers as migrants have several advantages," he said. "They have no nesting territories to defend, and they aren't as tied to ideal fishing perches, because of their ability to hover, a quality not shared by green or ringed kingfishers."

The three species seem to interact amicably, dividing up perch sites among vertical riverside forests by size—tiniest (green kingfisher) down low, middle-sized (belted) higher up, and biggest (ringed) highest up.

Something else about size seemed intriguing. Not all ringed kingfishers are large. A subspecies the size of a belted kingfisher inhabits far southern South America with temperate habitats, like Patagonia. Perhaps thirteen inches long is the right size for fishing and surviving the temperate versus tropical habitats of North and South America?

Tim was particularly intrigued by the northward movement of ringed kingfishers. "My favorite theory is ringed kingfishers hopscotched north along rivers coming from the mountains of nearby Mexico, including the Sierra de los Picachos," he said. The route would lead them to the Rio Grande below Falcon Dam, completed in 1953 and altering the natural flooding regime. That meant earthen banks are more stable for nesting kingfishers. However, the flood-dependent tall ash and cedar elm forests along the Lower Rio Grande are shrinking, which is grim for the nesting red-billed pigeon and Audubon's oriole.

Our conversation ranged far and wide, leaving me considering the intersections of highly evolved species and behaviors with habitats at risk from our thoughtless destructive acts. At the same time, our curious minds can lead us down tantalizing scientific pathways that are beautiful to witness. What is life without questioning, wondering, pursuing, and beholding?

I continued the ringed kingfisher hunt on foot and mountain bikes at Santa Ana National Wildlife Refuge; by kayak on a four-mile stretch of the Lower Rio Grande; on a pontoon boat called the *Riverside Dreamer*; and jouncing in a pickup truck with the hilarious Roy Rodriguez.

Then the only full-time Latino birding and nature guide in the valley, Roy now works for the Texas Parks and Wildlife Department. He's broad-shouldered, cheerful, and zealous about birds. Once, he took President Jimmy Carter birding, a story he recounted that day. The president was so anxious to add to his bird list that he ordered Roy to step on the gas and exceed the speed limit, followed by a racing escort of security vehicles.

"The ringed kingfisher is a jumpy bird," Roy said on our foray. "You watch one fishing and it's in this zen mode, just staring down. When another bird lands nearby, he's startled and almost falls off his perch." He'd come to know kingfishers by personality, praising the feisty green kingfisher for taking on birds three times bigger: "A green kingfisher will chase away a great kiskadee."

Roy was mystified when I asked him my red belt questions. So was Martin Hagne, director of the Valley Nature Center. I met him at one of the prime birding spots in the McAllen vicinity, Estero Llano Grande State Park. Near the town of Weslaco are reclaimed farmlands and old *resacas* (former oxbows of the Arroyo Colorado) forming a bountiful network of wetlands.

Martin and I watched a green kingfisher poised on a low branch much too close to a ten-foot-long basking alligator. The slender limb swayed, and so did the tiny bird, but not her head, which she held steady as she scrutinized the water. Her colors were green shimmers and creamy milk. In a blink, she dove to the water and was back on the perch pounding a chubby brown fish two times, flipping her meal like pizza dough, and swallowing the prey headfirst. The alligator slept.

I recognized magnetic family traits in all three kingfisher species, from a smack of a fish to the outsized head, and a bill like a blade. I wished I could find one feather of each, from a green, belted, and ringed kingfisher. If I were to choose, I'd pick one tuft of a malachite-shaded feather from the back of the green kingfisher. For the ringed and belted,

I'd select a reddish feather from females and ponder the subtle differences in hues.

Over five days, the intensive search for one bird and clues to a conundrum steered me to the full exuberance of threatened life on the border. At every turn, I met people striving to protect, restore, and connect the remnant native habitats of the Lower Rio Grande and willing to go the extra mile to show me kingfishers. Keith Hackland, a dapper gentleman and owner of the bird-friendly Alamo Inn, even provided mountain bikes for us to pedal to river access points scattered within Santa Ana National Wildlife Refuge.

There, at the edge of the Rio Grande, we rested among anacua trees and Mexican valley ash, breathing in the perfume of the huisache tree's butter-yellow flowers. We listened to the *click-click-click* of a green kingfisher scooting above the languid current to the Mexico side and back, invisibly threading the two countries and one precious river corridor with every jeweled wingbeat.

℘

I had a feather fascination that only grew in the presence of the red belt puzzle. I hoped the answer to the female's brilliance might lie somewhere in the art of seduction, avian style.

People are more like belted kingfishers. We'd be the odd ones in the bird world. While I've never figured out cosmetics, I delight in earrings, necklaces, and bracelets, often choosing turquoise, amber, and silver. For birds? Males are more akin to stereotypical women in our culture—at least when there's a difference in plumage between the two.

Ring-necked pheasant males strut by with their bodacious scarlet and green heads, while the tawny speckled females blend into the grass. Merganser males grow splashy feathers for the breeding season, their head feathers a green sheen like ferns in the rain. Some birds don't stop with feathers. In his seasonal quest to outshine rivals and bid for females, a male ruddy duck's beak changes color from black to baby blue.

Even as they molt and replace feathers, belted kingfisher females maintain their colorful edge over males. As John James Audubon wrote,

"Belted applies only to the female, the male being destitute of the belt or band by which she is distinguished."

Ah, the destitute male. There are those feather color shifts, however, from juvenile to adult plumage. The young males I watched at the pond had a tad of the feminine, with their coppery blue upper bands and a sprinkle of reddish feathers on both sides of their bellies and extending to a bit of their underwings. I wondered why they lose their cinnamony reds when growing adult plumage? I'd found nothing in the literature to suggest a reason.

Fanning through 470 pages of *The Sibley Field Guide to Birds of Western North America* (a prized possession signed by the author), hundreds of birds blurred by in a kaleidoscope. I paused on a random page. Even when the feather hues were the pastels of olive, slate, butter, and almond of flycatchers, the designs were sophisticated and artful.

Bird feathers fueled a lethal millinery fashion in the 1870s. Soon, one white egret plume was not enough. Like mad hatters, women vied for feathers of egrets, cranes, herons, and warblers. They wore multiple species on their haute headwear, from individual feathers to a whole bird, or even a mini aviary. The feather trade in Europe and America for outrageous bird hats peaked at the century's turn and continued until 1920, fifty years of slaughter.

William Hornaday, director of the New York Zoological Society, labeled London as the "mecca of the feather killers of the world." He wrote of the travesties in his 1913 book, *Our Vanishing Wildlife*. Examining three separate plume sales in London over nine months in 1911, he calculated a death toll of 223,490 birds: 120,168 egrets, 41,090 hummingbirds, 20,698 birds of paradise, 13,598 herons, and 9,472 other birds. For every ounce of plumes, six egrets died. The most coveted of white feathers came from egrets in the breeding season. That meant hunters slaughtered parents on their nests, leaving whole colonies of baby birds to suffer and die.

Under an illustration caption, "Beautiful and Curious Birds Now Being Destroyed for the Feather Trade," Hornaday listed "Belted Kingfisher, Greater Bird of Paradise, Victoria Crowned Pigeon, Common Tern, Superb Calliste, and Cock of the Rock."

New York City was awash with ostentatious plumes, too. In 1886, a naturalist named Frank Chapman stood on a street corner in Manhattan with pen in hand, tallying the birds he could identify on women's hats: three bluebirds, two red-headed woodpeckers, nine Baltimore orioles, five blue jays, twenty-one common terns, a saw-whet owl, and a prairie hen. In two visits, he counted 174 birds and forty species. One egregious hat sprouted egret feathers, owl heads, sparrow wings, whole hummingbirds, and five warblers. Other notables from his survey included twenty-three cedar waxwings, twenty-one northern flickers, and a greater prairie-chicken.

As feather hunters decimated bird populations, two women spoke up to save the birds. The year was 1896, more than two decades before women would have the right to vote in the United States. Harriet Hemenway and Minna Hall, cousins and members of Boston high society, championed a boycott of the plume trade. Harriet, a spirited birder, would live to be 102. The cousins hosted tea parties and enlisted nine hundred women committed to the boycott.

Their activism shepherded in a new era of environmental organizations lobbying on behalf of birds and their habitats, first the Massachusetts Audubon Society and ultimately the National Audubon Society. The alarm bell sounded. One state after another banned the sale of feathers. The Lacey Act of 1900 prohibited interstate commerce, to support the states that had enacted protective laws. Lawmakers soon expanded the act to prevent trade in exotic feathers. The carnage continued, however, until the passage of the much stronger Migratory Bird Treaty Act of 1918, protecting all native migratory birds.

Harriet and Minna deserve a monument for their bravery and ability to expose the horror of fashionable hats. Then, as so often now, they had to defeat a false narrative put out by industry to assuage women's guilt. Sellers often asserted the feathers were plucked from bushes and birds were unharmed.

Across the Atlantic in London in 1889, Emily Williamson founded the Royal Society for the Protection of Birds (RSPB) to stop the "murderous millinery." She was soon joined by Etta Lemon and Eliza Phillips. Their tireless efforts eventually led to the passage in England of the 1921 Plumage Protection Act. Today, the RSPB has become a global force in conservation.

These early women environmental champions—Harriet, Minna, Emily, Etta, and Eliza—were bold, tenacious, and unafraid to outshine their male counterparts. They remind me of female belted kingfishers.

❧

Another fatal trade arose in the 1800s: feathers for fly-tying. Elite wealthy men developed a zeal for fly-tying with exotic and rare bird feathers. They turned to one book in particular: William Blacker's 1842 *Art of Fly Making*. Within its pages, iridescent cobalt and cerulean kingfisher feathers from what Blacker called the Indian Kingfisher (maybe the blue-eared kingfisher) composed some of the elaborate flies. This demand for exotic feathers continues in a black-market trade, including one shocking heist of millions of dollars of rare bird study skins from the British Natural History Museum at Tring in 2009. The thief? A twenty-year-old fly-tying fanatic named Edwin Rist.

Feather fascination has a long history. In ancient China, people paid high prices for electrifying blue kingfisher feathers and even named an art style Tian-tsui, translated "dotted with kingfisher feathers." So high was the demand for Cambodian kingfishers that the trade contributed to the wealth of the Khmer Empire and resulted in a mass slaughter of kingfishers. The practice continued until the Chinese Revolution.

The Tartars of Eastern Europe and Central Asia sought the feathers of the common kingfisher as love talismans. They'd kill the kingfisher, pluck the shiny blue and orange feathers, throw them into the water, pick up the ones that floated, and use them to stroke the person they hoped would come to love them.

The rampant black-market trade in wildlife parts in our overpopulated world continues to threaten the future of many dwindling species. Javan and collared kingfishers of Indonesia are among the thousands illegally transported, traded, killed, and sold for supposed cures.

The plundering feather trades exemplify another western "civilization" divide from our animal kin. Yet, people do speak up for the birds. Within each one of us lies the tinder to be sparked in the presence of living birds, where an egret's plume glimmers in a marsh and a kingfisher's dive slices through sun rays in a blur of blue, white, blue, white, red, white, and blue.

Ah, that flash of the red belt. Why such pizzazz? My hair at birth was auburn. I'm the only one of my parents' three children to inherit red hair from my grandmother Rebecca Hallett on my father's side. I have a framed black-and-white photo of a teenage Rebecca hiking in the White Mountains of New Hampshire, wearing her thick long hair in two braids. Dressed in knickers, sturdy boots, and a wool sweater, she smiles at the photographer, her husband-to-be.

What I remember most from my grandfather of his courtship stories was how much he loved Rebecca's gorgeous hair. My son also entered the world with carrot-colored hair, the only one of my parents' six grandchildren with that propensity. No wonder I'm drawn to the female kingfisher's belt. We redheads must stick together.

&

Returning to Montana after the Texas trip, I had to admit the mystery would be tough to crack. I decided to call one of my experts.

"I think it is likely that the color and belts are important in sexual recognition," said Mic Hamas, recalling his observations of kingfishers in the Great Lakes region. "The rufous belt could reduce aggression, because a male would have an immediate visual cue."

He pointed to the solitary and territorial nature of belted kingfishers. For males, defending a nesting territory is imperative for breeding success. A diggable, vertical dirt bank that is safe from flooding and not too far from water is a hot commodity. When females return, males are ready and waiting. Seeing a flash of her vivid belt would be the male's instant cue to welcome a female rather than to chase her away as he would a rival.

Mystery solved? Not at all, said Mic. First, no one had conducted research to find out whether this premise was true. Second, he had a hunch there was more to the story.

Next, I turned to my ornithologist friend Dick Hutto, who savored any avian riddle and had the personal experience of watching the nesting Rattlesnake Creek kingfishers with Sue and their two sons. "There can be other cues besides color," Hutto said, noting that birds identify members of the opposite sex by vocalizations as well.

Geoffrey Hill fell in the visual marker camp. An Auburn University ornithologist and author of the 2010 book *National Geographic Bird Coloration*, he was a plumage specialist. When I called him, he speculated the female's belt could be like the black mustache mark of a yellow-shafted northern flicker, which is the one distinctive pattern setting the male woodpecker apart from the female. (Male red-shafted flickers, found in the western states, have red mustache marks.) A 1936 study demonstrated that when the researcher glued a fake black mustache to the side of a female yellow-shafted flicker's face, her mate mistook her for a male and drove her away.

"I suspect the kingfisher belt also could be a marker for sexual identity," Geoffrey said. "It's only a reversal of what you'd expect if you think of it as an additional color rather than a simple mark."

However, the male flicker had the showy mark, not the female. Unconvinced, I quizzed Geoffrey on the source of belted kingfisher feather coloration, another potential clue. Ornamental plumage coloration derives from either pigments or microstructures in feathers. The probable source of the rufous belt are melanins, the same pigments giving us hair color and skin tone. Melanins come in more than one form. Specifically, phaeomelanin produces earthy rusts, chestnuts, and golds, while eumelanin expresses in browns and blacks.

In contrast, carotenes supply the vibrant reds, oranges, and yellows in birds like orioles and tanagers. Carotenes originate in food that birds must find, eat, and transfer to their feathers. Geoffrey's research of house finches showed the healthiest males were those with the reddest feathers, derived from the best diet of carotene-rich foods. Females picked the brightest males as mates. Color vibrancy signals health and fitness.

Although female kingfishers do not derive their pigment from foods, something provocative about melanin came to light a few years after my conversation. In a 2017 study covering a sweeping nine thousand species of birds, scientists found that a third have complex plumage colors, and most patterns come from melanins, which birds control at the cellular level.

The analogy? If birds were artists, they'd paint bright swaths of color with carotenes and finer details with melanin. The melanin-derived patterns may convey information about individuals and play a role in sexual signaling. The finding opens the door to the possible role of a melanin-derived kingfisher belt in expressing some form of messaging.

Could a female's belt be her superpower? If so, she wasn't overt, like dominant female phalaropes. As Dan Albano pointed out to me early on, all three species of these intriguing shorebirds reveal a sex-role reversal, accompanied by brighter plumage in females. Red and red-necked phalaropes breed close to the Arctic Circle and winter in tropical oceans. The Wilson's phalarope nests in western North America and migrates to South America.

I remember watching a small flock of Wilson's phalaropes on a pond cupped within an eastern Montana prairie on a June day. The birds spun in circles to create whirlpools, which stirred up insects from the bottom and into the center of the vortex, where the phalaropes snapped up the protein-rich food with long slender bills.

A Wilson's phalarope female flaunts deep peachy feathers extending along her slender long white neck and washing onto her gray back, with a debonair dark stripe through her eye and down along her neck. In contrast, a male's feathers are muted grays and whites with a hint of peach. There, the reversal of coloration makes sense, since after the female lays her eggs, the male takes over. His colors blend with an open ground nest. In contrast, belted kingfishers nest underground, where camouflaged plumage is unimportant.

Phalaropes also practice an unusual mating tactic called polyandry—females mating with multiple males. Ornithologists theorize that polyandry plus males tending the young tips the survival edge in favor of females, who can depart early from northern climates for a southern migration. Competition among females for males can be vicious, with aerial chases and dramatic encounters on the water. However, I found nothing to suggest females differed in shades of bright colors, which could be employed to their advantage.

If I found similar competition among female belted kingfishers, would the size, shape, and brightness of their belts serve as status symbols? When I checked with Mic, he favored this line of inquiry, since he had anecdotally noticed differences among the sizes and patterns of belts and recorded chase scenes. He suggested I visit the Smithsonian National Museum of Natural History in Washington, DC, to compare female belts on study skins that date to the early 1800s. He knew James Dean, the bird collections manager, and promised an introduction. Who wouldn't want to meet someone with the name of the crushingly handsome actor, defying all stereotypes of some pasty-faced man with thick glasses in the windowless aisles of antiquity? I put the visit on a "must do" list. The puzzle-solving continued with three guiding questions.

First, did red belts of females differ in color, size, and patterning among individuals? That would take me in the direction of the Smithsonian.

Second, would a female display her red belt to hold sway among other females? If showier, then would she edge out other females for a male with the coveted nesting bank? I'd need to be alert to aggressive behavior in females toward other females in future nesting seasons and to compare their belts in the field.

Third, if her eye-catching belt served as a visual marker, would there be some evolutionary connection to explain why this fell on the female instead of the male?

ॐ

Before the upcoming season of the kingfisher watch, I contemplated the deeper meanings of my trip to the southern border. Through the lens of the returning traveler, I'd gained perspective on divisions and the free flow of birds linking two worlds.

Reflecting on one of my stops to scan for kingfishers, I revisited a particularly vivid scene. There, by the tiny town of Roma, a movie set for the 1952 film Viva Zapata (starring Marlon Brando as the Mexican revolutionary Emiliano Zapata), I had traced the path of a white pelican flapping to the Mexico side of the Lower Rio Grande. Cloud white wings billowed above a young woman in a multi-hued dress. She had waded knee-deep into the river with an armload of laundry to rinse clothes of scarlet, teal, orange, and yellow in the muddy water. Four children in frayed shorts and tee-shirts splashed beside her. A skinny, long-nosed, short-haired dog slinked along the shore. We could just see the edge of Ciudad Miguel Alemán, then home to more than sixteen thousand people, many suffering the violence of warring drug cartels.

An international bridge spanning the river served as a reminder of the long-standing family and cultural links between the two towns.

I felt sadness and a yearning I'd heard expressed by the Russian poet Yevgeny Yevtushenko, reciting to an overflowing audience at the University of Montana in the late 1980s: "Why is it that in folk songs of all nations and all ages people express the desire to become birds? Because birds know no borders."

When the ringed kingfisher fished from a tree branch high above the Rio Grande, I found my moorings, as if gazing into eyes uncannily like mine. Coming home to Rattlesnake Creek, I recognized "my" kingfishers as linked to a larger family. Connection. Commonality. Belonging. Always the feel-good belted kingfisher led me swerving around the bends of happiness—a laughing, teasing, and tantalizing bird dangling clues to a mystery that had become more than why the female wears the red belt.

Coming home, I embodied the migratory female belted kingfisher, flying north with my newfound strength and wisdom gained from my flight away without a mate. Coming home, I carried my father's steadfast belief in me. Pursuing the red belt mystery, I chased down a few female powers of my own, like independence, fortitude, and even bravery.

Interlude

"Kookaburra sits on the ol' gum tree. / Merry merry king of the bush is he. /
Laugh, Kookaburra, laugh, Kookaburra." Song lyrics by Marion Sinclair

CHAPTER 9
Greek Myth and Naming Kingfishers

> For seven days before the winter solstice, and for the same length of time
> after it, the sea becomes calm, in order that the kingfishers may rear their
> young; from this circumstance they have obtained the name of the halcyon
> days, the rest of the season is winterly.
>
> —Pliny the Elder, *The Natural History of Pliny*

The day I first told the Greek myth of Halcyon and Ceyx to Ian, he lit up like I would have at eleven when similarly enchanted by legends of magic, fantasy, mischievous gods, and animals, of timelessness, shapeshifting, and immortality. In second grade, Ian became an avid reader when words took shape into stories of dragons, schools for wizards, and talking animals.

A favorite view from my second-floor home office was my son reading within the bosom of our sprawling old apple tree. His nook, composed of several rough-hewn planks and reached by a rope ladder, reminded me of the maple tree outside our family's rented farmhouse near Westtown School, Pennsylvania. I remember the ease of that jump to catch the lower branch and scramble up to a comfy fork of the tree trunk. There, I read J. R. R. Tolkien's *Lord of the Rings* on drowsy summer days before entering sixth grade.

Sifting through books from the library, the myth of the halcyon bird surfaced in several places, including Edith Hamilton's classic *Mythology, Timeless Tales of Gods and Heroes*, in Thomas Bullfinch's *Mythology*, and in works by Pseudo-Apollodorus, whose ancient telling includes a twist. Simultaneously, I was delving into kingfishers of the world and scientific names with variations of Halcyon and Ceyx. It was time to know the myth inside out.

The book I settled on as the most expressive was not Greek but written by the Roman poet Ovid. Stowed away on Ian's multiple bookshelves, I found a copy of the worn hardback with a torn black cover: *The*

Metamorphoses of Ovid, a 1954 translation by A. E. Watts. Each chapter is part of a continuous narrative written in the meter of epics, like Homer's *Iliad* and *Odyssey*. Each myth reveals the universal theme of change that Ovid pronounces in the beginning: "Change is my theme. You gods, whose power has wrought all transformations, aid the poet's thoughts, and make my song's unbroken sequence flow from earth's beginnings to the days we know."

Reading Ovid's version of Halcyon and Ceyx more than once, I began to recite the story to Ian, my mother, and friends who seemed to be either attentive or humoring me. I embellished some of the details and changed a few names to reflect other translations that I liked. I chose Halcyon over Ovid's Alcyone spelling; Apollo (Greek) as the god of light rather than the Roman name of Phoebus; Hera (Greek) rather than the Roman Juno; and Ceyx as King of Trachis, instead of Trichina.

The full story, written by Ovid and altered by me (with apologies to the great poet), became a mantra that I'd also recite in the company of birds and flowing water.

Halcyon, daughter of Aeolus, God of the Winds, fell in love with Ceyx, son of Eosphorus (Lucifer), the Morning Star. Their love was rare, the kind where souls, spirits, and bodies entwine. They married and lived in harmony in the way that Ceyx reigned the kingdom of Trachis.

But all was not well. Ceyx had a brother named Daedalion, who was as warlike as Ceyx was peaceful, except when it came to his daughter Chione, whom he adored. For Daedalion, life dealt a crueler fate, in sharp contrast to Ceyx's joy.

Chione's ravishing beauty attracted two suitors in the form of Apollo and Mercury. After she bore twins, one from each god, Chione boasted that her stature rose higher than Artemis, goddess of the hunt and sister of Apollo. Infuriated by this act of hubris, Artemis killed Chione.

The bereft Daedalion threw himself from the cliff of Parnassus. As he fell, Apollo intervened. Daedalion's arms became wings, his nose a hooked bill, and his toes curled into talons. Once fierce as a human, he flew as the predatory hawk.

When Ceyx learned of all that had happened to Chione and his brother Daedalion, he grieved and grew fearful. The tragic loss of Chione combined with his brother's fate could well portend trouble for the tranquil kingdom. Ceyx approached Halcyon, telling her he must consult the Oracle of Apollo at Delphi and go by sea, since the overland path was then impassable.

Halcyon warned him of the dangers of turbulent winds, which she knew well from her father, Aeolus. Ceyx held her close and told her he would be careful, but that was not enough for her.

"Please, take me with you," she begged.

"I cannot. I must go with my crew while you remain safe on shore."

"No! Together, we will face the danger of the storm."

Ceyx listened, and his love burned strong. He promised to be home before two full moons had passed. They kissed, and their bodies melted into one another as the waves broke on the sea.

Halcyon watched the ship set sail. Her tears flowed as her vigil began, walking the shore day upon day. Her waist-long, auburn ringlets blew in the salty wind. Halcyon's turquoise dress rippled with the colors of the Aegean Sea. Often, she cast off her slippers and ran barefoot, splashing in the foam.

Once, she saw a kingfisher hover above the ocean. She held her breath as the resplendent bird paused in mid-flight, even as her own life felt on hold while the love of her life sailed far away.

Ceyx and his crew glided halfway across the sea toward their destination. It was then, as night fell, that whitecaps foamed on the waves. A southeastern wind blew and soon became a gale until the sea churned in a fury.

The captain called out to furl the sails, but the violence of the storm swallowed his words. The ship rose high to teeter on the summit of looming waves, then crashed into the valley depths, only to climb once more. Rain poured. Thunder boomed. Lightning struck. Water gushed into the vessel until the crew wept and called out for their families. Ceyx had one word on his lips, "Halcyon."

Without warning, a giant wave broke upon the ship, shattering the rudder and the mast. The splintered boat sank into the depths.

Ceyx, one of the few torn from the vessel instead of trapped upon it, clung to a plank, and spoke Halcyon's name one last time as a black wave curved down on him. Before the dawn lifted the gloom of darkness, the Morning Star dimmed in grief.

Meanwhile, Halcyon walked the sands and prayed at the shrine of the Goddess Hera that Ceyx might come home safe to her. Hera, wife of Zeus, listened to Halcyon's entreaties, yet even she could not change his fate.

Hera sent her messenger Iris, goddess of the rainbow, to the cave of Somnus, god of sleep. The glimmering Iris woke Somnus to ask if he would command Morpheus to take the shape of Ceyx and appear in a dream to Halcyon. Somnus lived with his three shape-shifting sons. Icelos represented four-legged creatures, birds, and snakes, while Phantasos mimicked soil, rocks, waves, and trees. Only Morpheus could take the form and even copy the pattern of speech and movement of humans.

Somnus agreed. Iris retreated before she, too, might succumb to the somnolent cave of deep dreaming. Morpheus then flew to the bedchamber of Halcyon, who woke to the specter of her Ceyx, dripping wet and pale. She cried out when she saw him, as he told her he had drowned.

Queen Halcyon ran to the sea, tears streaming. Hera and Zeus, in their pity, had made sure that the body of Ceyx would wash up on shore where Halcyon could at least enfold her king one last time. When she saw the body of Ceyx rolling on the incoming waves, she climbed up a rock jetty and leaped to join him in death.

As Halcyon fell, Hera and Zeus changed her into a kingfisher. Her leap became flight, and she cloaked Ceyx in her soft wings, touching his face with her horny beak in the only way she could kiss him. It was then that the Gods transformed Ceyx into a kingfisher as well.

The two birds flew away, feeling the newfound freedom and a love no longer bound by gravity. Each year, they nest upon the sea over the winter solstice, when Aeolus, father of Halcyon, lulls the waves for seven days before and seven days after the solstice, the time when the kingfishers brood their young upon the waters.

"Halcyon days" would come to mean more than a sailor term for calm days within a stormy season. To live in halcyon days is to know a fleeting utopia. To remember them is to glimpse the carefree days we long for.

Only in the version by Pseudo-Apollodorus do the lovers commit one travesty that never turns out well in Greek myths. Once thought to be Apollodorus of Athens (180 BC), this author was a mismatch for the era and lived during the first or second century AD.

Regardless, his mythological recounting traversed the centuries to our time, including his flourish of Halcyon nicknaming her husband Zeus, while he called her a pet name of Hera. Naturally, the Gods grew angry with the outrageous hubris and caused the terrible storm on the sea. Only after Ceyx drowned and Zeus and Hera witnessed his dying words did they soften and turn the lovers into birds. I've decided to reject this telling. Surely, Halcyon and Ceyx knew from Daedalion's fate that they would never risk offending the gods.

The love story wrapped me in a feathered daydream. The more I submerged in kingfishers on my home stream, the closer I felt to avian life and the possibility of slipping out of my skin and testing newfound wings.

ৄ

Since that fateful day when I first learned the definition of halcyon as kingfisher, I'd found halcyon references in literature and lyrics, even the original version of the anthem "America the Beautiful": "O beautiful for halcyon skies." Throughout classical literature, halcyon has found favor. Shakespeare referred to a warm spell in late Autumn as halcyon in *Henry VI*: "Expect Saint Martin's summer, halcyon days, Since I have entered into these wars."

Walt Whitman in *Leaves of Grass* wrote, "Then for the teeming, quietest, happiest days of all! The brooding and blissful halcyon days!"

Poet John Keats, in "Endymion," begins with immortality in the way of Halcyon and Ceyx: "A thing of beauty is a joy for ever"; and deeper into the poem is the halcyon bird: "O magic sleep! O comfortable bird, / That broodest o'er the troubled sea of the mind."

Herbert James Draper, a London artist of the Victorian era, painted the bereft Halcyon at the edge of the sea with an azure cloak that billows behind her bare bosoms and a wine-red sash that sets off her sea-blue skirt. A pair of kingfishers in the same watery hues fly behind her. Sea nymphs invite her into their magical sphere.

What does it mean for lovers in the shape of birds to nest over the winter solstice as our earth turns toward the light and days begin to lengthen? What is it to find a languorous sea in the stormy season? What is it to brood our young and, figuratively, the "troubled seas of the mind?" If I kept following the halcyon bird, I might come closer to knowing.

☎

Since first reading the scientific names of kingfishers of the world, I'd wondered why the Greek myth of Halcyon and Ceyx should be prevalent throughout the family and across the globe. In the eighteenth and nineteenth centuries, ancient Greek mythology formed the bedrock of education for many Europeans. So familiar were scientists with the pantheon of Greek gods and goddesses that their names inspired the naming of plants and animals.

I visualized Carl Linnaeus in 1758 working by candlelight, dipping his pen in ink, and writing in refined script: *Alcedo alcyon*, the original scientific name for the belted kingfisher for the tenth edition of his famed *Systema Naturae*. Later, a German naturalist named Johann Jakob Kaup would rename the genus *Megaceryle*.

Linnaeus, a Swedish botanist and physician, is considered the father of binomial nomenclature, which denotes each species with two names—the first the generic or genus descriptor and the second the specific epithet. Thus, *Homo sapiens* is our species name.

In seeking clues to the red belt mystery, I climbed the belted kingfisher's family tree. To know the bird of myth, I'd leaped squirrel-like to a separate limb. What I hadn't done was step back to view the entire kingfisher taxonomy. It was time to review the basics, including a recitation of the mnemonic device: Keeping Precious Creatures Organized For Grumpy Scientists (Kingdom, Phylum, Class, Order, Family, Genus, Species).

Kingfishers belong to the order Coraciiformes, along with bee-eaters, motmots, todies, hornbills, and hoopoes. Behind each name is a fabulous bird, like the turquoise-browed motmot. I once spotted this flamboyant tropical dweller with pendant-like feathers (rackets) at the tip of a long tail among a cavalcade of smaller birds feasting on an ant procession near the Mayan ruins of Coba on the Yucatan Peninsula.

Coraciiformes translates as raven-like, yet there's no genetic connection to ravens or any other corvid (including crows and jays). Meanwhile, there's one definitive anatomical feature—toes. Coraciiformes birds share a partial fusion of two of the three front-facing toes, a feature called "syndactyly." In belted kingfishers, the outermost digits are fused at their base to create a sole that's handy for kicking out dirt during excavation of a nest tunnel.

Kingfishers nestle within the family Alcedinidae that in turn divides into three subfamilies. As taxonomists confirm new species, the diversity grows. The 2021 tally from the IUCN Red List of Threatened Species records 120 species of kingfishers and includes nineteen genera. Eleven species are threatened, and two subspecies have gone extinct since 1600. More than a third (forty-two species) are of conservation concern. Many of those species reside in vulnerable places like islands or in the forests of Southeast Asia, where logging has decimated their homes and sea rise from climate change threatens all who live there.

The subfamily Daceloninae, tree or wood kingfishers, harbors the highest diversity, and includes the laughing kookaburra, stork-billed kingfisher, and many species of paradise kingfishers. There's plenty of flash and radiance, but few "fishers. Most seek their prey on land.

The subfamily Alcedininae are the river kingfishers, which include the Greek bird of myth (the common kingfisher, *Alcedo atthis*). Think rainbow, electric, lustrous, luminescent, and glitter. Even their names give a hint of their beauty: shining blue, azure, indigo-banded, and malachite kingfisher.

The Cerylinae subfamily or water kingfishers divide into three genera—*Megaceryle* (belted, ringed, crested, and giant kingfishers), *Chloroceryle* (American pygmy, Amazon, green, and green-and-rufous kingfishers), and *Ceryle* (pied kingfisher)—for a total of nine species. With my laser focus on *Megaceryle*, I noted a strange phenomenon. How could those four species be in the same genus when spanning three continents? The belted and ringed kingfishers overlap in the Americas, while the giant kingfisher inhabits Africa, and the crested kingfisher dwells in Asia.

In 2006, phylogenist Robert Moyle applied genetics to kingfisher evolution. His accepted work points to the cerylids evolving first in the Old World, likely Africa, and then the ancestor of the belted and ringed kingfishers crossing the Atlantic Ocean to the New World. His work suggested two dispersal events from the Old World to the New World within the past five million years. His findings also supported earlier taxonomists, who noted the close relationship of ringed and belted kingfishers. The two formed a superspecies (a group different enough from other species to be considered an entity) with giant and crested kingfishers. That led to changing the genus names of belted, ringed, giant, and crested from *Ceryle* back to *Megaceryle* in 2007. The pied kingfisher would remain the one species in the genus *Ceryle*.

In the New World, our paltry six species of kingfishers may reflect their latecomer status. The world they entered was well stocked with fishing birds.

ℯ

The cradle of kingfisher civilization was once thought to lie in the rainforests of Malesia, encompassing Indochina, Indonesia, Malaysia, and New Guinea. However, Moyle's research points to the Australian region, where kingfisher diversity is highest, including more endemic (found only there) species than any other area. Asia and Africa follow in that order as hosting the most variety. A fundamental problem with the Malesia origins theory is this: much of the archipelago did not exist until the early Miocene (34–23 MYA), long after kingfishers showed up in the Eocene fossil records in Europe and North America.

Paleontologists excavating in Germany's Messel Pit Fossil Site (the richest place for uncovering clues to Eocene evolution) unearthed the oldest kingfisher ancestor, dating to the middle Eocene (48–38 MYA). *Quasisyndactylus longibrachis* is no larger than an outstretched hand, with a top-heavy head and a flattened sword bill.

Most kingfishers live in forests or woodlands by water, yet many are not fishing birds. They lurk on a tree limb to snatch a scurrying insect or lizard on the forest floor. The belted kingfisher and others that hover over water and dive for fish indicate some higher level of sophistication, suggesting a more recent origin.

The laughing kookaburra (*Dacelo novaeguineae*) of Australia earns the record for biggest kingfisher—up to eighteen inches long and weighing one pound. In contrast, the belted kingfisher is about ten to twelve inches long and weighs about five ounces. At the petite end of the spectrum are members of the *Ceyx* genus, the dwarf and pygmy kingfishers—you could cradle one in your hand.

༂

My college friend Liza Gadsby lives near the last vestiges of rainforests of southern Nigeria. For decades, she's risked her life to save endangered primates, running the nonprofit Pandrillus with her partner Peter Jenkins. On one of her visits to her home city of Portland, Oregon, she gave me a gift of a mummified African dwarf kingfisher (*Ispidina lecontei*) she had found alive but could not save. The smallest kingfisher in the world (at just under four inches) is the size of a hummingbird and almost weightless.

Even in death, not all had faded. I ran my fingertips over the orange head and breast, the cobalt blue back, white chin, and black forehead, the scarlet bill, and toes. The wings open wide as if in one last flight from a rainforest vine.

༂

Although names in Latin sprinkle the Halcyon and Ceyx myth across continents, their true names belong to the people who knew kingfisher behaviors and spun their legends. As I'd learned, the Salish name for the belted kingfisher is čális (ts ah lease). On the southern coast of Oregon, linguist Patricia Phillips of the Miluk Coos, told me the name in the Hanis language is shjit'is (shi-jit-is) and in Siuslaw and Lower Umpqua it's ch'a'tii (chi-AH-ee). The pronunciations are best heard in sound files to hear consonant clusters not found in English, like "shj." "In languages around the world, bird names are often inspired by onomatopoeia," Patricia said. When I hear the kingfisher words in Salish, Hanis, and Siuslaw and Lower Umpqua, I'm reminded of the rush of waters, with the hard consonants like resonating sharp notes as a kingfisher begins a rattling phrase.

Linnean and indigenous taxonomy converge in defining a bird. Class Aves describes birds as warm-blooded, feathered, winged, beaked, egg-laying, and flying (most). As Latin and common names identify the bird by color, sound, pattern, or behavior, so do those of indigenous peoples. However, they would not name birds for individual people, a Euro-American tradition that suggests discovery and even ownership.

Changing offensive bird names has gained traction following the social reckoning of 2020—the year of George Floyd's murder, sweeping Black Lives Matter protests, and a white woman in Central Park falsely accusing a birder who was black of threatening her. Black Birders Week and the compelling prose of J. Drew Lanham calling for inclusiveness are welcome trends as birding becomes ever more popular, especially after the shelter-at-home times of the coronavirus pandemic.

McCown's longspur marked the first name to change. John McCown led campaigns against indigenous peoples and then fought for the Confederate Army in the Civil War. This demure and declining songster of the prairie now is named the thick-billed longspur.

Fortunately, the belted kingfisher has an excellent name, which pays homage to the female's swashbuckling belly band—bold, daring, and seductive. Names have power. By changing names to assure justice, will attention to overlooked birds lead to their protection? Naming and knowing can be a key step toward intimacy followed by action.

ॐ

Taxonomy focuses on what separates and what binds. The myth of Halcyon and Ceyx erases divisions in a common longing to experience feathers and flight. Animal transformation myths remind us of our intertwining fates.

Mythologist Joseph Campbell shared an intriguing story of trans-formation in reverse, of a kingfisher becoming a man—a myth of the Andaman islanders of Indonesia. The tale falls within a universal theme of fire theft. In the first of several variations, "Sir Kingfisher" attempts to steal fire from the deity Bilika, who kept a pearl shell and a red stone to strike together and create sparks. As Sir Kingfisher came close to her flame while she slept, Bilika woke and flung the shell at him, which sliced off his wings and tail. He dove into the water and bore the fire to the next in line for the relay. Bronze-winged Dove was last, and distributed the fire to all except Sir Kingfisher, who had been turned into a man.

In another transformational myth, the Chamorro people of the island of Guam tell of a village woman who talked too loudly and made trouble for everyone. She strode among the people in her cinnamon-orange ker-chief and blue dress with a white apron, stirring up things, until an angry *taotaomona* (ancestral spirit) had enough and turned her into the first Sihek (kingfisher). Her clothing became the colors of the female Sihek, and she cried "*sksh—sksh-sksh- kroo-ee!*" whenever people approached.

This story is part of a long oral tradition of the Chamorro people, verified by Pale' (father in the Chamorro language) Eric Forbes, histo-rian and author of the blog "paleric," which includes the story, "Cha'-mo tumattitiye i sihek yanggen chineflålågue hao" (Don't dare follow the *sihek* if it is whistling to you.)."

Today, you would hear . . . nothing. The Sihek, or Guam kingfisher, is extinct in the wild. Like a refugee waiting to return to a home that may no longer exist, this kingfisher clings to a precarious existence in zoos. In 1988, biologists captured twenty-nine of the once-common birds endemic to Guam. Without their foresight, the Sihek would be extinct, a victim of brown tree snakes that escaped onto the island after stow-ing away within military equipment on a ship from New Guinea. The predatory snake devastated the island's defenseless birds, sending twelve species to extinction. Today, Guam continues to struggle with eradica-tion. Still, there is hope for Sihek. The captive breeding program in zoos is a triumph of persistence and creativity that slowly has increased numbers to close to 140 birds. To hear the call of a wild Sihek in Guam would be a glorious day.

There's another form of recovery that Robert Macfarlane, the lyrical British nature author, addressed in *The Lost Words, A Spell Book,* a series of incantations to bring back nature words omitted from the 2007 edition of the *Oxford Junior Dictionary.* Those words included bluebell, acorn, wren, and kingfisher—to be replaced by the likes of broadband, voicemail, and celebrity. Every spell is meant to be read aloud. My favorite line from Macfarlane's kingfisher chant is "Gold-fare, wing-fan, whipcrack the kingfisher—zingfisher, singfisher!"

Why not pull out all the stops? In these precarious times for the future of life on earth, let's call forth every power to change the course—from science to myth to spells, and the greatest of all? Love.

Looking down from my office window on my son in the apple tree, I decided to join him. Monkeying up the rope ladder, I saw that Ian was reading the Earthsea trilogy by Ursula Le Guin, not just any version, but my yellowed paperbacks from childhood. He let me place an arm around him, and we escaped to the mythical realm of Earthsea, where names and language have the power to alter the balance of the world.

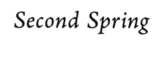

Second Spring

CHAPTER 10

Second Season, Second Chances

> Kingfisher courtship is a very noisy and spirited affair. One does not know
> just how many miles up and down stream it is considered proper for the
> gallant to pursue his inamorata before she yields coy acceptance, and it is
> difficult to perceive how the tender passion can survive the din of the actual
> proposal, where both vociferate in wooden concert to a distracted world.
> But la! Love is might and doth mightily prevail.
>
> —William Leon Dawson, *Dawson's Avian Kingdom*

The kingfishers were ramming the upper stream bank below the highest arc on April 17 of 2010. The pair took turns. One would hover from as far as twelve feet away and then fly full tilt into the adamantine wall of earth. *Bang!* The bird bounced back and staggered in the air before wobbling to a tree branch on the same side of Rattlesnake Creek. Then, the mate took aim and dirt flew when the sharp bill struck the steep bank.

I was reminded of the scene in J. K. Rowling's *Harry Potter and the Sorcerer's Stone* when young Harry screwed up his courage to run straight into a pillar as the only way to reach "platform nine and three-quarters" and the train to Hogwarts School of Wizardry. He pushed his shopping cart full of luggage through the post, which dissolved when he committed to the act.

For the birds, creating a nest and raising future generations of kingfishers proved a powerful motivator. For Harry, his first action would lead to changing the course of good and evil. Although one was reality and the other fiction, both required a leap of faith or, rather, a headfirst collision.

A commanding *rat-a-tat-tat(!)* shook my reveries. A pileated woodpecker pounded a dead pine tree searching for insects tunneling within the wood. Envision hurtling straight into a tree at 16 mph. To absorb the concussive force, the woodpecker's thick skull forms a natural helmet, and the cartilage at the base of the beak acts as a spongy shock absorber. Nothing about a kingfisher skull suggests a similar adaptation.

Smash! As aerodynamic as a fighter jet, the female kingfisher powered into the bank. The tip of her bill jammed into the soil. She bounced off. A few seconds later, she flew down to the shallow edge of Rattlesnake Creek and bathed in the bracing waters, droplets scattering. The rinse was brief. She flapped back up to a branch, wiped her dripping beak on one wing, and preened.

For three consecutive days, Lisa, Paul, and I watched the birds persevere. What started as a dent morphed into a shallow bowl and then a hole. The vertical surface lacked holds for kingfisher tiny toes to find purchase and no nearby tree limb for a handy perch. The dagger bill served as the primary tool. Not all the soil looked diggable; we could see embedded cobbled rocks. On the plus side, climbing predators would be stymied from reaching a hole placed about three feet down from the top of the bank and twelve feet up from the creek.

The first morning the kingfishers hit the wall with their bills as chisels, sending dirt flying. On the second and third days, we noticed they sometimes carried soil in their beaks. The male out-carried the female, eleven bouts to five. We couldn't be sure, but we think they opened their bills slightly to strike and snatch debris. Like all birds, the bony bill is protected by a thin layer of keratin, the same material as our fingernails and toenails. However, unlike most birds, the lower mandible can unhinge more than the upper, a useful adaptation for excavating a burrow or snagging a fish underwater.

We recorded the daring crashes into the bank from our vantage point about a hundred yards away on the rise above the floodplain. As usual, Paul was meticulous with time, gender, numbers, and concise descriptions. He counted 176 bill strikes in 180 minutes over the three mornings, with the male and female taking turns almost equally.

I discreetly wrote down their names of the previous 2009 season: Halcyon and Ceyx. Since my return from the lower Rio Grande, I'd observed the pair for a month preceding this astonishing drama. Although it was presumptuous to assume they were the same birds, this female's belt, like Halcyon's, didn't buckle. Both birds seemed familiar to

Lisa and Paul, too, in looks and most behaviors. However, what we were witnessing was bizarre—or was it?

Paul had a hunch our observations might well be the first to be recorded. Later, in 2013, he would publish a note in the *Wilson Journal of Ornithology* reporting the new find of aerial ramming. I'd be a coauthor with Lisa—published citizen scientists of belted kingfishers.

The act of citizen science is threefold: to observe, record, and then share the finding. Not every discovery need be earth-shaking. In this case, our observation was head-pounding. Each blow reinforced a fierce fidelity. Some birds, such as sandhill cranes, strengthen a lifelong mate choice with ritual dancing. Kingfishers may be loyal only one season at a time, yet the devotion we witnessed might exceed all other birds in chutzpah.

When Paul followed up on our observations to see whether other kingfishers in the world exhibited this remarkable behavior of beak-turned-battering-ram at a nesting site, he found reports of thirteen species. One was a member of the subfamily Alcedininae (the common kingfisher of Greek myth), and the other eleven species fell within Daceloninae. In all cases, both sexes participated. The belted kingfisher is the first documented aerial rammer of the subfamily Cerylinae.

Just three kingfisher species are exclusive bank crashers—the belted, the common, and the white-throated kingfisher (ranging from Turkey to the Philippines). The remaining ten ram termitaria (termite mounds), trees, or banks combined with other surfaces. The laughing kookaburra will fly at top speed from up to thirty feet away to bash a nest hole into the concrete-like surface of a termitarium. This bold behavior is not without danger. The forest kingfisher (*Todiramphus macleayii*), a bluebird-sized denizen of Australia and New Guinea, arrows at breakneck speed to dent a termitarium glued to tree limbs. Observers have witnessed at least one bird crash and die from the impact.

Dan Albano described belted kingfishers "stabbing" a riverbank to begin a hole. He joined other watchers over the past century noting belted kingfishers probing with their bills while clinging to an earthen wall with their toes. Sometimes the birds hovered from a short distance away to fly in to pick at the nesting bank, a far cry from a full-on slam.

While Paul had scoured the scientific literature, I found a reference in a children's story from a book my father read to us as children, *Mother West Wind "When" Stories*, written in 1917 by Thornton W. Burgess, a self-trained naturalist. In "When Mr. Kingfisher Took to the Ground," Little Joe Otter recounted how the ancestor of Rattles the Kingfisher came to nest in a stream bank hole. To my amazement, I read, "He flew straight at the spot he had selected and drove his big spear-like bill into it. Then he did it again and again. . . . In a little while he had room to cling with his feet."

Add a female to the scene, and our descriptions almost matched, except for the bouncing-off part. Not all naturalists' unusual sightings are documented and recorded in journals, but they should be. Every anecdotal account can shed light on a bird's problem-solving skills, intelligence, and individualism.

ℂ

Despite the thrill of a new find on Rattlesnake Creek, we worried. Could this head-banging be damaging? By day four, the kingfishers had excavated a hole big enough to squeeze inside. The aerial ramming was over.

As the going got dirtier, the female bathed more often, from two rinses on day 1 to four on day 2, and eight on day 3. She cleansed her feathers twelve times, compared to the male's two baths. Then, either late on day 4 or on day 5, the pair gave up. We found them at the lower part of the upper bank, reclaiming an existing hole closer to last year's nest.

ℂ

The breeding season had begun earlier than we'd observed the prior year. On March 24, the male had inspected several scruffy holes below the dam. Then, five days later, after fresh snow in the night, the female arrived. Like a practiced dancing couple, they flew to the same wire to replicate their courting. Their patterns suggested fidelity to each other and to place.

Dan Albano banded an impressive ninety-two breeding kingfishers, and fourteen came back to breed a second year on territories along the Connecticut River. He recaptured one female three years in a row, and another returning four years. His data gave some credibility to the possibility of Halcyon and Ceyx renewing their bonds.

Dan's research of banded juveniles revealed many disappearing after a dangerous first year, except for a handful showing up sixty miles away. Would I see any of the 2009 brood again?

ॐ

My time at the nest bank was not as consistent as I'd intended, yet a trip to watch Ian play soccer in Boise for three days in late March proved fortuitous. Cheering for the team, I could not take my eyes off my son in the midfield with his light step, soft feet, and zest for dribbling through opponents, like a kingfisher eluding every obstacle.

Between games, I strolled the Boise River Greenbelt with Jyl Hoyt, an Idaho National Public Radio reporter who had created a series on the natural world called *Off the Trail*. We'd become friends since meeting in a graduate school class called Reviewing the Arts. She'd walked right into one of Missoula's grittiest bars, the Oxford, and wrote with hilarity about her meal of brains and eggs and the old railroad men who camped out on stools.

We scanned for kingfishers along an unpaved, wilder trail section, named in honor of Bethine Church, who continued the legacy of her late husband Frank Church as a leader in Idaho's conservation of wilderness. Trails on both sides of the Boise River serve as a corridor for walkers, runners, and cyclists on the mostly paved stretches. The city's protected greenbelt extends seventeen miles, an act of foresight dating to the 1960s.

Golden currant bushes waved sunny blooms below leafless cottonwoods. Within five minutes, we heard the first belted kingfisher, a male silhouetted in a tree across the river. He tilted his head, flipped his tail twice, and then began his chatty commentary. Within minutes, a female sculled past him at eye level, greeting him with a swift and soft trilling.

The following morning, I ran ten miles on the river to tally five kingfishers, spaced about every mile and a half or so. They fished by the weirs, where waters flow calm above and tumble below. I'd be lucky to see a single kingfisher if I ran a similar loop on Rattlesnake Creek. I dubbed this waterway the River of Kingfishers.

One male clung to a branch as winds rumpled his thundercloud crest. With the next gust, the slender limb swayed. He shifted his weight like a sailor on a heaving deck. Then, he stretched forward into an elongated weapon, uttered a one-phrase war cry, and dove. *Splash!* He rose with a slippery fish pincered in his beak. After a couple of smacks on the branch, he spun his quarry around the right way, tipped back his head, and slurped in the three-incher like a slimy oyster. For the finale, he lifted his tail and sent whitewash sailing into the river. His next *Kkkkk . . . kikkikikik* softened into a purring.

Here, the birds coexisted with a stream of people on foot. I was humbled again by the birds teaching me to be careful in labeling behaviors. Skittish? Not so much here. The riverside forest is a mecca for black-capped chickadees, lesser goldfinches, yellow warblers, and song sparrows crooning a suite of melodies. Mule deer step past sagebrush, incongruous within the lushness, and a reminder of the surrounding arid landscape.

Forced within a confined channel on its journey through the city, the river cannot wind and flood at will. A dam that stores water for irrigators impacts the flows. Even so, the River of Kingfishers does overflow the banks in spring after a good winter, and wood ducks bejewel the backwaters.

My father once wrote an essay for a local conservation newsletter in North Carolina about serendipity, musing on wildlife adjusting to our artificial structures in unintended ways. For instance, chimney swifts in the east and Vaux's swifts in the west flutter down into brick chimneys to roost. The chimneys help substitute for the loss of enormous older or dead trees with hollowed tops opening to the sky—the ones we've cut down by the millions.

Our task becomes to notice where wildlife adjusts to us, honor the gift of their presence, and be willing to yield and flex to their needs. I once knew a woman who left her truck parked in her barn, waiting for a house wren to finish raising her chicks in the nest woven in the tailpipe. Our greater work is to rewild and renourish what we've taken away and to protect all that remains intact.

છ

From late March to the April aerial ramming days, I often saw the pair at the lower and upper banks of Rattlesnake Creek. Bracing for bitter winds and blinking away snowflakes brought a certain exhilaration. Without the motive of hunting for birds, I'd have hunkered down inside waiting for fair weather. By venturing forth no matter what the forecast, I often glimpsed the pair and, once, a roller coaster of courtship flight high above me.

One day by the pond, I listened to the skipping-stone notes of a kingfisher pinging across the reservoir. Six sleeping goldeneye ducks floated on the windless pond in a halcyon daze, one male and five females. On a rock ledge, a Canada goose incubated her eggs. Her long neck swiveled to rest on her back of soft tan feathers dusted with snow.

The kingfisher's call aroused all who slumbered. Speeding in from upstream to the head of the pond, Ceyx circled and landed on a shrub below the goose. He preened, wiping each feather, clean and oiled for the day.

Halcyon whooshed in without a word an hour later to join Ceyx. I could hear her soothing chitter. The pair flew in unison downstream. Running after them past the pond, past the entrance to the buildings, and arriving at the first 2009 observation point for the courting birds at the lower bank, I stopped by the old friend of the ponderosa pine that had hidden me so well. Scanning across the now taller tangled willows, dogwoods, and alders to the earthen bank, I saw the cycle repeated—at once familiar and new.

The kingfisher duo eyed each other, two feet apart on the wire stretching between the rickety, red-roofed shed and a metal pole. Ceyx turned toward Halcyon, who allowed him to sidle up closer than I'd seen before, but still not touching. He opened his wings as if to embrace the daughter of Aeolus, god of the winds. She gazed back. Motionless.

At midday on April 2, I crept behind the ample trunk of a Douglas-fir close to the upper bank. My stalwart dog Luna napped on the cone-littered ground. Within a couple of minutes, Ceyx streaked by with wingtips glancing on water coursing with the colors of green, purple, gold, and brown rocks. I heard his purling warble. Halcyon trilled a tuneful phrase of clickety consonants. Then, the two birds skirred upstream, with the creek song serenading every winding turn, and stirring a memory.

I was with my father and my then five-year-old son, hiking up a trail in the Canadian Rockies that wended through an alpine meadow of blooming beargrass. White pollen filtered sunlight. Ian was leading the way when a long-tailed weasel gripping a vole jumped in front of him. Three miles up, we stopped at a lake to eat sandwiches on a flat boulder. Hoary marmots whistled from the rocky talus slope. I urged Dad to hike alone to the upper basin, while we'd rest and pick ripe huckleberries. He gave us a sunbeam smile and strode away as I took note of every strong step. It would be his last mountain trek before cancer claimed him four months later.

Dawn of April 5 marked one of several new landmarks of the second season—and this one was X-rated. In below-freezing temperatures, I hastened up the main trail through the cottonwood, pine, and fir gallery, pausing by the lower bank without seeing birds. Continuing north, I headed off-trail into the floodplain forest with the hidden arc of nesting holes. Hopping over the ditch and onto the island, I faced the boulder that knew the tap of kingfishers. I saw them.

The pair shared an exposed Douglas-fir root with a dip in the middle and overhanging the creek a bit upstream from the 2009 nest burrow. For once, they nestled close. Then, Ceyx leaped onto Halcyon's back in a mating event lasting a few seconds. As soon as he dismounted, she flew off to the closest branch and preened. He was all stillness. Nonchalance? Or postcoital thrill?

Two mornings later, under woolen skies and showers, I returned to the "mating root" and trained the spotting scope on Halcyon. A half hour passed until Ceyx circled the tallest pines. He closed his wings, stooped, stalled, pulled up, and parked a body-width away from Halcyon, who had followed his crochet-hook pathway with her bill. Their beaks opened and shut in a secret chortling.

Sidling so close their feathers touched, Ceyx raised and lowered his head. Halcyon flicked her tail twice. Then, he mounted her, his wings flailing and his bill holding hers for balance. She cocked her tail to the side to receive the cloacal kiss. That's the official term for a male bird fertilizing a female's ovum as he presses his cloaca, a posterior opening, on her cloaca to transfer sperm.

The sexual act did seem perfunctory. Mating was a far cry from my vision of Ceyx and Halcyon of Greek myth in their nuptial bliss. The transformation into kingfishers by the gods gave them the bodies and feathers of brilliant birds and the gift of flight, yet could they still be sensual? Whether in the form of a common kingfisher of the Greek myth or a relative here on Rattlesnake Creek, they might miss their human bodies. Kingfisher copulations are short and abundant, as I observed multiple times that spring.

∞

Second chances. Two days before the bank ramming of April 17, I spotted a female kingfisher out of place. At 9 a.m., there she was, high on a cottonwood limb by the open meadow with the viewpoint north toward the boulder and the provocative, well-favored root.

I'd never seen a kingfisher in this particular spot, about sixty yards inland from the creek. Her lengthened posture emanated alertness. From my vantage, I could not see if her chili-pepper swash of a belt met in the middle or not, but I knew she was unfamiliar. Her ratcheting call rose like a question as she spotted the distant Ceyx, who had landed on the mating root across Rattlesnake Creek. I trained binoculars on him. He appeared agitated, with head raising and tail snapping. Would she join him? No. Ceyx speared his way farther upstream to land on a pine branch.

The outlier female flew to him, and again he fled. The next scene would feel devastating if I were in her feathers. There he was, roping the banks in flight with another female, the real Halcyon. I was ready for drama between the two females, but there was none. Halcyon ignored her rival, perhaps contented Ceyx had committed to her as they flew in and out of an old hole. At one point, Ceyx bathed in the creek and then preened on a branch for ten minutes before rejoining Halcyon.

After an hour and a half of waiting, the rejected female shambled downstream on despairing wings. Would she find an available mate? I never saw her again.

This sighting of two females in season two did not advance a red belt theory of female aggression, but did add a milestone to the kingfisher spring watch.

In snow, sleet, ice, and a tad of fair weather, I kept up morning forays to the lower bank by the dam and the upper bank of last year's nest. Luna stayed close and never chased a deer or even a squirrel. The two of us fused with the streamside.

After the aerial ramming day, Paul, Lisa, and I were worried. The pair had settled on an existing burrow about twenty-five yards upstream of the island. The hole appeared far too visible to human intruders, like the ditch tender who checked the diversion of the creek separating the island from the mainland. I made a note to alert him. The hole also seemed too low on the creek bank, susceptible to flooding and predators.

Halcyon and Ceyx kept up steady improvements, perhaps lengthening the tunnel and reshaping the nest burrow. There's something universal about a desire to remodel a home, whether a shake-up expansion or a fresh coat of paint and rearranged furniture. The array of choices can expose stark differences of taste. Inevitably, remodeling an old house leads to unforeseen obstacles. For kingfishers, a barrier could be a root or a rock. A roof collapse is possible, too, if the soil isn't the right texture.

Seeking a place to put up the blind, I gave up because of the problematic ditch trail. I'd be much too visible to people, even if few came this way. Instead, I hid behind willows, dogwoods, and mock orange bushes. On April 26, Ceyx entered the hole for twenty minutes. Halcyon was inside. How did they manage the tight space? For the next few days, snow alternated with rain. The kingfishers continued to show their zeal for copulating on the fir root above the sexy flow of the creek. On May 10, Ceyx mounted Halcyon four times in half an hour. He often grasped Halcyon's crest with his bill as he clung to feathers on her back.

❧

Returning to Boise for another soccer tournament in the first week of May, I found time to stroll the river trail with Jyl. Immersed in her sweet yet strong radio voice and our girlfriend conversations, I wasn't prepared for the battle that was soon encircling us like a winged tornado.

A female kingfisher chased another female. One bird closed the gap as they whisked into the cottonwoods.

It was far quieter by Rattlesnake Creek. I walked to the lower bank on May 18 as the first blooming arnica flowers pleated the needle-strewn forest floor. The creek had swelled to a frenzy as temperatures climbed into the 60s. The pond overflowed the low concrete wall where last year's credulous fledglings had liked to rest. Rain came in drizzles, downpours, and mists for eleven days, with bursts of sun and no kingfisher sightings. I hoped they were incubating eggs, but couldn't be sure. Where were the dawn exchanges? Still, every return invited a new wildflower bloom, a warbler's arrival, or a shift in the creek's tempo.

The second season would be interrupted by a month-long trip of a lifetime. On June 7, I began counting the days—six until the trip to South Africa. Paul and Lisa vowed to observe when they could. I was off to a continent of kingfishers. This would be the first time the World Cup had come to Africa, the real draw for Ian's dad, whose passion for soccer rivaled mine for birds.

We were ready with a car rented, camps and lodges reserved, and four World Cup soccer matches on the docket. Ian showed no sign of teenage angst of being with his parents. We would be there in the winter season, a drier time, when the wildebeest, impala, zebras, warthogs, and water buffalo paraded into water holes. I'd studied up on the ten king-fisher species dwelling in South Africa, with my dream bird at the top of the list—the giant kingfisher.

A year earlier, on June 7, Ceyx and Halcyon had toted fish to their young. This time? We saw no sign of fish deliveries at the refurbished burrow. Even as anticipation for South Africa grew, so did my concern for the pair's chancy hole. At the same time, I'd chalked up a few satisfy-ing firsts of this second season. Whenever I had spied on Halcyon and Ceyx mating kingfisher style, I felt ecstatic and a little apologetic as the voyeur.

The aerial ramming? I had a secret hope at the beginning of the quest that I might find something new. Paul, Lisa, and I had done it. The ramming also added to our observations of kingfisher gender roles. Their fifty-fifty effort tipped the scales even more in favor of an egalitar-ian relationship.

The Boise River kingfishers showed that even skitty birds could be tolerant of people when fish were abundant. That wild chase? The two females circumvoluted the cottonwoods while we stood in the eye of the storm.

I was ready for another second chance, too. Rattlesnake Creek and kingfishers tendered a welcome escape from a certain unease permeating my marriage. Before this peregrination to the exotic continent of Africa farther away than I'd ever traveled, I felt the same mix of trepidation and thrill as when observing the kingfishers blasting headfirst into the bank. There would be no holding back. Trust the fall.

CHAPTER 11
World Cup for the Birds

When I was a child, I liked to copy the calls of the birds and they would come to me.

—Joseph Gumede, personal communication

Bleary after a thirty-six-hour journey, I opened the shades at the Woodpecker's Inn, set in a suburban neighborhood of gated homes. We felt the fear as soon as we landed in Johannesburg. Our hosts had advised us to take a taxi from the airport, rather than the cheaper public transport vans that never seemed to carry a white person. Racism appeared raw and closer to the surface than in my home country.

Stepping out on the balcony into the glare of morning sunshine, I heard a ghoulish laugh: *Ha-da-da! Ha-da-da!* Streaming over the treetops were silhouetted dark shapes the size of geese, with long necks and scythe-like bills. Every bird on the first day in South Africa was a rarity. We would see the hadada ibis often, whether in this city of fifteen million or within the secluded wetlands of Ndumo Game Reserve, bordering Mozambique.

With each passing day, we let go of fear. Yes, the troubling shadow of apartheid was there, but unity and pride pervaded the country. The 2010 World Cup had come to South Africa. For the three of us—my then husband Dave, Ian, and me—we, too, had a coming together.

Invariably, I would scout for kingfishers, each new species a wonder and each sighting a form of belonging. Everywhere, people of all backgrounds asked us how we liked their country. The answer? We loved South Africa. Our one regret? We couldn't stay longer. The World Cup soccer proved as magnetic as the kingfisher quest, with the best players on the planet dribbling, passing, and scoring as we blew ear-shattering vuvuzela horns in a cheering stadium. Even at a park camp, we'd join dozens of fans around a modest TV set up outdoors.

In our twenty-six days, we traveled to state-of-the-art soccer stadiums in Johannesburg and Durban, to birding guesthouses in Creighton, in Eshowe, and outside Polokwane and Dullstroom. We roughed it in superb wildlife protected areas: Imfolozi, Ndumo, and Mkhuze Game Reserves in KwaZulu-Natal; Kruger National Park; and the Golden Gate Highlands, the one place where we could walk freely without the danger of predators like lions. Still, we felt a prickling sensation of what might pounce from the shade or darkness.

On our trek in the Golden Gate Highlands, Ian climbed a high rock overlooking the expansive sandstone range and valleys of the Drakensberg Mountains, where J. R. R. Tolkien grew up and drew inspiration for the Lord of the Rings trilogy. Just as Ian opened his arms to the winds, a dragon-like bird glided ten feet above him. To this day, Ian remembers the secretarybird as his favorite of all the exotic avian species we witnessed, from lilac-breasted rollers to southern ground hornbills, grey crowned cranes, and African hoopoes. He did not know the secretarybird is rare, holds the record as the longest-legged predatory bird, and is a fearsome hunter of snakes. What he knew was an intimate connection with a gigantic bird in a wild place, as if he'd crossed a time threshold into the Jurassic or a fantasy door to Tolkien's Middle Earth.

A few days after the Golden Gate Highlands and our second World Cup game (the Netherlands versus Japan in Durban), Dave drove on the left along the dusty entry road to Mkhuze Game Reserve in the KwaZulu-Natal region. He pointed to the stacks of firewood along the way. "We should stop to buy some before we get to the reserve." As he slowed, six barefoot children came racing down from a thatched rondavel (hut) on the hillside dotted with acacia trees. After paying for a bundle, Dave asked them if they'd like to pose for a photo. Eagerly, they each picked up a piece of firewood to balance on upheld hands, and one asked to hold the South Africa flag we had in our car. That night, the wood burned long and hot, throwing sparks to the stars outside our safari tent at Mantuma Camp.

At Ndumo Game Reserve, a wildebeest snorted a few yards away during the night. This campground was unfenced. Anything might come by our tent. There, we hired Joseph Gumede, the park's experienced local bird guide. Within the first five minutes of our walk, he pointed to a striped kingfisher, motionless and camouflaged in a tree at eye level. This most diminutive of the *Halcyon*-genus birds, *Halcyon chelicuti*, dove for grasshoppers with the same sizzling plunge as a belted kingfisher twice the size.

Joseph carried a gun to protect us from dangerous predators. We walked in single file behind him along the fig-tree-lined Pongola River, until I headed off to investigate a bird by the river. Right away, his soft tenor shifted to a sharp command, ordering me back from the crocodile-laden waters. Even ten feet away was too close. After that, I never strayed. Joseph grew up in a local village and spent his childhood calling in birds by the names of his language. He told us his oldest son was training to become a bird guide, an esteemed profession in game reserves.

On another day in Ndumo, two pied kingfishers hovered above a pan, a shallow lake. Like waving white-and-black handkerchiefs held up by invisible hands, their wings blurred in the diaphanous light. The pied kingfisher, *Ceryle rudis*, is the lone species within a genus that joins *Megaceryle* and *Chloroceryle* to form the subfamily of Cerylinae.

I'd met another relative and a supreme hoverer. With eyes locked on prey far below, and head held still, the bird's wings stroke down and up about eight times per second. The fanned tail is the rudder. The dive is stupendous. When the black, arrow-shaped bill strikes and slides into the water, the tip sends shock waves that may be picked up by sensitive hairs on the fish. The dive must be precise, or the pied kingfisher's meal will escape. The difference between success and failure is just one-fiftieth of a second reaction time from that of the prey.

Vertical dives from thirty feet above the water could damage a pied kingfisher's eyes, but a bony plate connected to the prefrontal bone of the skull slides across their eyes upon impact, a design engineers have employed to improve high-impact shielding in the fields of aerospace, plumbing, and transport.

Pied kingfisher genders are similarly patterned in black and white, but the male has a second lower breast band and the female does not. I pondered this pattern, reversed from my home birds. Even if there were no color differences between genders, did the male's second band play a role?

When it comes to nesting within holes on vertical sandbanks, pied kingfishers assemble in social colonies that may reach a hundred pairs. The nonbreeding kingfishers (first-year birds) serve as helpers to fish and feed the young in the burrows. The chicks hatch asynchronously, an adaptation to life where prey can be abundant or spotty. The parents start incubating after the first egg, which hatches first and gives an edge to the chick as the oldest and biggest. In a lean year, the smallest chicks starve.

⁊⊃

My list of African kingfisher species expanded. Brown-hooded kingfishers (*Halcyon albiventris*) surveyed the mayhem of snorting warthogs at waterholes. The size of blackbirds, their orange bills, and the splash of turquoise on wings and tail, added flamboyance to the cream, tawny brown, and black feathers. Sit-and-wait predators, they dove from branches or wires to pounce on grasshoppers and other crunchy prey.

The malachite kingfisher (*Alcedo cristata*) eluded my camera every time, a teasing apparition in sapphire and metallic green head feathers, scarlet bill, indigo back, and gold-red chest. I often spotted one near water, an ultramarine splendor jeweling dense shrubs. Like the green kingfisher I saw on the Rio Grande, this tiny piscivore dives for small fish or crabs, prawns, tadpoles, frogs, and water beetles.

⁊⊃

Our trip finale was Kruger National Park, also our best chance to find *Megaceryle maxima*. Here, the giant kingfisher dwells along languid rivers near the tree of life, the baobab that can live for three thousand years.

The day we drove to the Pafuri Picnic Area on the Mozambique and Zimbabwe border, the farthest northern point in Kruger National Park, Dave and I felt conflicted. We'd looked forward to this premier birding destination on the Luvuvhu River, yet Ian dozed in the back seat. He had awoken feverish and subdued, far from our lively boy who had passed a soccer ball to a zebra, juggled the ball two hundred times while I birdwatched, and exclaimed over the tallness of giraffes and the immensity of the bull elephant that approached our rental car. We hoped he had some

Giant kingfishers

harmless twenty-four-hour malaise, but we were in South Africa, where diseases could be severe. Was it malaria? We'd taken all the precautions.

At Pafuri, we met one of South Africa's premier bird guides, Frank Mombasa. He confirmed the presence of giant kingfishers and then mimicked a jay-like *KEK* call. When the birds are disturbed, the *kek* can become a resounding, high-pitched, wind-up *kek-kek-kek-kek!* Like the belted kingfisher, they have softer greeting calls, like a *kah-kah-kah*. I kept my eyes mostly steady on the river as hippos rose and snorted in the turgid brown waters lined with sycamore figs, but I often turned away to check on a flushed Ian, who had by then fallen asleep.

Here, where the Luvuvhu River meets the Limpopo River, forming the border of South Africa, Zimbabwe, and Mozambique, are convergences far from harmonic. The history is thick with poachers and other villains escaping police in one country by crossing into another, a reputation leading to the name Crook's Corner in the nineteenth century.

Luck! A male giant kingfisher landed on a fallen tree that had washed to the edge of the Luvuvhu River. Just below him, standing on the cracked riverbed, was a nyala, an African antelope with antlers curving back above a chocolate and golden head with a dash of white below his eyes. Double glamour.

Colossal in the satiny light, the largest of all kingfishers in Africa shone with his wide dagger of a black beak, crest, and upper breast the coppery sheen of cinnabar. Black feathers on his back speckled in white resembled a starry night. A female's similarly reddish feathers would form a fashionable skirt on her lower belly. If seen side by side they'd be the color-coordinated couple heading out to a party.

Like belted kingfishers, the pair excavates a hole in an earthen bank, but the nesting tunnel can extend as far as a record-setting twenty-eight feet deep. Fall is the height of the breeding season. After the young have fledged, the female steps up to feed them for three weeks. Is she the more dedicated to her offspring? The prey for giant kingfishers includes more than fish. To nab a crab, the giant kingfisher juggles the wriggling invertebrate for a firm beak grasp, and then knocks the meal hard on the nearest surface until the pincers come off.

Meanwhile, Ian's fever worsened. We left in a hurry to reach the nearest health clinic two hours away. Closed. We drove another hour out of Kruger National Park to the closest town and into a dirty waiting room crowded with sick people waiting for a doctor who might not show up for another day—a sobering reminder of all we take for granted. Finally, we had no choice but to return to the park. Our fortune changed at the campground, where a vacationing doctor examined Ian and assured us he had strep throat. All he needed was penicillin, which we had in our medical supplies. Ian's health turned around within a day, and we continued our sojourn of World Cup and kingfishers with an underlying disquiet.

Near our camp at Shingwedzi in Kruger National Park, we saw one more giant kingfisher, this bird within stomping distance of elephants tapping the dry riverbed with their feet to locate water. A few days later, at Shrine Bush Camp, a park ranger named Phanuel Maluleke told me the name for the giant kingfisher in his language of Tsanga: *thungu-nununu* (pronounced toon-goon-oo-noo-noo).

Packing up to go home, I basked in all that was hopeful. Cars festooned in South African flags were as bountiful as the mopane trees of the veld. At World Cup matches, international visitors cast politics aside for the beautiful game. The feeling of unity extended mostly to our marriage, too. Like those undercurrents of racism, some overt, we could not erase our troubles, but we brushed them aside in mutual gratitude. This was Nelson Mandela's country, and his words rang true: "Part of being optimistic is keeping one's head pointed toward the sun, one's feet moving forward."

On our seventeen-hour flight from Johannesburg to Atlanta, a minor headache grew to a migraine. The tick that had burrowed into my ankle on one of our last days in Kruger National Park had left a small crater, which grew infected, itched, and swelled. The skin in the middle became necrotic. I covered it with a bandage.

By the time we'd arrived back home in Missoula, I could only curl up on the floor of the bathroom in a fetal position, moaning as what felt like ten ice picks jabbed into my head. The merest blink sent the picks deeper into my skull. I had the tick-borne parasite *Rickettsia africae*. Once diagnosed and taking the correct antibiotic, I was restored enough for a light-headed walk to the kingfisher bank on Rattlesnake Creek a couple days later.

℘

The nest across from the ditch tender's trail had failed. This year, there would be no fledglings crash-landing on the pond. Feeling sad, I longed to tell my bird friends the stories of kingfishers in Africa—the pied, brown-hooded, striped, malachite, and the resplendent close relative, the giant kingfisher.

As my list of kingfisher species edged upward, I noticed an enriching of my home community, as if the deep roots trellising the banks of Rattlesnake Creek extended to the Luvuvhu River and the Rio Grande, too. Across the planet, freshwater pours sustenance to quench the thirst of an astounding biodiversity that kingfishers remind us to treat with a reverence. Listen to the messenger.

My Africa travels were only dips in the sea, yet they opened my eyes to our fragile planetary diversity and to the struggles and generosity of people I met. By venturing to the outer ripples of a concentric circle, I experienced Rattlesnake Creek anew. When a rattling belted kingfisher sped by, my quickening heartbeat pounded like African drums and ears rang with the shocking exuberance of vuvuzelas.

Heading East

CHAPTER 12
Ghost Kingfishers

> Truth walks toward us on the paths of our questions. . . . As soon as you
> think you have the answer, you have closed the path and may miss vital new
> information. Wait awhile in the stillness, and do not rush to conclusions, no
> matter how uncomfortable the unknowing.
>
> —Jacqueline Winspear, *Maisie Dobbs*

Pulling out a drawer of belted kingfisher study skins, I rubbed my eyes
under the fluorescent light glaring on the pea-soup-green metal cabinets,
stacked three-high and almost to the ceiling. Within the sixth-floor back
chambers of the Smithsonian National Museum of Natural History in
Washington, DC, rests a treasure trove of birds—more than 645,000
preserved birds, representing the rare, the common, the exotic, and even
the extinct. The third-largest bird collection in the world houses 85 percent of the earth's more than ten thousand species represented. It was
late September of 2010.

Like a library, the birds are cataloged. All cabinets and drawers are
arranged by taxonomic order. The birds are the books, each with an
individual tag bearing a number, the collector's name, location, and date.
The numbers link to an extensive database and sometimes to written
journals tucked away into obscurity, yet bearing witness to bygone eras.

I had come to discern patterns in female red belts, looking for hints
or pathways to answer the ever more perplexing question, "Why are the
females brighter than the males?" This day would also mark my first time
holding a belted kingfisher alive or dead—not one bird but hundreds.
Specifically, I looked forward to comparing red belts among individuals.
If females could out-dazzle other females with a brighter, more prominent belt, this feature might give them an edge.

The belted kingfisher assemblage at the Smithsonian tallies 395
birds, with 258 prepared as study skins. Rows of these stuffed birds

lie belly-up in a drawer, wings tight against their bodies, tiny feet tied together, cotton in their eye sockets, and bills pointed up and back, the better to fit flat in a drawer. A handwritten collection tag is tied to each bird's petite foot. Entering the back corridors felt like a pilgrimage to a sacred tomb, one that happens to contain 145 million artifacts. All it took was a single phone call a few days earlier to James Dean, who'd managed the bird collection of the Natural History Museum for thirty years.

I'd walked in blustery rain from a Metro stop, crossed Constitution Avenue, and halted before the marble steps leading up to closed doors, working up my courage to go through the door marked Staff and Research Only. Opening the heavy metal door, I stepped inside. A guard scrutinized my driver's license, checking it for a match with the day's scheduled researchers.

Clipping on a visitor badge in the stuffy anteroom off to the side of a cavernous hall, I waited to be escorted to the bird collection by none other than James Dean. I couldn't stop thinking of the namesake actor with the greased-back hair, a cigarette hanging from his lip, and a Porsche roadster waiting in his staff parking spot. Instead, James was square-shouldered, quiet, and unassuming, with a salt-and-pepper beard, scholarly glasses, and a mild smile. I traipsed after him to an elevator taking us to the sixth floor and into an echoing room of looming cabinets in rows. Each one was secured with a latch and contained rows of wooden pull-out shelves.

James opened the first cabinet for me, the lowest one, and pulled out a tray of males. To look at all the shelves with belted kingfishers would take climbing up a six-step ladder in the aisle. "When you pick one up, be gentle," he said. "Some are quite old and not in good shape." I should take care to lift them by the whole body and never by the tail or wing or bill. I was free to take photos and stay as long as I wanted. Then, he faded away into the murkiness, reappearing every hour or so for a curt nod in my direction as he walked by carrying eagles and woodpeckers.

What lay before me represented an esteemed collection available for all who want to learn from what these still bodies and handwritten tags may offer. Study skins do not depict birds in natural poses. Instead, their purpose is to provide a record: day, month, year, location, and name of the collector. Once specimens are cataloged, the investigative possibilities continue to expand, as James had explained to me in an email exchange:

To me, one of the greatest values of bird collections is their value as documenting the natural history and biodiversity of the planet. Each specimen with its associated data is unique and represents one point of reference in our ability to understand that species and the biodiversity of the particular place and point in time of where the specimen was collected.

Despite a mummified look, most plumages remain rich in color and patterns. Each bird had all internal organs and tissue removed. If collectors prepared specimens well, the skins should last several centuries with intricate feathers intact. Until the mid-1970s, they treated the inside of the bird skins with an arsenic compound to fend off insects. As recently as ten to twenty years ago, the museums, too, applied insecticides. Collection managers now inspect the birds for any signs of insects, using sticky traps to monitor any stray bugs within the yawning back rooms of the Smithsonian. Freezing the new specimens before adding them to the collection helps, too.

I studied the arrangement of kingfisher shelves, organized by sex, and by season. I'd planned to examine female birds, but I couldn't resist opening one drawer after another. I also inspected the tray of males James had pulled out, starting with a bird collected in 1855 in Bodega, California. The breast feathers appeared as yellowed as an old book, a sign the collector who stuffed the bird had not cleaned all the fats from the skin. Bodega remains a town of about eight hundred people, on the coast of California and not far from Point Reyes, where I had spent two weeks running after kingfishers and musing at a Mesa Refuge writing retreat in the fall of 2008 at the onset of my quest. Maybe this bird once flew along Salmon Creek, which weaves through Bodega, or winged out on the Pacific Ocean's bays and wetlands, all homes of the Coast Miwok people. His stuffed body now serves as a historical marker staking out a territory in time.

I placed the 155-year-old bird from Bodega back into the drawer to nest next to a bird from Clarkston, Washington, shot a century later, in 1955, his snowy feathers as lustrous as if he had flown the day before. In 1957, the Dalles Dam on the Columbia River would drown Celilo Falls, one of the greatest salmon fishing places for many tribes.

Reading the tags with their neat, cramped handwriting and collector names was like scouring grave markers in a cemetery, but this time, instead of encountering a tombstone, I held the preserved body.

The 1950s also marked a continuing practice of shooting kingfishers, considered pests to anglers. Specimens to stuff were plentiful in a period when fishermen set steel traps on favorite perch sites. As A. C. Bent had lamented,

> The most serious enemies of the kingfisher are the selfish fisherman, who wants all the fish for himself and begrudges the poor bird an honest living, and the proprietor of a trout hatchery, who is unwilling to go to the trouble and expense of screening his pools to protect his fish. The former shoots every kingfisher he can with misguided satisfaction; the latter either shoots or traps any that visit his pools.

Opening the first drawer of females, my hands tightened on the rim. I whispered, "It's true." The reddish feathers forming the belts differed on every bird. Imagine if a painter daubed cayenne-hued paint across the breast to form a horizontal band and then smeared down the outside edges. Sometimes, she pressed hard to imprint a bold design. On others, her brush trailed off at an angle or left a white space for an incomplete belt.

I cradled a kingfisher with an almost full belt from the Jefferson River in south central Montana, shot on September 15, 1888, by Chas. W. Richmond. Later, I would search and find the exact reference in *The Auk* (the leading bird science journal then and now, under a new name, *Ornithology*):

> *Ceryle alcyon*. Belted Kingfisher—Very common along all the streams. Several were noted at Mystic Lake. At our camp on the Jefferson River, we found the fish infested with long, slender white worms which were coiled up in the flesh on the sides and the back. A Kingfisher shot at this camp was also found to be infested with these worms, seven of which (some of them nearly a foot in length) were found among (not in) its intestines.

The tag became the launch point for an unanticipated find. This kingfisher had lived with a stomach full of parasitic worms. Reading Richmond and F. H. Knowles' accounts of their explorations, mostly in Gallatin County, I caught a glimmer of the bird's former home, when Bozeman was a town of about two thousand people (compared to more than fifty thousand today).

Richmond and Knowles documented 111 bird species, of which they shot ninety-three, and collected seven hundred specimens. Their bird assemblages and journals offer a barometer for gauging former wildlife abundance. Clouds of sage grouse once burst from the sagebrush. Sharp-tailed grouse flocks sheltered in native bunchgrass. Bobolinks feasted on wild sunflowers. Kingfishers still thrive, but not the sage grouse, sharp-tails, or bobolinks. Their populations plummeted with diminishing habitats and incompatible practices, including grazing, haying, and encroaching subdivisions.

I picked up another specimen, a juvenile female, and read the tag of a "Chas. H. Townsend," who collected this kingfisher on the Farallon Islands, September 6, 1884. The feathers of the upper breast band were burnished copper, a sign of juvenile plumage.

Charles Haskins Townsend, 1859–1944, was in his twenties when he headed out on the US Fish Commission steamer, *The Albatross*, from San Francisco to the Gulf of California. During the fall and winter, he shot 226 birds, of ninety-two species, heralding eleven as new species.

The Farallon Islands, off the coast of Point Reyes, are dark, jagged, and imposing. Upon closer look, they're teeming with seabird colonies. To get there, kingfishers had to fly about thirty miles from the shore. The tag bearing Townsend's admirable script led to yet another eye-opener. Later, I would locate a current bird list for the Farallon Islands. Sure enough, the belted kingfisher is a winter visitor.

Studying tags and pensive about earlier times, I placed a 1900 Indiana bird next to a diminutive Alaska bird collected in 1885 on the Koowask River. The midwestern bird was a full two inches longer, a surprise when Alaska has a reputation for animals bigger than those in the lower 48 states, at least when it comes to grizzly bears.

Does diet influence the size of birds or not? Looking into this question a decade later, the current Smithsonian bird collections manager

Christopher Milensky told me belted kingfisher sizes are variable across the range. He also pointed to another factor called "preparator bias." By filling a study skin with a little more cotton, the specimen might appear longer or chubbier than when alive.

Whenever a Montana bird showed up in the collection, I felt my heart skip a homesick beat. Two months after returning from South Africa, our family of three (plus our elderly dog Luna) had packed up our Subaru and driven across the country to Washington, DC, for Dave's teaching-year sabbatical, a fellowship for him, and another second chance for us.

While missing Missoula and the West, I was happy to live on the outskirts of the capital city in Takoma Park, close to my younger brother Rob and his wife Cynthia and their three children. Ian attended middle school with his cousins at Sidwell Friends School, where an inspiring science teacher often had the students outside documenting pollinators in native gardens. My mother was a seven-hour drive away in North Carolina.

I had more than the Smithsonian lead to follow in those nine months on the east coast. Mic Hamas had given me this tip as well: "Go to Chincoteague Island in winter, and you'll likely see many kingfishers there fishing in the bays," he said. He was intrigued by how well the normally solitary and territorial kingfishers tolerated each other.

On the Smithsonian day, I would learn from the dead—such as the juvenile female from Hilger, Montana, a sleepy town in the center of the state, where water runs in rivulets and prairie potholes. Harry Mallets collected the bird on July 30, 1919, a year marking the continuing flu pandemic that broke out in 1918.

Earlier in Montana, Captain Thorne had roamed the remote terrain east of the divide to Lame Deer, now part of the Northern Cheyenne Indian Reservation. There, on August fifth of 1892, he shot a belted kingfisher female. She was stuffed with her head sideways instead of upward. Her belt was like Halcyon I'd followed on Rattlesnake Creek, with her signature breast band narrowing and then not quite meeting in the middle.

೫

A few years later, I would read more history within the belted kingfisher entry in the 657-page 2016 book *Birds of Montana*. George Bird Grinnell, who had translated stories with kingfisher totems, collected a bird on Cut Bank Creek near Glacier National Park in September of 1885, but the specimen is missing. Morton J. Elrod (a naturalist, University of Montana professor, and photographer) prepared a specimen from Missoula in September of 1897. I liked to think the kingfisher was an ancestor of at least one of the birds we followed on Rattlesnake Creek.

೫

The female belt sizes and intensity of colors diverged, but was there any rhyme or reason for the variations? I scrutinized one shelf containing eighteen birds, all collected between January and April. That should minimize the chance of confusing juvenile and adult plumage, or so I thought.

I moved the study skins around on the tray, arranging the kingfishers by gradations of red belts, and then returning them to their original positions. I gave a slight edge to larger females bearing bolder reddish belts. One big Panama juvenile bird's belt was thick and straight, with no narrowing in the middle. A few females showed only a glint of the russet feathers, like gesture drawings.

The birds with the most bronze in their upper bluish bands came from tropical locations, including Panama in January, Puerto Rico in February, and the Bahamas in April. Juveniles from hatching through December of their first year retain many rufous-tinged feathers. However, second-year birds can still show bronze shading through at least January and even into October of their second year. Despite plumage marking the birds as still youthful, they are ready to court, mate, and raise a family the next spring after hatching.

After four hours in the stark white light, breathing in slight fumes from bird preservation, I retreated. Six floors down in the main hall of the Smithsonian, I flinched at the contrasting clamor of families and school groups exclaiming over the famous taxidermy African elephant.

At fourteen feet tall and twelve tons, the elephant loomed Godzilla-like above the ant-like crowds as if to trumpet a silent message: "Remember your place in the world; it's not about you."

&

Later, I spoke on the phone with Geoffrey Hill, the feather coloration expert.

"Here's the problem," he said. "There's no way to know the ages of the birds when they were shot, except for the young ones. If you can't tell if a bird is one, two, or three years old, it's tough to compare feather colors." He suggested I return with calipers to measure variations in bird and belt sizes. An important clue might emerge. I wanted to be a committed citizen scientist, but I kept resisting the trip back to the catacombs.

The belly-up birds showed reddish belts varying in thickness and patterns, and at least some larger females sporting more dramatic belts and sashes. Those snippets served as a beginning for more research in the field.

Heading into the Smithsonian with one purpose in mind, I had uncovered something else. The stuffed birds were a conduit to history, to collectors and naturalists who also bushwhacked along streams like Rattlesnake Creek.

The other epiphany? James Dean waxed eloquent on the biodiversity significance of the collection, as well as practical applications that might even save human lives. Researchers learned how to mount miniature cameras on eagle backs by taking measurements of the skins in the collections, he wrote in a lengthy note after my visit. Hummingbird skins aided engineers in their design of robot drone devices carrying cameras into dangerous places. Biopsy samples from fluid-preserved birds dating to 1920 assisted infectious disease specialists studying avian influenza viruses from the 1918 pandemic. A skeleton collection serves as a field guide for archeologists for identifying bones in ancient village sites.

The study skins, combined with the oral history of the native peoples, tell us of a world we must remember if we are to value the meaning of wildness. Many of the specimens dated to the late 1800s and early 1900s, when "shotgun ornithology" was at its zenith. Author Scott Weidensaul coined the term in his book, *Of a Feather, A Brief History of American Birding*. Shooting birds for identification, research, and museum collections might sound barbaric now, but consider the tools available. Roger Tory Peterson would not revolutionize popular birding with his field guide until 1934. Low-cost binoculars only arrived on the birding scene after World War II. Zoom lenses for film cameras were still in the design phase in the 1950s.

In today's era, with endless possibilities for studying and documenting birds up close without killing them, collecting has dropped off. Instead, ethical debates over continuing the practice often ensue among ornithologists. When the public chimes in, the controversy can be fierce. James Dean made a compelling case for collections.

Scientists take a few thousand birds per year for study—inconsequential compared to outdoor cats killing an estimated 2.4 billion birds a year in the United States alone. On the other side is the question of ethics, especially when so many birds are struggling to find toeholds in depleted habitats. As I perused the collections, I noted several newer tags offering the compromise of collecting and stuffing birds that had died from other causes. The handwritten notes seemed apologetic: "struck a window" or "found on the road."

I left the Smithsonian with a funereal feeling. For some extinct species like the Carolina parakeet and the passenger pigeon, their tangible record of existence lies in preserved skins. We're inhabiting a world where the kaleidoscope of life is growing dark at our hands. Extinction indeed is forever. Yet, I'd also learned the value of our catalogued historical past as a link to the abundance of earlier times and to applications that may save birds and humans.

After examining hundreds of scientific study skins from so many parts of North America, I had a visceral need to be in the company of living kingfishers. I wanted to be outdoors like the angling bird, eyes seeking the movement of fish, with every sense in synchrony.

CHAPTER 13

Song of Sharpening Stone

Adults patrol their district, crying out, prompting Ojibwa to call it *o-gish-ke-mun-ne-sa*, the bird that calls like the noise made passing a knife over a sharpening stone.

—Robert E. Nichols Jr., *Birds of Algonquin Legend*

Running on the Sligo Creek pathway in Takoma Park, Maryland, on a fall colors day in 2010, I was on the alert. Scan. Don't trip on a crack. Pause. A red-shouldered hawk shifted on an oak branch as an eastern phoebe pegged a flying insect from her perch on a maple, shimmering with cardinal-hued leaves. A volley of kingfisher notes echoed from oak to oak, linking me to Montana in what would become a pivotal nine months away from Rattlesnake Creek and home.

Despite this creek's burden of plastic jugs and bags wedging between stones and the occasional wafts of sewage, native birds persevere within a highly urbanized watershed. The wildlife has a strong ally in Friends of Sligo Creek, which engages neighbors, families, and school groups to "sweep the creek" of litter, pull invasive weeds, monitor water quality, and delve into native plants and animals. Sligo is a haven for the human spirit, too.

Tumbling and sliding over smooth rocks, Sligo Creek flows nine miles to the Northwest Branch of the Anacostia River, which merges with the main Anacostia and into the Potomac River to finally enter the Chesapeake Bay of the Atlantic Ocean.

Worrying about polluted waters, I recalled my interview with Dr. Jeff Kelly in 2009, before the first season. When we spoke, he and fellow biologist Eli Bridge had nearly completed a two-year study of sixty-nine kingfisher nests on New York's Upper Hudson River. They hoped to determine whether PCBs (polychlorinated biphenyls) harmed the birds' ability to raise their young. They compared river sections above and below a historic PCB source.

Despite the ban of the toxin in 1979, these industrial chemicals still persist in the environment. As top predators in aquatic ecosystems, kingfishers can accumulate toxins, from PCBs to mercury. Pollutants concentrate as they work their way up the food chain, from phytoplankton to insects to fish to piscivorous birds. In fact, kingfisher eggs collected in 2002 and 2004 in their study area had elevated levels of the known carcinogen.

With concern, I learned that the lower Anacostia River was laden with PCBs. What might be the impact on birds? Later, in 2013, I would read Jeff and Eli's published study results that demonstrated how complicated it is determine harmful effects of PCBs on kingfishers.

Many factors influenced the birds' ability to raise a new generation, including quality of nesting habitat, easy access to fish, and parental ability to raise a brood. The authors finding of slightly higher nesting success downriver from the PCB site also correlated with superior habitat, likely claimed by experienced mates.

To secure a grant, scientists improve their chances when studying species for which extinction looms or when researching a bird might shed light on a human health question, like PCBs. However, the expansive territories and ever-wary behaviors of kingfishers pose serious challenges. Even sixty-nine nests offered a limited amount of hard-won data to analyze.

∓

To find kingfishers, I often biked five miles upstream along Sligo Creek to the University Ponds—two stormwater-gathering reservoirs ringed by cattails and hardwoods and close to the freeway roar. There, pileated woodpeckers threshed dead trees standing tall and whitened, the last of their bark slipping away. Sharp-shinned hawks whizzed in, sleek as race cars ruling the aerial freeway. Canada geese taxi-honked. Butterflies tossed like wind-blown slips of paper. Dragonflies helicoptered by. A great-blue heron froze, long neck extended in the predatory stalk.

A female belted kingfisher winged in with the happy chatter of a best friend. Her rufescent belt fastened in the middle. Five minutes later, a male jaunted in with a prattle that switched to a higher pitch and volume. No friendly encounter here. The female gunned for him. They lapped the pond once, twice, and thrice. She was right in his slipstream and gaining. In a desperate move, he shot into the layered forest. A tree branch snapped as he scuffed a wing on a dogleg turn. The female flew away and then back—alone.

From her perch on a tree stump protruding five feet from the water, she gave me a look, which I labeled as "victorious." Scribbling down another observation of female domination, I noted she was the city-smart tough bird on the block.

Her ancestors lived among the Algonquin-speaking peoples, consisting of twenty-four tribes, including the Piscataway of present-day Maryland. The Algonquin inhabited a great swath of lands, from Virginia to the Rocky Mountains and north to Hudson Bay.

In *Birds of Algonquin Legend* is a story of "O-gish-ke-mun-ne-sa," the bird that calls like the sound of a knife passing over a sharpening stone. Kingfisher flew back and forth close to a crying man named Nanaboso, who had dreamed an animal living in the water had killed his uncle. Soon after, his uncle did not come home from a hunting trip. As Kingfisher zipped by, an aggravated Nanaboso snatched him by his head, wet all his feathers, and rubbed them the wrong way so they stood up. Next, he threw the bird aside.

A bedraggled and admonished Kingfisher then informed Nanaboso in a low voice that he knew of his uncle's fate. A now pleased Nanaboso offered him the fur he wore around his neck in exchange for assistance. He smoothed down the roughed-up feathers and wrapped the gray fur with red on front around Kingfisher's neck, which is why he has "that mark around his neck today."

Kingfisher told Nanaboso that a *manito* (a spirit) shot up from the river, twisted a tail around his uncle, pulled him from his canoe, and killed him. To find the *manito*, Nanaboso should go to the island where the *manito* lived with two sons. Nanaboso eventually slew the *manito*. As in the earlier stories, the kingfisher was a messenger and helper, even if not the most forthcoming one.

O-gish-ke-mun-ne-sa. This is the bird of the beak lancing the water and calling like a knife sliding across a sharpening stone. I wasn't sure about that comparison, but with a light circular touch of knife blade on stone, you can induce a series of tinkly slurred notes rising and then falling away.

As time, culture, and technologies change, our sound analogies evolve, too. For example, A. C. Bent in the 1940s wrote of the kingfisher call:

> It consists of a series of harsh, wooden, rattling notes of great carrying power. It has been likened to the sound made by an old-fashioned policeman's or watchman's rattle, a very good description for those of us who are old enough to remember such out-of-date sounds; but it may remind the younger generation of the sound made by certain noise-making instruments used at get-together dinners, political rallies, or other joyous gatherings.

Noise-making instruments? Some party sounds never go out of style—from spoons banging on pots to party blowers. Kingfishers do have a spritely way of lifting spirits.

A decade later on the Oregon coast, I would marvel at two male kingfishers keeping up a constancy of vocalizations for two hours while chasing, swerving, hovering, sparring, and possibly playing. After all, the heavy fog had just lifted after a week and the bay dazzled in sunlight. Once, a third kingfisher joined in the fray and tripled the intensity of chatter. The birds arced through the sky above the rippling cobalt waters of Coos Bay.

ॐ

By September's end, belted kingfishers from the north were migrating down the Atlantic coast to escape the oncoming ice. Some would stay put, as Dan had observed on the Connecticut River, where males toughed out the coldest nights in earthen nest burrows.

Favorable winds triggered their flights guided by internal compasses. When the birds collided with strong easterly trade winds, they ascended to higher altitudes of calm air. On occasion, storms might blow the migrants out to sea, as far as four hundred miles off the coast. Would their sharpening-stone calls slice the clouds?

Thanksgiving with my mother and family in North Carolina offered a prelude to coastal kingfishers, which I hoped to see in relative abundance a month later at Chincoteague National Wildlife Refuge in Virginia, following up on Mic Hamas's tip.

Kayaking among marshes and open water on the bayside of Topsail Island, I soon spotted three belted kingfishers hovering high above tidal channels. They also claimed wooden stakes placed in the shallower waters by oyster farmers to mark their shellfish spots. There were fish, fish, and more fish. Why not share the bounty? Here, the territories for kingfishers had shrunk from a mile to a hundred meters, yet they defended their space with bold forays and calls like torrents of rain.

I saw more males than females as notetaking gave way to exhilaration each time a kingfisher rode the salt air down to the sea and escalated up to a favored oyster stake with a southern shine of a fish.

Before returning north, I made one solo pilgrimage to the old milldam across the marsh behind my parents' former home. I sat on my father's bench, where tree leaves flickered orange and burgundy above the tidal stream. A red leaf of the sweet gum tree sailed on the golden fingers of the outgoing tide. A pileated woodpecker cocked his scarlet crest from a sturdy limb. Carolina chickadees bantered. Two hooded mergansers—resplendent in their white and black fan-shaped head crests—floated by the muted yellow reeds.

Then I heard the unrolling of notes, of naming, of *o-gish-ke-mun-ne-sa*, as the kingfisher's scooping wingbeats gathered up rays of morning sun. The bird and my father's spirit converged where salt mingled with freshwater, birth met death, and decay fostered renewal. I edged toward the kingfisher poised on driftwood, her belt of autumnal reds glowing like the forest.

An ocean-stirred zephyr blew loose strands of hair into my eyes. My father's last walk was here, a few days before he died, and I was with him, and it was December, and always there were birds.

 howe

I chose the time deliberately: Chincoteague on the winter solstice of 2010, when the mythic birds brooded their young on the seas, calmed by Halcyon's father, the wind god Aeolus.

Dawn broke on a bitterly cold December 20, marking eight years since my father had died. On that day, I had awakened at 3:30 a.m. The moon was full. Rain mingled with tears as I ran on the North Carolina beach at high tide, trapped between the living and the dying and yearning for Dad's spirit to skim the waves with the pelicans. At daybreak, I drove the ten miles from our family friends' beach house to join the bedside vigil. His breaths rose and fell like slow breaking waves.

The views from the townhouse window overlooking the Chincoteague marsh now reminded me of my father's vista in those final days. I'd insisted on cranking up the hospice bed high enough for him to see the tidal rivulets suffusing the cordgrass.

These comparable channels threaded the gold-brown cordgrasses reflected in icy calm waters. A vulture glided on tilting wings. Hooded mergansers ghosted past, dark shapes catching the breath of the day ahead. The island lighthouse still beamed a blinking spotlight to sea. Somewhere, a herd of wild ponies awoke and a kingfisher shook her wings.

I had a sensation of Dad's spirit close by. The lighthouse beam clicked off at 7 a.m. Then, all wraiths retreated and yielded to the living. Sunshine brought ice-melting heat.

A kingfisher spurted past the balcony and claimed a pier post. The first-year bird leaned forward with those impossibly tiny feet clutching the post. His eyes were shiny black and round. I admired his dapper plumage of navy-blue head and matching brassy-bluish neckband dipping to a point on his white chest. Not your statue-still fisherman, he arched up, scrunched down, and turned his head to the right, left, and downward and flippered his tail once, twice, and three times. Without warning, the spunky angler dropped headfirst into the water. Splash. A quick winging up to another pier post, and he was empty-billed.

Diving again, he nabbed a fingerling fish flashing like a star and swallowed without the usual thwack. A third dive. A miss. A shake of water droplets from feathers. His crest rippled down the back of his head like a Chincoteague pony's mane. Then, he lifted his tail and a white arc of kingfisher excrement squirted away from his feathers. A salty headwind flattened his head crest. Opening his bill wide, out dropped a pellet—a tidy capsule of fish bones.

He was as restless as a second grader stuck behind a desk with recess five minutes away. The young male stared forward, skyward, downward, and over one shoulder. When serious about fishing, his keen eyes scoped the waters below. I listened to his ringing, stone-sharpening calls.

I'd come to Chincoteague to experience flocks of kingfishers and found only one bird and a song of solstice trailing through shadows and into the light.

Common kingfisher

CHAPTER 14
Bird of Myth in London

> I watched the female kingfisher speed bullet-like over the weir and up the
> Court field stretch. She shone like a blue jewel against the brown murk of
> the swollen river and the drab dead reeds that sulked in clumps along its
> edge. She whistled as she rounded the corner at the end of the stretch.
> —Charlie Hamilton James, *Kingfisher: Tales from the Halcyon River*

I could have come to London for the changing of guards at Buckingham
Palace, the British and Tate Museums, Parliament, Big Ben, Westmin-
ster Abbey, St Paul's Cathedral, *The Lion King*, or to imbibe British ales
at pubs with names like the Bag O' Nails. Or even to buy trinkets in
advance of the royal wedding of Catherine and William. Instead, I came
to London in April of 2011 to find the common kingfisher of ancient
Greek myth.

The invitation coincided with my personal upheaval over the New
Year. The stint back east close to family proved momentous. I'd taken a
kingfisher-like dive to leave my husband after years of difficulties. It was
time to find sure footing. There was no turning back.

With the heartache came a feathery lightness. Ian and I would live
the rest of the school year within the welcoming and lively home of my
younger brother, sister-in-law, and their three children in Takoma Park.
In June, Ian and I would load up the car, our aged dog Luna, and drive
the 2,300 miles home to Missoula, Montana.

"If I can get you over here using frequent flier miles, would you come?"
Willa asked via email on a gray January day. Willa is a redhead, a tennis
player, and a capable Missoula friend, then residing with her husband
and son for the year in London. We'd known each other since our sons
were in daycare. She suggested a week when she'd be alone and would
love the company. Stunned by Willa's generosity, I accepted and warned
her of my quirky avian desire. Willa—always up for a challenge—took

up the research right away. Her rented flat was positioned in an ideal location, only blocks from the storied Hampstead Heath, with its rambling hills, forests, and ponds.

At the end of March, she sent me this advance report:

> I was walking across Hampstead Heath the other day and saw a maintenance guy filling the bird feeders, so I stopped and asked if he ever saw kingfishers in the area, and he said yes! He told me they usually arrive in April—with luck, we won't be too early. It is gorgeous here, 60 degrees and pure sun, flowering trees, and tons of birds.

I would enter an orchestra of birds, and many would be new. I'd traveled to Europe only once, decades earlier. At last, I would be courting the halcyon bird on Hampstead Heath—at 790 acres, a protected green space almost as vast as New York City's Central Park. Brits often refer to their one species in a proprietary way as *the* kingfisher. After all, the common kingfisher, *Alcedo atthis*, is the most resplendent of British Isles birds.

The English have both glorified and persecuted their ravishing bird. The "kingfisher" name stems from the king's fisher, an appellation from the 1500s in England, which pays homage to the royal blue feathers of the common kingfisher as worthy of a king's cloak. Fisher is a tip of the hat to the angler.

Long ago, a dead kingfisher could be used to serve superstitious purposes. Dangle one by the bill inside the house and the bird's breast would turn in the direction of the winds to come. Tuck a mummified bird in a wardrobe to repel moths. Today? The common kingfisher holds a place of high honor. As British naturalist, author, television presenter, and nature documentary director Simon King wrote in the foreword to Charlie Hamilton James's book, *Kingfisher, Tales from Halcyon River*, "The kingfisher is a world-ranking dandy of a bird" and "one of the most kaleidoscopic on the planet."

I would have to agree. Turquoise feathers flare from back and wings; the chest is fiery, and flame feathers seem to crackle behind the eye. The dainty toes are scarlet. Only a close-up view of beak colors can reveal the gender. The male's lower mandible is black, while the female's is orange. The call is a thin whistling high *cheeee*.

"As kingfishers catch fire, dragonflies draw flame," wrote the poet Gerard Manley Hopkins—one of my favorite lines of all poetry. If he'd written instead of a male belted kingfisher of cool blues, whites, and grays, he might have penned, "As kingfishers catch rain, dragonflies draw mist."

Like the belted kingfisher ranging over most of North America, the common kingfisher rules the northern latitudes through Europe, including Greece, and extending as far as northern Africa, Asia, Japan, and the islands of Indonesia. A male and female will pair up in fall, rather than in spring. However, they keep separate territories all winter until ready to mate and nest. From March to July, the birds may raise as many as two to three broods. The population in Britain is estimated to be between 3,800 and 6,400 pairs.

Their fragile future hinges on clean and protected waterways for fishing and nesting. The Royal Society for the Protection of Birds points to long-term declines in Britain since 1970, stemming from polluted rivers. Other risks include collisions with windows, heavy machinery destroying nest banks, and predation.

Survival, even in the cleanest of environments, is far from easy. Studies in Britain show about half the fledglings make it through the first couple weeks, and a quarter live to breed the following year. Frozen rivers in severe winters can be deadly for northern birds. In the infamous winter of 1962–1963, fifteen of the sixteen pairs on thirty-two kilometers (twenty miles) of the Thames succumbed. The oldest common kingfisher on record lived to be seven and a half years old.

What were my chances of finding even one bird in one week centering on Hampstead Heath?

ᙎ

Our first full day in London, on April 6, dawned cloudless, a phenomenon in a city where residents are ready for drizzle. According to Willa, Londoners reach for their pair of "wellies" before a walk on Hampstead Heath.

Lacing up my running shoes, I scoured the map and prepared to navigate the streets of Highgate, which wound uphill and down to the Heath, about a mile away. I'd read on the website of the London Bird Club that three kingfishers had recently appeared on the Highgate chain of ponds on Hampstead Heath after a winter on the coast. Promising.

I closed the triple-locking door of the bottom-floor flat on a street of upscale, historic row houses and jogged up a cobbled narrow street. Schoolboys in white shirts and dark jackets jostled each other. In clipped British accents, mothers urged young children not to dally. Running down the main street of Highgate for a block, I paused as a shiny red double-decker bus roared by on the left.

Dodging traffic and pedestrians, I spied the lane to the Highgate trailhead and trotted downhill to the Heath. Spacious pathways wended over dewy meadows and woodlands, around a pond, and up a gentle hill of green lawn—a civilized British park. Hampstead Heath has felt the tremors of generations of people strolling, running, or riding horses ever since entering the history books as Hemstede in the year 986 AD.

On this morning, dogs outnumbered people, about four per person. Every dog appeared well behaved. You could have any of them over for tea. Turning right from the emerald meadows onto a wooded path, which paralleled the chain of ponds, I stopped at a fork. The trail to the left was marked: Welcome to Highgate Ladies Bathing Pond (Ladies Only). I slowed to a walk past bike racks, a ping-pong table in the trees, an elfin lakelet, and arrived at the two ponds. Trees rang with the bewildering refrains of chaffinches, tits, English robins, and blackbirds. The Olympic-sized lake is for swimming, with a wooden dock, a shed, and a lifeguard on duty year-round. The second pond is for contemplation.

A hale Londoner in her mid-sixties was breast-stroking across the swimming pond in the company of ducks. By the second secluded pond, a woman about my age sat on a bench in the sun. Trying not to disturb her, I tiptoed to the water's edge. A silhouette leaped out like a golden apple within tangled branches. The cobalt, turquoise, and amber living gem perched on a dangling limb only a few feet above the quiet waters.

The common kingfisher of myth basked in the solitude of the Ladies Bathing Pond. After a couple minutes, I turned to the woman on the bench and pointed. She smiled.

"Oh, how lovely! This is the first kingfisher of the spring we've seen."

We luxuriated in the moment. The breaststroker strode over from the swimming pond, dripping wet, her one-piece sensible bathing suit pulled down off her shoulders to her waist, her breasts bared in the privacy. The three of us communed with the lone kingfisher. A few minutes later, the halcyon bird fanned away to the far side of the pond and into the forest.

The two women told me of swimming when a kingfisher skimmed so close over their heads, they could have touched a feather. Tempted, I dipped my fingers in the frigid water and chose to stay on land.

When I left the forest trail, I was the gamboling horse, exhilarated and light-footed. Three more times I returned to the Highgate Ladies Bathing Pond, and never immersed in the bracing waters. Where's the bravery? Once, a mute swan flexed her curvy long neck into the reeds to pluck stems for her nest. Another morning, a red fox hesitated before a hedge, his ears pricked, and eyes inquisitive.

The kingfisher did not appear again. If I was to have one glimpse, I could not have chosen a more ideal place than in the company of bare-breasted women. Revisiting the Latin name for the common kingfisher—*Alcedo atthis*—I found a translation of a lyric poem Sappho wrote for Atthis with words of love, wreathing past and present centuries in universal longing:

Beyond all hope, I prayed those timeless
days we spent might be made twice as long.
I prayed one word: I want.
Someone, I tell you, will remember us,
even in another time.

I could imagine Sappho and Atthis emerging from the waters as a kingfisher haloed above their sensual selves. Plato called Sappho (who lived between 615 BC and 550 BC) the tenth muse. I wonder whether, in the many lost fragments of her poems, there are praises for kingfishers? The birds still bedazzle the shores, ponds, and waterfalls of Lesbos, an island in the Aegean Sea not far from Turkey.

Like Sappho and Atthis, the love story of Halcyon and Ceyx lives on in this bird. But the reality of the common kingfisher's life history is not all romance. The British subspecies (of seven divvied up by plumage shades) is aptly named *Alcedo atthis ispida*, meaning bristly, as in easily antagonized. When it comes to irascibility, the female is so territorial she can be violent on the rare occasion. I know this from evidence in the 2002 film, produced by Charlie Hamilton James and his wife Philippa, called *My Halcyon River*, the fictional name for an actual stream in the English countryside.

My conceptions of a "halcyon" bird were shattered in one fatal scene: A pair of females skirmish for precious nesting territory. The flying birds crash into the currents. They tussle until one kingfisher snaps her bill shut on the head of the other and forces her underwater. Blue feathers spin downstream.

Ispida. Bristly. This might also be a useful character trait for weathering the rain, fog, and blustery squalls of Great Britain—something I missed in my weeklong visit. Instead of pulling on wellies, I lifted my face to the sun. Willa walked the Heath with me and made sure I did ride a double-decker bus, visit the British and Tate Museums, taste British ales, see a play, and at least look at trinkets for the royal wedding.

The zenith? The bird of transformation appeared among strong women, right when I needed that vision most. Shedding my old skin was painful. Ahead? I would try out wings to fly—leading me westward and home to the kingfishers of Rattlesnake Creek.

Coming Home

CHAPTER 15
Rattlesnake Creek Return

What makes a place special is the way it buries itself inside the heart, not whether it's flat or rugged, rich or austere, wet or arid, gentle or harsh, warm or cold, wild or tame. Every place, like every person, is elevated by the love and respect shown toward it, and by the way in which its bounty is received.
—Richard Nelson, *The Island Within*

A shriek creased the morning calm. I'd opened the car door at my usual parking spot along the entry road to the Rattlesnake National Recreation Area. Something was up. Hearing the kingfisher alarm far from the upper nest bank marked a first. It was April 23 of 2012, the fourth season.

After arriving home to Missoula with Ian ten months earlier, my life had become freer and more challenging. The trips to the kingfisher bank offered respite and, on this day, an unsettling vivacity.

Running down the needle-strewn trail to the secret cutoff, I stopped short. Two emphatic rattles burst from above the tallest pines. I glimpsed only the flaring white patches on a kingfisher's piceous wings, as if kindling the air. On this path, I had come to predict where a pine squirrel would palaver and natter from a high western larch. I anticipated the nasal *yank-yank-yank* of a red-breasted nuthatch, and pine and fir trees exhaling the jingling keys of dark-eyed juncos.

From the halcyon bird, I have learned never to be complacent and always open to the shattering of preconceptions. On this day, the trail belonged to kingfishers in a state of ferocity. For the past nine mornings in a row, I had witnessed a courting pair by the stream. Not here in the upper forest. Not high in the sky.

I hurdled a log and sprinted down the faint deer trail to the upper overlook of the nest bank. Below me, the alder and birch trees crested like waves pummeling the ponderosas. Wrapped cottonwood buds burst with desire. The forest floor glinted with yellow glacier lilies. Three kingfishers whipped by. One screamed. If lightning had a voice, it would be this electrifying, brief, and rending undulation. Their wings lacerated the air as one bird accelerated to touch the other's tail with a beak. The leader pulled away.

For the past week and a half, all had seemed copacetic with the apparent couple of the season. I was again the voyeur as the male hopped on top of the accepting female with his wings flapping for balance. After mating, he dove into the creek for a refreshing bath. The duo sampled potential nests like newlyweds choosing an apartment. I remained uncertain and mesmerized by the annual ritual. Then, everything shifted.

Ten feet overhead, a female swung by on pumping wings and stalled to a landing on a cottonwood branch below me. Her ratcheting intensified in rate and higher pitch. A series of rapid notes fired from her bill into the morning chill. She lifted off, banked right, and was gone. A few seconds later, two female kingfishers catapulted across my field of view. Each bore the rouge of belts upon white bellies. One looked decidedly unbuckled. Could she be the original Halcyon of the 2009 first season?

Time sailed on bird wings. Every few minutes, kingfishers encircled the forest in a ring of outcry. One high-pitched phrase from downstream wavered across the greening woods, tattooing every note on my forehead. Striding toward the sound along the floodplain rim, I crossed the meadow to the lower viewpoint, where I had peered upstream to see kingfishers mating on that sensual bird swing of a root above the rapids.

Repeated consonants hailed down from a dead cottonwood by the creek. There he was, splendid in his sheeny blue bandana. The male pointed his bill to the treetops as if to mark his high-stakes territory. Or maybe he simply felt relief. After all, he had escaped the two females stampeding after him.

Could he be cheering for his mate of the season as they duked it out? From an evolutionary sense, a dominant female might better withstand the rigors of nesting and raising young. In that case, he'd switch mates without a shrug. Was there loyalty? The value of shared experience? Love?

I sketched him in my journal, drawing bold squiggling lines of his distress. The two females flew in with matching fierce cries. Their flight felt as dizzying as a dust devil. The hunter crashed into the tail of the hunted, bounced off, and then landed on the branch by the male. Off he flew. In a few seconds, all three vaporized up the creek.

As I considered my second encounter with an outsider female at the onset of the nesting season, I could not be sure who was chasing whom. Would the size, brilliance, and pattern of a flashy red belt play a role in the outcome? The chase scene supported the premise of females willing to battle for rights to this coveted male, holder of a premier nesting bank.

Even with missing puzzle pieces, the detective work had led me to places I might never have gone otherwise—from examining study skins in the Smithsonian to canoeing the Lower Rio Grande.

Six minutes passed. When a bald eagle lumbered by with slow wing-beats, I gasped at the refulgent white head and tail lit by morning sun rays. I waited in the quiescent meadow. All remained calm.

Later, Paul and Lisa came to the upper vista to watch a kingfisher pair working away at nest holes as if nothing had gone down. No aerial chases. No second female. What would we know if we lived and breathed this place around the clock? When I asked Paul what happened in the afternoon, he replied in an email:

> In fact, quite a bit. They started exploring sites in that upstream half of the bank. Possibly as many as half a dozen holes were rammed or entered. It seems they have yet to choose THE SITE. They did some vocalizing too.

Had the scuffle among three birds renewed the nest digging vigor? Paul believed the female could be our original 2009 mate, with her distinctive broken belt and familiarity with the nest holes. I decided to forgo the temptation to call her Halcyon, even as I questioned whether belted kingfishers should be labeled as "seasonally monogamous." Without having banded our original pair, we could not be sure.

We believe Halcyon did return in 2010, the season of a failed nest. In 2011, Lisa and Paul could not locate an active burrow and reported only glimpses of kingfishers on the creek. When I returned from the east coast, elated to find my center on Rattlesnake Creek, I saw no sign of a nest or fledglings that summer. Yet, every call and flash of kingfisher wings felt like a welcoming-home party.

Rain settled on western Montana. The creek heaved with the weight of water, and the trickle of winter wren song was the pianist tinkling the highest keys. I left town for a few days in mid-April for work, and Paul and Lisa sent a favorable report:

> I get the impression that the male has made a burrow choice and is trying to get the female to commit. We saw him reenter the old burrow he was in for 6 min on 19 April. This time we timed two of his entries at 11 min and 9 min. The female flew up to the bank nearby (<0.5 m from the burrow) while he was in, but we saw her land at the burrow only once, remaining at the entrance for about 3–4 seconds. I think we are getting close to having a specific burrow to watch. She's fickle, though.

Huddled at the upper viewpoint, often in drizzling rain, I regularly saw the pair conversing and perusing among holes of the upper nest bank—all the way to the end of April and into early May. They seemed a bit soggy and unenthused.

Cumulus clouds swung across the rising sun on May 7. At last! A female kingfisher burst from within a hole high in the bank's upper end. I marked the watch spot with sticks to position the spotting scope upon return. A few minutes later, the pair breezed out of view as if to defy any conclusions. Then, they came back.

By the creek's edge, I ran my hands over the corduroy bark of the shielding Douglas-fir as the female on the bank pecked at a hole to widen the entry. Her short tail clicked back and forth like a pendulum. She entered, and soil sprayed from the burrow, a sign she was digging with her tiny trowel toes. I had longed to see that fountain of dirt Mic Hamas had described so long ago. The sight was as bracing as a waterfall.

Six feet down from the top and in the center of the arcing bank, the new hole featured a potato-sized green rock jutting below the entrance, an easy identifier. Of course, the female then changed her mind. From a tree perch, she eyed the bank like a writer facing a blank page. Quick flaps to the right of the hole. Her wings papered the earth for a few seconds, and her bill was the stippling pen. Then, she flounced away as if in a huff. From downstream, I heard her calls brushing the willows in bursts of syncopated poetry.

The next day, positioned at the lower vantage point, I stared up the winding narrow creek for any glimmers. Yellow warbler song laced the dew-laden air. A chipping sparrow sewed the seams of the morning. Then, kingfisher wings splintered the mist above a set of rapids. Landing on the mating root, she flew up to a fir limb. The male joined her. Their tandem flight formed a wrinkle on the brow of the stream. The seasonal clock was ticking. The couple's appearance together throughout May was not a good sign. If incubating, I'd see only one bird at a time. As spring unwound with yellow blossoms of arnica flowers spackling the forest floor, I wondered if the pair would nest at all.

Still, the frequent sightings of kingfishers lifted my spirits. When the male flew up from a dive empty-billed, his crumpled crest was hilarious; I wanted to come over for haberdashery rescue. When his mate scratched her head with her teensy foot, she was ungainly. It was like seeing a queen and king off duty, with crowns put aside and all pretense of pomp and circumstance gone.

෨

My June sojourns to the creek were hopeful, with views of only one bird, suggesting the other was incubating eggs—very late. On the morning of June 26, I lounged at the lower viewpoint under a blueberry sky, breathing in a juicy day. Something stirred in the willows that wickered the creek.

An American redstart hopped from twig to twig, probing for insects with his thin, precise bill. I felt a pang. Certain warblers were so . . . my father. A year after his death, I was in the Yucatan with my mother, seeking the birds he'd listed in pencil and all-capital letters. Walking alone on a cloistered trail leading to a Mayan ruin, I glimpsed a fleck of a warbler. Tropical leaves like outstretched hands hid every songbird, and the trees shivered with their gleaning of insects.

"Please help me a little here, Dad," I said. As if on cue, an American redstart popped up on an exposed branch at eye level only six feet away. He fanned his tail to reveal a lustrous black fringe on orange, the same bittersweet color as the Mercury Coupe of Dad's courtship days. The redstart of the Yucatan cocked his head as if to say, "You called?"

The redstart of Rattlesnake Creek had come far from his wintering home, likely the west coast of Mexico or even Central America. Joining him, a calliope hummingbird needled a mayfly rising vertically from the currents. Both birds migrated thousands of miles to come to this place of nesting, this home. The day before, a storm struck Missoula with quarter-sized hail. High winds toppled trees. The calliope hummingbird must have pressed tight on a sturdy limb as a sheltering tree bent and swayed.

&

As a single mother shepherding Ian through his freshman year in high school, I found hardship spurred new growth, like willows budding after a battering winter. There's resilience in newfound independence and in the interdependence among friends and nature. Whenever I entered the community of this creek, I felt my limbs interlacing with the pollinators and the pollinated. When I faltered, I turned to the kingfisher, ever the helper.

One evening, a storm cooled the July air where I was weeding a flower bed in the backyard. When a rainbow spanned the upper valley, I dropped my garden tools and headed toward the anchoring place on Rattlesnake Creek. Sure enough, two kingfishers curved past the nesting bank that marked the pot of gold.

&

The tropical perfume of mock orange blossoms permeated the forest at the upper nest bank on the last day of June. Everything dripped water from yet another night's storm. My feet were sopping wet, so why not jump the ditch to the island and bushwhack through alders and tansy ragwort weeds?

Déjà vu. The male flew into view with a fish, landed on an alder branch, and proclaimed his ardor in a triplet of *Kkkkkk . . . Kkkkkk . . . Kkkkkk* calls. His mate alighted on a second branch. The minnow size of the fish suggested the young must not be more than a week old. Lisa,

Paul, and I had caught act 1, missed act 2, but were there for act 3 and the finale—with luck.

This new hole was two feet down from the top of the bank, not far from the island's northern tip, and shaped like a squashed grapefruit because of a rock obstacle. A roundleaf alumroot added a decorative look. Wavy green leaves clustered at the base of the plant, and a spiky frond of creamy white flowers adorned the nest entry.

Ꮼ

I watched whenever I could, but I'd stepped up my contract writing to better support Ian. The more I came to the creek, the more well-being flooded into my core. Where kingfishers nourished chicks, I could flap my arms and imagine my toes lifting off the ground.

Luna was no longer with me for the 2012 kingfisher watch. In her last week of life, the prior October, she'd mustered a creaky run toward a white-tailed deer below the apple tree. A couple mornings later, I called her from the yard and she could not rise. A friend helped me lift her into the car and I drove her to the veterinarian. The X-ray showed a broken leg and cancer riddling her bones. There was no choice. The vet told me she had only one slot for the appointment, at four o'clock, an hour after the start of Ian's Junior Varsity soccer game. I never missed a home match. At least I'd catch the first half.

As I turned to leave the field, Ian and an opposing player collided on the far side. Ian writhed on the grass, holding one hand in pain. Paralyzed and teary, I stood there on the sidelines, helpless. "Just go be with Luna," my friends said. "We'll take care of Ian." And they did. While a doctor wrapped Ian's two broken fingers, I cried with my head buried in Luna's still-luxuriant golden fur. She'd lived to be sixteen and a half.

I ached for Luna at the burrow watch and sometimes reached down to pet her imaginary head pressed against my knee. Over three hours on the eleventh of July, I noted several fish deliveries, with male and female taking turns as expected. The lateness of nesting made observation an indolent activity. Ponderosa pines exhaled vanilla and brown sugar. A cordilleran flycatcher—startling with a white eye-ring on olive feathers—landed as a kingfisher flew up to the burrow.

On the sixteenth of July, a fuzzy dipper begged for food on a creek-polished rock midstream. The fledgling flapped, gaped, and emitted a high-pitched and beseeching "feed me!" The parent preened and dipped. Another juvenile flew in, and the adult stuffed their beaks with protein-rich insect larvae. The dippers appeared to have raised one brood and now this second one. Meanwhile, kingfishers came and went with fish for their young.

The lethargic kingfisher watch shifted on July 28 with a sky-shattering holler aimed at me. I knew what it meant. The parents were luring their young into the world. Sure enough, a chick took one cautious look at the sky from the hole entry and backed into safety. Vigilance prevailed.

But we had a problem. This year, Lisa, Paul, and I could not set up a blind because of the hole location. Despite a screen of shrubs between us and the burrow, the watch would be far too disruptive. I respected the birds and missed the fledging, yet I was at peace. For some baffling reason, I did not see the juveniles bellyflopping into the pond. Throughout the rest of summer, I watched several young kingfishers in various Rattlesnake Creek haunts like Greenough Park, Tom Green Park, and the Bugbee Preserve.

ॐ

Fast forward to the spring of 2013. I had spent hours reviewing field notes from multiple seasons, circling and starring intriguing behaviors since 2009. The kingfishers often nixed every new conclusion with a 180-degree shift, like the 2013 female arriving at the burrow bank on the fourth of March—a month earlier than anticipated. Long after I assumed the 2009 hole would be inhabitable, this pair chose the original one. Had the male or female perhaps hatched from an egg deep within and felt a magnetic pull, like salmon following the scent of their birthplace stream?

On June 14 of this fifth season, at 8:20 p.m., I hid behind the alders on the island. A male fired up to the trusty hole with a fish the size of a pocketknife. Then? Both the male and the female emitted war cries splitting the evening sky, where a cloud gathered into the shape of two kingfishers nuzzling.

I whispered apologies for my intrusion. On my way out, I almost stepped on a ropy scat filled with deer fur, large enough to be deposited by a wolf. The winter before, my naturalist neighbor had observed two wolves chase an elk across Mount Jumbo. When cross-country skiing a mile up from the nest bank, I'd encountered big canine prints, which a biologist confirmed as a wolf. Humbled, I felt a sharpening of senses within the presence of big predators resuming their rightful place.

Two days later, the midday heat felt punishing, a time when all animals ought to be taking a siesta. The kingfishers? They paid no heed. Back at the bank, I counted sixteen fish transfers in two hours—another new record. The male and female proved equally energetic.

The pair's efforts paid off. I was optimistic. At last, I would catch those wondrous few seconds of a chick launching into the air from the lip of a burrow and feeling the rush of first flight. Unfortunately, I tore my quadricep muscle during overly ambitious marathon training. I'd struggled to get to the nest hole on crutches, cried, swore, and gave up. Ian shook his head over this latest, worst running injury, asking me why I continued to train for marathons? He pointed out that if I would be less competitive, I might make it to the starting line. He was right. Even though I ran for joy, I also ran for speed, and the fitter I became the faster I would run—to my detriment. While the kingfishers helped me in the art of slowing down and stillness, they also fostered my love of rocketing flight.

ॐ

Death came to Missoula after a massive snowstorm in February 2014. The day began with a youthful snowboarder climbing up Mount Jumbo, apparently unaware of the winter closure to protect the elk herd. At the top, the thrill seeker chose a deadly path down the sheer, open slope. Cutting fresh tracks, he set off an avalanche, which burst down a gully and accelerated to speeds of more than 120 miles per hour—slamming into the home of a prestigious fisheries and genetics professor and his artist wife, who were sipping tea by a fireplace. He survived. She died. The snowboarder rode the slide down and joined in rescue efforts. Two weeks later, I heard volunteers were needed to shovel away the snow and retrieve belongings. I didn't hesitate.

Dig. Dig. Pause. Wipe the tears from my eyes. I cried for these good people, and for personal losses. The pain seared as I thrust, heaved, and tossed with all my strength. I'd chosen a snowbank away from the original location of the buried main house, where dozens of people labored. Here, only one young man from the neighborhood and I toiled. I doubted we'd find much, and I was wrong.

The force of the avalanche had knocked the house off its foundation and pushed individual rooms far away. We struck the artist's bedroom closet, exposing a rainbow of her hand-sewn clothes. Our work became the chiseling of archeologists. We called for help, and others joined us. With each dress and blouse sparking rays of emerald, turquoise, magenta, or sunflower yellow, I felt her spirit sending this message: Go be colorful. You never know when life will end.

ℴ

Spring of 2014 could not come soon enough, the melting, the flooding, and the first yellow glacier lilies sunning on the forest floor. The kingfishers returned for their annual cycle of dig, dig, and pause to excavate a nest for the next generation. The circle continued.

"In attending to this wilderness . . . I knew myself to have been instructed for life." I repeated Henry Bugbee's words so often, his quote inscribed on the Bugbee Preserve boulder became a mantra. Listen. The kingfishers have a lesson to impart.

On the seventh of May in 2014, the female kingfisher excavated with extraordinary vigor. Her feet scrabbled, and half her body snugged inside. Dig. Keep going. Dig. She was soon joined by the male, and together they fashioned a new burrow below the highest arc of the upper bank in a horizontal stretch of softer sandy soil and between two cobbled layers. I was pleased. The hole would be safe from both floods and predators. What could go wrong?

A gang of rough-winged swallows crowded the bank in mid-May— and all hell broke out. The roguish birds could have checked out the vacant holes for nests. Instead, they poked their heads often into the active burrow.

One swallow gawking at an incubating kingfisher could be ignored—but two? Too much. At 11:15 a.m., the female erupted from the hole. Like Diana the huntress, she chased them off without a sound. A couple of minutes later, she flew back inside to warm her clutch of eggs. The swallows wasted no time. Six pesky birds circled the hole, giving buzzy calls. Their light bellies were the color of pale mushrooms, contrasting with the earthy brown of their slim pointed wings. Every few minutes, the kingfisher scooted to the entry, her bill poking out far enough to send the swallows off. If that failed, she hustled after them.

Paul recorded similar action on his trips over the next few days, until the swallows gave up. Watching the incubation period of about twenty-two days at varying times gave us the chance to note the comings and goings of the birds, at more frequent intervals than the literature suggested. The idea that nothing happens when the birds incubate for hours proved far from the case. Field observations once again showed the kingfishers had their own ideas.

On May 21, in the middle of the day, a kingfisher flew out of the hole and downstream. When he winged back to balance on a branch too close to my hiding place, his crest was wet. He preened his feathers. Then, he slipped back into the hole after a three-minute absence. A half-hour later, the female arrived with a trilly greeting. She had a fish! I watched as she entered the burrow and backed out empty-billed.

Tenderness? Diligence? Love? Again, I knew the stir of excitement of a new find. Dan Albano had observed a male feeding a female during courtship, an act common enough in the bird world to be termed "allofeeding." But this? The female was feeding her mate during incubation. And why not, I think? He was hungry during a long shift. The behavior was also risky, possibly alerting predators to the nest.

ॐ

I had a bit of extra nurturing to do myself. This was the summer that Ian and I hosted a nineteen-year-old Polish student for a month. To be with Mateusz Piesiak was to spend days with a young Audubon toting a camera. He set up hummingbird feeders in strategic photographic spots in our wild backyard of the home I'd rented for Ian's last two years of high school. After pangs of wanting to stay in the house Ian had known all his life, moving out as part of the divorce settlement had proven liberating. Like kingfishers choosing a new hole, I was renewed and ready.

We inhabited a cozy bird's nest a half mile from Rattlesnake Creek and tucked on the slope of the North Hills with a grand view of the saddle of Mount Jumbo. The morning sun coursed onto the east-facing front balcony in spring. Songbirds rustled in the wild plums, marking a wildlife-rich zone between our backyard and the bunchgrass hills. In winter, a pygmy owl splashed in the birdbath. Once, a kingfisher graced a locust tree twenty yards away as I wrote in my journal about the myth of Halcyon and Ceyx.

Mateusz gave me hope for the future. His parents bought him his first camera at age five to document the songbirds he followed even as a toddler. No matter the family lived in Wroclaw, the fourth largest city in Poland. Mateusz set up elaborate feeders to look like natural perches in community gardens and snapped photos for hours. As soon as he was old enough to drive, he left the city whenever possible to explore wilder destinations. By the time I met him, he had won international awards for bird photography.

To my delight, Mateusz and Ian helped me erect the blind, set well back from the creek, a tricky feat so far into nesting season, but we chose midday and escaped the birds' wrath. A few hours later, Mateusz was with me, and photographing kingfishers.

I cherish his detailed image capturing the instant before the male would fold his wings to enter the burrow. The male's plumage is the color of a nimbostratus cloud backlit by the sun—misty blues, grays, and hints of violet and moss green. The tail fans to show polka-dot patterns on the outer feathers. His spread wings reveal arcs of frosty white.

The chicks fledged on July 6 and 7, the two days when Mateusz could not be there. Sandra joined me instead, always a shining time when our geographic distance closed within a hand's touch. There we were, the audience of two, silently clapping at the crescendo of the season, squeezed into our blind, a bit like fledglings gawking at the light.

The parents enticed the chicks. They shook the silvery fish. We cheered for each tentative black bill probing the air from the darkness. Then, an emboldened youngster teetered on the edge and retreated.

And . . . we missed the actual fledging. I know. It's hard to admit, and I'm not sure why. We tried. Yet, there it was: zero for six seasons, but who's counting? What I did count were at least five juveniles at the pond, and one day tallied a stunning seven kingfishers. Their wings stenciled the reflecting waters.

In my deep dive into kingfishers, I tapped into all their mythic powers as messengers, helpers, healers and protectors, transformers, and bringers of joy.

&

The next year, it was time for Ian to fledge. He graduated from Hellgate High School in 2015 and chose the University of New Mexico to attend. I would miss our pesto pasta dinners at our kitchen counter bar, or finding him down along the Clark Fork River in the spring of his senior year, where he volunteered for the Watershed Education Network. I would miss his quirky humor and the big-heartedness that is my son.

Yet, like the kingfisher parents, I was ready for him to fly from the nest. I could have pointed out to Ian that even baby kingfishers knew how to keep things tidy in their burrow. Instead, I concentrated on the hugs. We have a similar tendency to move on from arguments within minutes.

The spring of Ian's graduation, Lisa, Paul, and I continued the annual nest-hole-guessing game. On April 27, Paul spotted a female drafting the wings of another female. A week later, we observed the male dive into a hole and reappear with a single pebble in his bill, which he dropped into the creek from a perch. The female flew in and out with her stone and released it into the stream. Soon after, the pair mated twice. Pebble foreplay? And another new find for the long watch over the seasons.

Paul and I separately saw courtship allofeeding that 2015 spring, too. The romancing did not always go well. Once, I watched as the male called his intended with an enticing fish outside a burrow, where she hid for forty minutes and resisted his pleading from a tree perch. At last, he ate the fish.

We found the active hole up high on the bank with surprising ease. The birds did not dilly-dally. Paul and Lisa set up their blind in May.

With seven years under our belts, we could almost pin down the timing of incubating eggs, feeding the chicks throughout June, and fledging on about Independence Day. This season I would miss the event for a vagabonding reason.

છ

The 2015 summer marked the end of my arc of watching on Rattlesnake Creek and the beginning of a year-long foray as a roving naturalist in a pop-up camper, which would lead me to settle back in Oregon. Setting anchor first in La Grande in the northeast corner, I would join my conservation comrades of Greater Hells Canyon Council in saving forests and rivers. I chose the region where I'd researched my master's thesis, a journalistic investigation of environmental controversies surrounding the deepest gorge in North America.

Meeting with old friends brought back a wash of memories from my thesis days in the late 1980s. I'd interviewed a hundred people, capsized while rafting Granite Rapids of the Snake River, and joined harrowing horse and mule trips on precipitous trails under the leadership of Loren Hughes, the bigger-than-life conservationist from La Grande who saved countless big trees and wild places, appealing timber sales with handwritten letters and five-cent stamps.

On one Loren Hughes trip, I rode a big black horse on a perilous trail below the rim of Hells Canyon. The disaster happened without warning. My horse cut the switchback to head for the mule he spotted above me, almost straight up the near-vertical slope. As my horse grappled for footing on rock scree, I threw myself forward and clutched the saddle horn. From behind, I barely heard the command from the experienced rider Mary McCracken: "Let go of the reins!" I did. All I could do was to hold on to this thundercloud heaving his way upward.

Mary has told me since she was sure the horse and I would fall over backward and die. I remember getting off with knees wobbling and shaking. Clearly, I'd demonstrated the worst riding skills ever. I owe that horse my life, and Mary, too, whose voice had rung through the chaos— "Let go of the reins!"

Those words. If I lived in Greek mythology, then I'd wonder if some god had willed the big black horse to defy gravity. The wild rivers and streams tumble with the same message. During my rambling months, I was like a fledgling learning to trust my wings.

Under the high peaks of the Wallowas in 2016, I would meet the kind and good man I would marry. I would also unofficially change my name from Deborah to Marina in honor of my great-grandmother Marina Waite. The lilting syllables flowed like the waters I'd come to know: *Ma . . . ri . . . na.*

In that prior year, I'd traveled with the protection of a pair of clay sculpted kingfishers and the living birds, which sometimes showed up in surprising places, like the spunky queen exulting within the spray of Devil's Churn on the Oregon coast. Winter storm waves curled like herds of horses with manes of frothy whipped cream through the narrow inlet lined by volcanic basalt cliffs. Foam blew into the air. The surf funneled into the chasm as if shot through a high-pressure fire hose and then exploded into a geyser. Right in the fury, a kingfisher appeared in defiance of storm and surf. She landed on an otter-sized boulder on the far side of the chasm's entry. The waves broke two feet away. Her starfish-hued belt was the one color in a black-and-white scene. Without flinching, she fished a tidepool with neat dives to catch tiny sculpin.

"Halcyon," I called, and my words joined a striking wave. Of course she was there, at home in the winds governed by her mythic father Aeolus. Versatility. Bravery. Focus. Calmness within the maelstrom.

ॐ

Traveling far, I followed Salish elder Louis Adams's adage, of not rushing when everywhere is home. Often alone with plenty of time within my solar-powered camper, I sifted through Rattlesnake Creek field journals to seek more patterns and meanings.

I was pleasantly startled by the number of "firsts" and felt a kindred connection to all naturalists who deepen what we know and bridge the canyon of our separation from nature.

Why does it matter that kingfishers hover and ram banks, carry pebbles in their beaks in courtship, and chase swallows away instead of staying put on eggs for hours? Why care about the meaning of the rare gender reversal of color? What's the significance of females chasing females, and all the variations of belt size and color I found in the Smithsonian? Why travel afar to sleuth the closest relatives—the ringed kingfishers of the lower Rio Grande and the giant kingfishers of South Africa?

I believe our kinship with all life is at stake. Unless enough of us spend time in the field immersing, noticing, reveling, and wondering, we won't act in time to save ourselves. We don't have to be biologists; we only have to be curious.

When it comes to belted kingfishers, their trilling, consonant-rich calls above waterways send a message the Salish people have known since time immemorial. Water is life. Treat wild waters as you would an elder. Listen to their wisdom. Honor the complex web of riparian plants and forests vital to shading, cooling, and nourishing thousands of species converging on these living ribbons of lush green.

I'd come to know the kingfishers on one stretch of a home creek as family. Their well-being mattered in the way of love that is reciprocal, supportive, and essential.

Recording and passing on what we know to the next generation is a gift, a legacy, and another expression of love. My mother compiled more than thirty family photo albums with captions and often with accompanying lively narratives, which have become our family's most treasured possessions.

Thoreau's journals are revered for his insights on nature and living. His phenology demonstrates that human-induced climate change is interfering with the exquisite timing of bloom and pollinator, insect hatch, and nesting birds.

Saving my stacks of field journals and then sharing findings is one form of reciprocity for the generosity of the kingfishers on Rattlesnake Creek. Over the seasons of searching, I had walked, run, crawled, sat, shivered, stared from a blind, hid behind trees, and scratched notes. Within Rattlesnake Creek, the melodies and rhythms of wildlife formed an ever-changing symphony. Studying my field entries, I noticed a mix of musical tempos, from largo to allegro, and a thundering crescendo of kingfisher wings.

In March, the trees are leafless and the migrant songbirds absent, yet the resident nuthatches, juncos, chickadees, song sparrows, and dippers are present. Geese and ducks float on the pond. A lone male kingfisher protects his nesting bank and awaits the arrival of a female.

In April, the neighborhood rouses with the singing of dippers, juncos, song sparrows, and the prattling of pine squirrels. Buttercups bloom and then freeze. Canada geese nest on the cliff above the pond. Pussywillows signal the beginning of budding and leafing. An overwintering mourning cloak butterfly tests velvety maroon wings, fringed in sapphire dots and framed in pale yellow. The creek swells with more rainfall, a clear innuendo of floods to come with the snowmelt. Even then, Rattlesnake Creek often swirls transparent as antique glass over a montage of sage, amber, gold, and russet stones.

The kingfishers are courting in April. Ospreys return from Baja, Mexico. By the third week on a sunny day, pussywillows brim with bumblebees, solitary bees, a checkerspot butterfly, and a blue butterfly. That's when balsamroots wave their showy yellow flowers on the bunchgrass hillsides, while glacier lilies and yellowbells ruffle the forest floor like saffron taffeta.

May enters with the drumming of ruffed grouse and the unfolding of red osier dogwood and wild rose leaves. Ospreys and common mergansers patrol for fish. The kingfishers get serious about mating and nest excavating. The creek rises and, on a sunny day, radiates olive green and frosted whitewater. Glacier lilies still bloom.

The frequent rains dousing the Douglas-fir trees portend the hastening pace of sprouting, budding, and blossoming. Mayflies are hatching, their ephemeral lives cut even shorter by wild trout at the creek's surface and songbirds in the air. The migrants are returning, like Hammond's flycatchers, yellow-rumped warblers, and all the swallows—tree, violet-green, and rough-winged.

Next, the nodding purple bells of clematis twine around dogwoods. Elfin green needles star the larch tree limbs. May is leafing time. The snowberry follows gooseberry and currant bushes, but the red osier dogwoods are slower, with buds like praying hands even in mid-May, the time of dippers feeding their fledglings. Scents of wild onion permeate the floodplain forest dotted with Oregon grape, blooming in yellow clusters. Wild turkeys swagger among wild strawberry flowers the size of nickels with five-petaled white petals.

Cutthroat trout fin upstream to spawn as the creek runs even higher, yet still clear. The interlacing roots and forests of the mostly protected watershed prevent the erosion and mud found in logged and roaded stream valleys.

June is the month of fecundity—of mating, nesting, raising, growing, hatching, fledging, transforming, flowering, and singing. The neighborhood is in full swing. Lazuli buntings attract females by singing songs of ever-greater complexity. Spotted sandpipers perform knee bends along the creek edge and guard their speckled eggs, camouflaged on a pebbly beach. A pair of red-tailed hawks circles overhead, not far from their stick nest high on a fir on the creek's west side. White-tailed bucks grow velvety antlers. Arnica blankets the forest floor in yellow blooms. Native bees converge.

By mid-June, the blossoming multiplies with white clusters of ninebark shrubs and the purple pillars of penstemons and lupines. MacGillivray's warblers, Wilson's warblers, and American redstarts perform arias from their well-positioned posts within the layered forest.

Calliope hummingbirds sip from flowers and snip insects above the creek, not far from a kingfisher nest hole, where furrow marks etch deeper with the prints of the parents entering and exiting as they deliver fish to the chicks.

If June is fecundity, July is the parenting month. Warblers spend far more time hunting caterpillars to feed chicks than proclaiming territory in song. Mock orange scents the air with desire. Kingfisher fledglings learn to fish at the pond in the company of wheeling flocks of violet-green swallows. Swainson's thrushes sing longer than most other birds, their honeyed chords tremoring up and into the heart-shaped leaves of cottonwoods. Not one day is alike. Here, the pressed grasses outline a deer bed. There, coral fungi bursts from a decaying log after rain. In spring, I'd note the whumphing of a ruffed grouse drumming, which would quiet with the onset of nesting.

Part of attuning to the wild is to notice the silence as much as the sound. "The silence, the pause, is as important as the words," said Oregon poet laureate Kim Stafford, in describing poetry as our native language.

ℬℭ

Kingfishers were still confounding, but I found them more reliably with each passing year, from 2009 through 2015. Even a seven-season summary needs tempering. There's no absolute surety with birds.

I tallied five successful nests with juveniles fledging from mid-June to mid-July. Absent banding the adults and chicks, we could not be confident how many chicks fledged, or their genders, or how many years our original pair returned. Halcyon may have come back four years in a row. Still, my notes led to some potential conclusions for the era before the small dam came down, freed the creek, and washed away the fledglings' training pond. As savvy birds, they would eventually find another pool, perhaps one created by beavers.

In the seminal first season of 2009, with by far the most hours logged, the three youngsters we observed fledged on June 26. The second season highlight? Aerial ramming and our citizen science contribution. The kingfisher pair appeared exceptionally diligent, yet in late June of 2010 their nest failed. In 2011 (the summer of my return from the east coast), our records were scanty. Lisa and Paul believed the birds tried without success again.

The season of 2012 proved to be a late nesting triumph with a handful of fledglings roaming the creek by the end of July. In 2013, the birds remodeled the first 2009 hole, and the young fledged in mid-July. In 2014, I set up the blind midway through the breeding season, facing a new hole in the midsection of the bank. At least five juveniles launched from the burrow in the first few days of July. In 2015, the birds selected yet another new hole. Paul and Lisa set up their blind, and once more, the birds fledged in early July.

The pair tended to court at the lower bank below Mountain Water Dam in March or April, and then move to the upper bank. Courtship commenced with the aerial circus and show-off quarrying. Mating was popular on the Douglas-fir root. Conjugal relations, hole selection, and excavating took several weeks, a maddening time when the birds chose a burrow and then changed their minds. April also seems prime time for the arrival of a second female to vie for the male.

By mid-May, the couple had typically settled into incubating eggs within the chosen hole. If so, the chicks hatched in early to mid-June, and the parents geared up for high-stakes fishing to feed the hungry young.

The chicks fledged in late June to early July, and like Brownian motion, they pinged their way downstream to the pond. By late July, the young kingfishers filtered through the lower reaches of Rattlesnake Creek, facing the perils of Cooper's hawks.

The female likely migrated south by late fall, while the male shed wildness for urban life on a wire high above the Clark Fork River in Missoula. Lisa and Paul, who live in the lower Rattlesnake Valley, have seen (more than once) a wintering kingfisher flying diagonally above Greenough Park toward the river.

Within the yearly cycle, the kingfishers continued to baffle us with their timing, failed nests, and unseen fledging. With every passing season, they remained a source of continuity and conundrum, and as skittish as ever.

On visits to Missoula, I pay homage to the arching nest bank on Rattlesnake Creek, and sometimes a kingfisher will grace me with his or her presence. Lisa and Paul continue to document the annual ritual of nest selection. Their camouflaged turkey hunting blind like mine has become weathered from use. Only once did Paul notice any sign of a human visitor, and that one left a business card.

Lisa saw a chick fledge—again. Once, Paul encountered two females poised a few feet apart on the same branch. One lifted her wings as if in warning, and yet they stayed in restless uncompanionship.

Naturally, Paul and Lisa applied their curious minds to a new question: How frequently do kingfishers rattle near their burrow? They kept track over six active nesting seasons from 2014 to 2020 (there was no nest in 2017). They could vouch for at least two fledglings per season, and likely there were more. Their data came from observing 109 nest approaches and 105 departures.

The parents rattled most during chick-raising and the least during incubation, but overall? They were far from quiet. They chattered 93 percent of the time upon arriving and 56 percent upon leaving. Alerting a mate or chicks hidden within the burrow might be the equivalent of calling, "It's me and not an intruder. Don't jab me with your beak!" But why not be silent upon exiting? My hunch? Their language is much more nuanced and complex than we think.

The kingfishers chose the same nest burrow in 2016, 2018, and 2019—a hole on the high upstream side of the bank. Paul saw a third female on the scene several times. In the 2020 courtship, he confirmed a new female with a more pronounced white gap in her russet belt.

But in 2021? After initial flights in and out of the same burrow as the prior year, the pair was nowhere to be found—likely overwhelmed by the disruptions from the City of Missoula removing the dam and associated buildings, the creek reconfiguration, tree plantings, and surveys up and downstream for bull trout. We hope their absence is temporary, and as restoration activity subsides the birds will reclaim their upper nest bank. Paul did find kingfishers five or six miles up the Rattlesnake near flourishing beaver ponds.

In July of 2021, on a wildfire-smoke-laden day with temperatures in the 90s, my son Ian and I pressed through wild rose, cow parsnip, mock orange, and alder to jump the ditch to the island. There, we took off our shoes and waded across slick round rocks of the low-flowing cold creek to the boulder of kingfishers. Where Swainson's thrushes duetted, a western tanager perched above Ian's left shoulder, and Rattlesnake Creek glassed over a tessera of stones glowing in heady hues. We lingered in our hideaway.

Why return year upon year? Why keep looking for kingfishers in my Oregon terrain, too? I echo naturalist Bernd Heinrich's sentiments from his 2020 book, *White Feathers, the Nesting Lives of Tree Swallows*:

> But the lure of seeing something new or unexpected is powerful, and this usually requires being at the wrong place at the right time or vice versa, mucking around in one's much-loved places and situations.

Where kingfishers pitch their calls to the wild rivers, I find my song in the harmony of water, sky, earth, and bird. Seeking the halcyon bird, I've come closer to wildlife than ever before, like one afternoon in late September of 2011, seated by the upper nest bank, drinking in the domain of kingfishers with no real purpose. The creek bubbled over a glossy rock with a gulp and glug, and maroon dogwood leaves shook in a slight breeze.

Then, like a river phantom, a sinewy mink flowed over my outstretched bare legs. Feeling the rippling of chocolate-hued fur, I knew the meaning of becoming one with the wild neighborhood.

At last, too, I understood my father's infamous slide shows, a wellspring of family hilarity whenever we show them. In most slides, my mother, brothers, and I face away from the camera, tiny in comparison to the majesty of a mountain, waterfall, forest, or grassland. We were never the centerpiece, at least when it came to landscape. We were always well-loved.

Grieving for my father, I found his spirit residing close by on the stream's edge, where I tapped into his belief in my abilities to navigate a new course. The longing for his presence will never go away, yet I've come to a place of peace with this invisible touching of hands or raising binoculars. In my son, I see glimpses of his grandfather, from endurance to the way Ian hugs me, firm yet gentle.

My mother died in her sleep on June 11 of 2020, drawing her last breath to the tune of the dawn chorus filtering through the sliding door I'd opened a few minutes before. No longer would those big, brown eyes open wide to the waterfowl on the nearby pond, which had become a favorite place within her Collington senior living community in Maryland. She'd moved there from North Carolina eight years earlier to be closer to my younger brother's family.

In regular trips east to see my mother in her declining years, I'd often observe a kingfisher presiding among herons, turtles, and flocks of Canada geese and mallards. During the difficult months of isolation when the coronavirus pandemic forced Collington to isolate, my mother's aide would call from the pond dock, and I'd listen to them exclaiming over ducks paddling by.

On that sad morning, I knew the kingfisher's chattering phrase would unfurl over her halcyon pond reflecting oaks, maples, and all we cannot know when eyes close for the last time. What our family did know was this. The day before, my brother Rob was by her side when she stopped breathing for too long, until she opened her eyes and looked at him in confusion, "Where's Dave? I was just with him." For years, our mother had referred to our father as "Dad" to us, but this time? Dave. Maybe they are like Halcyon and Ceyx, flying forever as kingfishers—or brown pelicans.

℘

The kingfisher of the Arikara origin story laid a great beak across a canyon for people to cross to a better world. Today, the mythical beak invites us to traverse from despair to hope, and from passivity to action on behalf of nature that is us. Like people harmed by terrible injustices and healing only with tender support, the natural world has a way of renewing, given a chance.

Free a pine tree from barbed wire cutting deep into the bark and come back to see the vibrant new needles. Clear the way of invasive plants and in the soil lie native seeds waiting to sprout. Close ditches that diverted life-giving waters into suburban lawns and the stricken creeks will again brim with insects and fish. Take down artificial dams with care and restore beavers to their natural keystone role of creating pools and watch them store water, nurture fish, and attract my favorite bird.

We can't restore extinct species. We can't bring back centuries-old forests after logging, and we can't give up. My esteemed conservationist friend Brock Evans often rallies the younger generation to embrace "hopeless lost causes" and points to the victories of wilderness, wild rivers, and protecting ancient forests and endangered species. He likes to share a favorite quote he adapted from architect Daniel Burnham: "Dream only large dreams, for they have the power to fire people's souls."

Our waterways give and we must give back. Our wilderness-fed streams and rivers are essential. These are the waters that can best weather the climate chaos if we honor their rights to flow clean, clear, cold, flooding, and free to merge with wetlands and intact forests, which store carbon, exhale oxygen, and sustain life. Every native bird, animal, and flower interweaves within a community of cooperation.

The kingfisher's rollicking, rolling, ratchety, staccato calls signal our awakening. Attend. To be alive is to spread our wings and see where they take us. To be alive is to immerse in our animal selves. With every headfirst plunge, the bird of transformation calls us to be bold.

With the help of Lisa and Paul, I learned to be a better citizen scientist of my wild neighborhood. In our modern world, we have far more people and far fewer naturalists. We need them. My observations build on all those who came before me who had the keen ability to notice and record details of our changing climate.

Studying kingfishers in the field is to paddle a twisting river with ears trained on the rattling call and eyes following the flight of wings bearing colors of sky, snow, and stone.

The Boise River kingfishers taught me to suspend conclusions gathered too soon. Once, I embarked on a solo run of sunshine and storm. At my turnaround past the heron rookery and past the trotting red fox with a plumed tail brushing the sunlight into shadow, I heard the dueling voices of kingfishers. As hail bounced off the river and pounded tender cottonwood leaves, the ardent pair copulated on a branch above the rainbow-struck currents.

The belted kingfisher is a bird of quickening and calm. The bird that mates below a rainbow urges us to chase desires, care for family, excavate the recesses of dreams, fears, and spirit, and to be on the lookout for fleeting beauty.

If we live within nature's embrace, will we return to spinning the ancient stories of animal transformation? We will not hold ourselves apart any longer. We will not be so lonely. Myths of becoming animal can take our feet back to the forest, the riverbank, and to a place of belonging.

I remain a student of the belted kingfisher, teaching me to honor this miraculous planet at every level, to respect all living creatures, and to enter the world each day with senses receptive to the heat of sun, throb of hail, and numbing bite of cold. Every time I hear the ringing call, I'm one with the music of flowing waters. The answer to the halcyon quest is right here in this one beautiful bird. From hours watching the nest hole, I found the confluence of observation and dream. Whenever a kingfisher flew in with a fish, all dropped away to one precise point.

One night during the all-encompassing first field season, I'd dreamed that a kingfisher flew by at eye level in my backyard, so close I could hear the swish of feathers. She flipped over and flew upside down, a raven trick I'd seen before. She righted herself, wheeled around, and landed on my outstretched right hand.

"You know me," I said.

"Yes, I do know you," comes the bird rattle from a sharp, long bill, and we are speaking as if two kingfishers sharing a perch.

"How did you fly on your back like that?"

"It's easy. I'll show you."

I woke with the touch of kingfisher toes on my hand and a wing feathering my face. In that dream, we talked and understood each other in the language of birds.

N

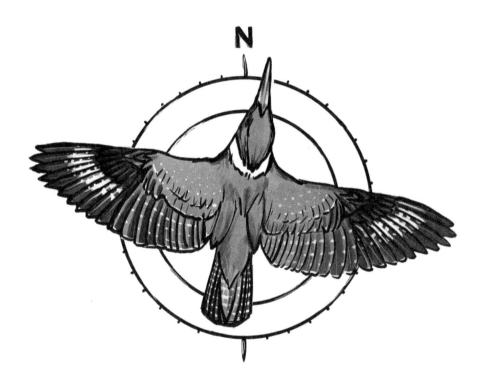

Acknowledgments

I begin with humble gratitude for the people who have known the belted kingfisher in Missoula since time immemorial, and with a land acknowledgment written by the Séliš-Q̓lispé Cultural Committee for the City of Missoula and the University of Montana:

> We acknowledge that Missoula falls within the aboriginal territories of the Salish, Kootenai, and Kalispel people, and honor the path they have always shown us in caring for this place for generations to come.

Our future depends on honoring their path and the deep wisdom attained by attending to intimate rhythms and relationships. I am grateful to the late Salish elder Louis Adams (1934–2016) who taught me the meaning of "everywhere is home," and of living in ways that nourish lands, rivers, and the animal people.

Out of respect for the kingfisher and all beings, I've strived to avoid the impersonal pronoun "it," which is typically applied when unsure of gender. Robin Wall Kimmerer, author of *Braiding Sweetgrass*, proposes new pronouns of "ki" for an individual and "kin" for plural. In her Potawatomi language of animacy is a word that that means "a being of the earth," or Aakibmaadiziiwin. From this name, she chose *aaki* (meaning land) and then shortened to ki, as a being of the living earth.

Change takes time, and until ki and kin flow more easily off my tongue, I've simply written the name—kingfisher, chickadee, mink, wolf—or crafted a sentence differently when not knowing the gender. I did have a recent epiphany. Drop the "g" and kingfisher is kinfisher. Family. Relative. Loved one. I'm fond of calling females the queen fishers.

I thank the wonderful team at Oregon State University Press: director Tom Booth (a fellow kingfisher enthusiast); acquisitions editor Kim Hogeland for believing my book worthy of publication; OSU Press marketing manager Marty Brown; and editorial, design, and production manager Micki Reaman, who selected the copyeditor and linked me with my delightful indexer Stephany Wilkes (author and professional sheep shearer).

My gifted and discerning copyeditor Susan Campbell opened my eyes to the pitfalls of untethered modifying, while honoring my style of writing. Susan is the best editor I've ever had and a kindred spirit, too.

I am grateful to artist Ram Papish, whose talent, bird knowledge, and creativity illuminate his kingfisher drawings, which open each chapter, and the three-dimensional map of the Rattlesnake Valley.

Donna Erickson and Beth Judy of our Missoula writing group, Rockin' R, offered more than a decade of loving support, reviews, and insights. During our writing retreats to cabins, we'd outline our books in progress on flip charts, solve dilemmas, and read out loud. We continue to cheer each other on.

Author Laura Pritchett's guidance, review, and belief in me were critical to bringing the book to the finish line. I'm thankful for her mentorship. Taking a weekend poetry class from Oregon Poet Laureate Kim Stafford helped me pay closer attention to the rhythm, flow, and power of language.

Lisa and Paul Hendricks fell prey to the allure of kingfishers, often joining me in the field or independently observing the nesting pair on Rattlesnake Creek over the seasons. Paul is an accomplished zoologist and a classical naturalist. From him, I learned the value of accurate notes, yet could never rival his precise shorthand, gained from years of field observations. Lisa and I watched kingfishers within a camouflaged blind for hours at a time. She's an educator whose infectious joy for birds cultivates future ornithologists. Thanks to Paul, we have a published natural history note documenting our first-time observations.

Sandra Murphy accompanied me on many a kingfisher watch and is always there for me, as I am for her. Jyl Hoyt, another dear friend, shared her River of Kingfishers—the Boise River. Chris Paige led me to kingfishers on the Bitterroot River. Chris Brick clarified the Missoula area geology and origins of the colorful mudstones of Rattlesnake Creek. Mateusz Piesiak took photos of kingfishers at the blind and opened my eyes to his inquisitive and talented passion for bird photography that he continues today.

Biologists and friends Colleen Matt and Larry Aumiller believed in my book and put me up whenever I landed back in Missoula during the year of living out of my camper. Friends Maureen Riley and Pete Hettinger were the ones who rescued Ian from the soccer field with his broken fingers. It does take a village to raise children.

ॐ

"I've always had a sweet spot for kingfishers," Dr. Dan Albano told me the first time I called him. Dan, now a biologist for a wind energy company, investigated the jaunty charmer of North American waterways for five years on the Connecticut River, leading to his PhD dissertation, "A Behavioral Ecology of the Belted Kingfisher." My well-thumbed copy served as the vital reference during my field quest to find and study a kingfisher burrow. From afar, Dan was unfailingly generous in sharing his knowledge, and encouraging whenever I tripped in my fieldwork.

Dr. Michael (Mic) Hamas, the preeminent kingfisher expert, lent an encouraging ear at several points along the way and, at times, seemed downright wistful not to be out there with me taking on the list of questions he still wants to answer.

My thanks go to scientist Dr. Jeff Kelly, who studied winter kingfishers and toxin connections and helped in my initial nest search questions. Dr. Richard Hutto, ornithology professor emeritus at the University of Montana and researcher, entered the red belt mystery search with intriguing ideas and explanations. Researcher Jim Davis informed me about kingfisher vocalizations. Dr. Bret Tobalske of the University of Montana illuminated the pattern of kingfisher flight and hovering mechanics.

David Liberty shared his Umatilla tribe's kingfisher lore and generously reviewed my manuscript. Salish tribal member and fluent speaker Aspen Decker provided the Salish word for kingfisher of čális (ts ah lease). Linguist Patricia Phillips of the Miluk Coos shared the Hanis and word for kingfisher of *shjit'is* (shi-jit-is), and in Sha'yuushtł'a uhl Quuiich (Siuslaw and Lower Umpqua) it's *ch'a'tii* (ch-ah-ee). Wilbert Fish, Blackfeet herbalist, told me the Napi boulder story. Nathalie Pereda, archivist for Guampedia (nonprofit affiliate of the University of Guam) researched sources for the Chamorro Sihek kingfisher source—not an easy task.

I honor and thank Byron Weber (1945–2010) for teaching me to perceive a world of insects in a single bush. Sue Reel's clear-sighted perceptions at the kingfisher watch steered me in the right direction. Mary Manning, friend and botanist, identified plants and taught me riparian ecology. Willa Craig made it possible for me to witness the bird of Greek myth, the common kingfisher, on Hampstead Heath in London.

Brock Evans, my mentor in environmental conservation, cheered me on throughout the ups and downs of finding a publisher and continues to remind me that I have more to offer as a conservation spokesperson and writer.

James Dean, bird curator of the Smithsonian National Museum of Natural History, introduced me to the back halls and drawers of kingfisher study skins. In 2021, his successor Christopher Milensky reviewed the relevant part of the manuscript and offered important insights. Ornithologist Geoffrey Hill, an authority on bird feather coloration, weighed in on the kingfisher's red belt and offered relevant studies.

I owe the trip to the lower Rio Grande to Nancy Millar, then vice president of the McAllen Convention and Visitors Bureau. She arranged for the stellar guides Keith Hackland and Roy Rodriguez, and a field visit with ringed kingfisher expert Dr. Timothy Brush, along with the opportunity of meeting Martin Hagne, director of the Valley Nature Center. In South Africa, I appreciate all the people who opened my eyes to kingfishers, notably guide Joseph Gumede in Ndumo Game Reserve and guide Frank Mombasa in Kruger National Park.

Dan Burke (University of Montana assistant director of Disability Services) helped me "see" the world from the perspective of those who do not see with their eyes, and thanks to his friend Eric Wahler for permitting me to publish his kingfisher poem.

I'm grateful to Jan Hodder and Mike Graybill for offering their coastal home for house-sitting, where I revised the manuscript, inspired by frequent sightings of kingfishers plying the bay.

I thank Liza Gadsby for her kingfisher gift, and for all she has done for the betterment of wildlife in this world, and urge people to support the nonprofit Pandrillus, so vital to the future of primates in Nigeria. Jeff Fair provided insight into the sharpness of kingfisher bills and recommended me to the Mesa Refuge writers retreat in Point Reyes, California. I'm grateful to the two-week stay there that launched this book. Similarly, I owe much to Summer Fishtrap Gathering of Writers in Oregon for the insights I gained from studying with Laura Pritchett in July of 2016.

By drawing out the writing of this book long enough, my world changed at Fishtrap, where I met Wes Pyne, who confirmed the power of transformative love if two people are willing to take the plunge of a kingfisher. I thank him for his unconditional support, his pithy way with words, and the inspiration he gave me to reach the finish line.

Throughout, my son Ian always believed in this grand project to write about kingfishers and the halcyon myth. I appreciate the support of all my family—brother Rob Richie and sister-in-law Cynthia Terrell and their daughters Anna and Becca, and son Lucas; and brother David Richie and sister-in-law Hilary Stunda and sons Sam and August.

My mother Catherine Richie encouraged the book and listened to many passages that I read to her in person and over the phone. An English major and a fellow writer and reader, she was unfailingly supportive up until her passing in 2020. I credit my father Dave Richie for my love of birds and my passion to conserve nature.

The final acknowledgment must go to every kingfisher in this one sweet world.

Further Reading

Throughout the book, I've referenced certain key sources.

Albano, Dan. "A Behavioral Ecology of the Belted Kingfisher." PhD diss., University of Massachusetts, 2000.

Bent, Arthur Cleveland. "Belted Kingfisher." In *Life Histories of Familiar North American Birds*, 111–129. Smithsonian Institution United States National Museum Bulletin 176, 1940. https://www.birdsbybent.com/ch11-20/kingfish.html.

Billerman, S. M., B. K. Keeney, P. G. Rodewald, and T. S. Schulenberg, eds. "The Cornell Lab of Ornithology: Birds of the World." https://birdsoftheworld.org/bow/home.

Fry, C. Hillary Kathie Fry. *Kingfishers, Bee-Eaters & Rollers*. Princeton, NJ: Princeton University Press, 1992.

Kelly, Jeffrey F., Eli S. Bridge, and Michael J. Hamas. "Belted Kingfisher (*Megaceryle alcyon*)." Cornell Lab of Ornithology: Birds of the World. Version 1, March 4, 2020. Text last updated 2009. https://birdsoftheworld.org/bow/species/belkin1/cur/introduction.

Woodall, Peter. "Family Alcedinidae (Kingfishers)." In *Handbook of the Birds of the World*, Vol. 6, *Mousebirds to Hornbills*, ed. J. del Hoyo, A. Elliott, and J. Sargatal, 130–249. Barcelona: Lynx Edicions, 2001.

Additional Sources by Chapter

INTRODUCTION

Komunyakaa, Yusef. "Yusef Komunyaka Shares Poems from His New Collection." Interview by Scott Simon. NPR, June 12, 2021. Audio, 6:00. https://www.npr.org/2021/06/12/1005833517/yusef-komunyakaa-shares-poems-from-his-new-collection.

CHAPTER 1: HOLE QUEST

Baicich, Paul, and Colin J. O. Harrison. *A Guide to the Nests, Eggs, and Nestlings of North American Birds*. 2nd ed. San Diego, CA: Academic Press, 1977.

Blanchan, Neltje. *Birds*. New York: Doubleday, Page, 1926.

Bridge, Eli, and Jeffrey F. Kelly. "Reproductive Success of Belted Kingfishers on the Upper Hudson River." *Environmental Toxicology and Chemistry* 32, no. 8 (2013): 1855–1863. doi:10.1002/etc.2263.

Davis, James W. M. "Acoustic Recognition in the Belted Kingfisher: Cardiac Response to Playback Vocalizations." *The Condor* 88 (1986): 505–512.

Hamas, Michael J. "Human Incursion and Nesting Sites of the Belted Kingfisher." *The Auk* 91, no. 4 (1974): 835–836.

Hamas, Michael J. "Ecological and Physiological Adaptations for Breeding in the Belted Kingfisher (*Megaceryle alcyon*)." PhD diss., University of Minnesota, 1975.

Hamas, Michael J. "Territorial Behavior in Belted Kingfishers, *Ceryle alcyon*, during Fall Migration." *Canadian Field-Naturalist* 119, no. 2 (2005): 293–294.

IUCN. "The IUCN Red List of Threatened Species." Version 2021-1. https://www.iucnredlist.org.

Kelly, Jeffrey. "Ecological Response to Variable Resource Distributions: Effect of Prey Availability on Belted Kingfishers." PhD diss., Colorado State University, 1996.

Kroodsma, Donald E. *The Singing Life of Birds: The Art and Science of Listening to Birdsong*. New York: Houghton Mifflin, 2005.

Lane, Oksana, David Evers, Dan Albano, Terry Haines, and Robert Taylor. "Belted Kingfishers (*Ceryle alcyon*) as Indicators of Methyl Mercury Availability in Aquatic Systems." Maine Department of Environmental Protection, 2004.

Maclean, Norman. *A River Runs Through It and Other Stories*. Chicago: University of Chicago Press, 1976.

McLeod, C. Milo, and Douglas Melton. "The Prehistory of the Lolo and Bitterroot National Forest: An Overview." USDA Forest Service, Northern Region, Lolo and Bitterroot National Forests, 1986.

Moore, Kathleen Dean. *Riverwalking: Reflections on Moving Water*. New York: Houghton Mifflin, 1996.

Northwest Power and Conservation Council. "Grand Coulee Dam: Impacts on Fish." https://www.nwcouncil.org/reports/columbia-river-history/grandcouleeimpactsonfish. Accessed June 28, 2021.

Plateau Peoples' Web Portal. "Bitterroot Valley and Place Names Lesson (Séliš u Qlispé): Nł?ay Place of Small Bull Trout: The Missoula Area and the Séliš & Qlispé People." https://plateauportal.libraries.wsu.edu/digital-heritage/bitterroot-valley-and-place-names-lesson-s%C3%A9li%C5%A1-u-ql%CC%93isp%C3%A9-curriculum. Accessed June 22, 2021.

Rosenberg, Kenneth V., Adriaan M. Dokterl, Peter J. Blancher, John R. Sauer, Adam C. Smith, Paul A. Smith, Jessica C. Stanton, et al. "Biodiversity

Loss: Decline of the North America Avifauna." *Science* 366 (6461): 120–124. doi:10.1126/science.aaw1313.

Salish-Pend d'Oreille Culture Committee and Elders Cultural Advisory Council, Confederated Salish and Kootenai Tribes. *The Salish People and the Lewis and Clark Expedition*. Lincoln: University of Nebraska Press, 2005.

The Condor. The Editor's Book Shelf 6 (May 1904): 80.

Wells, Diana, and Lauren Jarrett. *100 Birds and How They Got Their Names*. Chapel Hill, NC: Algonquin Books, 2001.

White, H. C. "The Eastern Belted Kingfisher in the Maritime Provinces." *Bulletin of the Fisheries Research Board of Canada* 97 (1953): m1–44.

Winkler, D. W., S. M. Billerman, and I. J. Lovette. "Kingfishers (*Alcedinidae*)." Cornell Lab of Ornithology: Birds of the World. Version 1.0. . https://doi.org/10.2173/bow.alcedi1.01.

CHAPTER 2: COURTING KINGFISHERS

Kennedy, Fergus. "Second Sight: The Incredible World Only Animals See." *Bang! Oxford's Graphically Gorgeous Science Magazine*, January 2014. http://www.bangscience.org/2014/01/second-sight-the-incredible-world-only-animals-see/.

Kroodsma, Donald E., and Jared Verner. "Marsh Wren (*Cistothorus palustris*)." Cornell Lab of Ornithology: Birds of the World. Version 1, March 2020. Text last updated 2013. https://doi.org/10.2173/bow.marwre.01.

Leopold, Aldo. *The River of the Mother of God and Other Essays*. Edited by Susan L. Flader and J. Baird Callicott. Madison: University of Wisconsin Press, 1992.

Miller-Rushing, Abraham J., and Richard B. Primack. "Global Warming and Flowering Times in Thoreau's Concord: A Community Perspective." *Ecology* 89, no. 2 (2008): 332–341. http://www.jstor.org/stable/27651546.

Muir, John. *Our National Parks*. Boston: Houghton, Mifflin, 1901.

Primack, Richard P., and Abraham J. Miller-Rushing. "Uncovering, Collecting, and Analyzing Records to Investigate the Ecological Impacts of Climate Change: A Template from Thoreau's Concord." *BioScience* 62 (2012): 170–180.

Schwab, I. R., and N. S. Hart. "Halcyon Days." *British Journal of Ophthalmology* 88, no. 5 (2004): 613. doi:10.1136/bjo.2004.045492.

Sudbury Valley Trustees. "Gowing's Swamp, Concord." https://www.svtweb.org/properties/page/gowings-swamp-concord. Accessed June 22, 2021.

Thoreau, Henry David. *Thoreau on Birds*. Edited by Francis H. Allen. Boston: Beacon Press, 1993.

The Journal of Henry David Thoreau. "The Walden Woods Project." https://www.walden.org/collection/journals/. Accessed June 29, 2021.

CHAPTER 3: LOST BURROW

Alt, David, and Donald W. Hyndman. *Roadside Geology of Montana.* Missoula, MT: Mountain Press, 1991.

Alt, David. *Glacial Lake Missoula and Its Humongous Floods.* Missoula, MT: Mountain Press, 2001.

Finley, William Lovell. *American Birds; Studied and Photographed from Life.* Pennsylvania: General Books, 2009 [1907].

Murphy, Alexandra. *Graced by Pines: The Ponderosa Pine in the West.* Missoula, MT: Mountain Press, 1994.

CHAPTER 4: NEST WATCH

Birkhead, Tim. *The Most Perfect Thing: Inside (and Outside) a Bird's Egg.* New York: Bloomsbury, 2016.

Mousley, Henry. "A Study of the Home Life of the Eastern Belted Kingfisher." *Wilson Bulletin* 50, no. 1 (1938): 3–12. http://www.jstor.org/stable/4156690.

Prum, Richard O., Eric R. Dufresne, Tim Quinn, and Karla Waters. "Development of Colour-Producing β-keratin Nanostructures in Avian Feather Barbs." *Journal of the Royal Society Interface* 6 (Suppl 2, 2009): S253–S265. doi:10.1098/rsif.2008.0466.focus.

Skutch, Alexander F. "Incubation and Nestling Periods of Birds." *The Auk* 62 (1945): 8–37.

Skutch, Alexander F. "Life History of the Amazon Kingfisher." *The Condor* 59, no. 4 (1957): 217–229.

Wheelock, Irene Grosvenor. *The Nestlings of Forests and Marsh.* Chicago: A.C. McClurg, 1902.

Wheelock, Irene Grosvenor. *Birds of California: An Introduction to More Than Three Hundred Common Birds of the State and Adjacent Islands.* Chicago: A.C. McClurg, 1904.

White, E. B. *The Trumpet of the Swan.* New York: Harper & Row, 1970.

CHAPTER 5: FLEDGING

Campbell, Joseph M., Bill D. Moyers, and Betty S. Flowers. *The Power of Myth.* New York: Anchor Books, 1991.

Michener, James. *Centennial.* New York: Random House, 1974.

Sibley, David Allen. *What It's Like to Be a Bird.* New York: Alfred A. Knopf, 2020.

Waters, Frank. *Book of the Hopi.* New York: Penguin Group, 1963.

CHAPTER 6: ART OF FLYING AND FISHING

Ask Nature. "High Speed Train Inspired by the Kingfisher." https://asknature.org/innovation/high-speed-train-inspired-by-the-kingfisher/#. WxhYOlMvyis. Accessed August 14, 2021.

Benyus, Janine M. *Biomimicry: Innovation Inspired by Nature*. New York: William Morrow, 1997.

Bralliar, Floyd. *Knowing Birds through Stories*. Los Angeles: HardPress, 2014.

Carson, Rachel, Nick Kelsh, and Linda J. Lear. *The Sense of Wonder*. 15th ed. New York: HarperCollins, 1998.

Enzensberger, Hans Magnus. *The Number Devil: A Mathematical Adventure*. London: Picador, 2000.

John J. Audubon's *Birds of America*. "Belted Kingfisher." https://www.audubon.org/birds-of-america/belted-kingfisher.

Kilham, Lawrence. "Biology of Young Belted Kingfishers." *American Midland Naturalist* 92, no. 1 (1974): 245–247. doi:10.2307/2424222.

Lanzone, Mike. "An Unlikely Target—Cooper's Hawks vs. Kingfishers." 2012. http://www.nemesisbird.com/birding/bird-sightings/an-unlikely-target_coopers-hawk-vs-beki/. Accessed August 14, 2021.

Parrish, John W., James. A. Ptacek, and Kevin L. Will. "The Detection of Near Ultraviolet Light by Nonmigratory and Migratory Birds." *The Auk* 101, no. 1 (1984): 53–58. https://doi.org/10.1093/auk/101.1.53

Sibley, David Allen. *The Sibley Guide to Bird Life & Behavior*. New York: Alfred Knopf, 2001.

Sibley Guides. "Wings, Above and Below." March 2013. http://www.sibleyguides.com/2012/03/wings-above-and-below/.

Tobalske, Bret W. "Hovering and Intermittent Flight in Birds." *Bioinspiration & Biometrics* 5, no. 4 (2010): doi:10.1088/1748-3182/5/4/045004.

Tucker, V. A. "The Deep Fovea, Sideways Vision and Spiral Flight Path in Raptors." *Journal Experimental Biology* 203 (pt 240, Dec 2000): 3745–3754.

University of Montana. "College of Humanities and Science Flight Laboratory." http://hs.umt.edu/dbs/flightlab/default.php. Accessed July 12, 2021.

CHAPTER 7: WINTER STORY

Bugbee, Henry. *The Inward Morning: A Philosophical Exploration in Journal Form*. 1st paper ed. Athens: University of Georgia Press, 1999 [1958].

Bugbee, Henry. *Wilderness in America, Philosophical Writings*. Edited by David W. Rodick. New York: Fordham University Press, 2017.

Chandler, Kaitlyn, et al. *The Winged: An Upper Missouri River Ethnoornithology*. Tucson: University of Arizona Press, 2017.

Keats, John. *Endymion*. Book One, 1818. London: held by British Library.

Grinnell, George Bird. *Blackfoot Lodge Tales, The Story of a Prairie People.* Lincoln: University of Nebraska Press, first printing 1962.

Grinnell, George Bird. *The Fighting Cheyennes.* East Bridgewater, MA: J.G. Press, 1995 [1915].

Grinnell, George Bird. *The Cheyenne Indians, Their History and Lifeways.* Edited by Joseph A. Fitzgerald. Bloomington, IN: World Wisdom, 2008.

Linderman, Frank B. *Indian Why Stories, Sparks from War Eagle's Lodge-Fire.* New expanded edition. Lincoln: University of Nebraska Press, 2004.

Salish-Pend d'Oreille Culture Committee. http://csktsalish.org/index.php/about/culture.

Shakespeare, William. "Henry VI." *William Shakespeare Complete Works.* Edited by Jonathan Bate and Eric Rasmussen. New York: Modern Library, 2007.

Thompson, Terry, and Steven M. Egesdal, eds. *Salish Myths and Legends, One People's Stories.* Lincoln: University of Nebraska Press, 2008.

Weisel, George. *Ten Animal Myths of the Flathead Indians.* Missoula: Montana State University, 1959.

CHAPTER 8: RED BELT MYSTERY

Blacker, William. *Blacker's Art of Fly Making* (London: George Nichols, 1842). Project Gutenberg, 2011. https://www.gutenberg.org/files/35752/35752-h/35752-h.htm.

Brush, Timothy. *Nesting Birds of a Tropical Frontier: The Lower Rio Grande Valley of Texas.* College Station: Texas A&M University, 2005.

Brush, Timothy. "Ringed Kingfisher (*Megaceryle torquata*)." Cornell Lab of Ornithology: Birds of the World. Version 1, March 4, 2020. Text last updated 2009. https://birdsoftheworld.org/bow/species/rinkin1/cur/introduction.

Chng, S. C. L., James A. Eaton, Kanitha Krishnasamy, Chris R. Shepherd, and Vincent Nijman. "In the Market for Extinction: An Inventory of Jakarta's Bird Markets." *TRAFFIC*, September 2015. https://www.traffic.org/site/assets/files/2466/market_for_extinction_jakarta.pdf.

Ehrlich, Paul, David S. Dobkin, and Darryl Wheye. *The Birder's Handbook: A Field Guide to the Natural History of North American Birds, The Essential Companion to Your Identification Guide.* New York: Simon & Schuster, 1988.

Galván, Ismael, Jorge García-Campa, and Juan J. Negro. "Complex Plumage Patterns Can Be Produced Only with the Contribution of Melanins." *Physiological and Biochemical Zoology* 90, no. 5 (2017): 600. doi:10.1086/693962.

Hill, Geoffrey. *Bird Coloration.* Washington, DC: National Geographic Publishing, 2010.

Hornaday, William T. *Our Vanishing Wildlife: It's Extermination and Preservation*. New York: Charles Scribner's Sons, 1913.

Howe, Marshall A. "Social Interactions in Flocks of Courting Wilson's Phalaropes (*Phalaropus tricolor*)." *The Condor* 77, no. 1 (1975): 24–33. doi:10.2307/1366756.

Jackson, Beverly. *Kingfisher Blue: Treasures of an Ancient Chinese Art*. Berkeley: Ten Speed Press, 2002.

Johnson, Kirk Wallace. *The Feather Thief*. New York: Penguin Random House, 2018.

Moyle, Robert G. I. "A Molecular Phylogeny of Kingfishers (Alcedinidae) with Insights into Early Biogeographic History." *The Auk* 123, no. 2 (2006): 487–499.

Noble, G. K. "Courtship and Sexual Selection of the Flicker (*Colaptes auratus luteus*). *The Auk* 53 (1936): 269–282.

Remsen, J. R., Jr. "Community Ecology of Neo-tropical Kingfishers." *University of California Publications in Zoology* 124 (1991).

Sibley, David Allen. *The Sibley Field Guide to Birds of Western North America*. New York: Alfred Knopf, 2003.

Skutch, Alexander. "Kingfishers: Sovereigns of the Watercourses." *Nature Magazine*, 1952.

Souder, William. "How Two Women Ended the Deadly Feather Trade." March 2013. http://www.smithsonianmag.com/science-nature/how-two-women-ended-the-deadly-feather-trade-23187277/?no-ist.

The Royal Society for the Protection of Birds. "Celebrating Over 100 years of Saving Nature through Campaigns." https://www.rspb.org.uk/about-the-rspb/about-us/our-history/celebration-of-the-rspb-founders/.

Weidensaul, Scott. *Of a Feather: A Brief History of American Birding*. New York: Harcourt Books, 2007.

Yevtushenko, Yevgeny. *Divided Twins, Alaska and Siberia*. New York: Boyd Norton, 1988.

CHAPTER 9: GREEK MYTH AND NAMING KINGFISHERS

Bullfinch, Thomas, and Richard P. Martin. *Bulfinch's Mythology*. New York: HarperCollins, 1991.

Campbell, Joseph. *The Way of the Animal Powers. Part 1: Mythologies of the Primitive Hunters and Gatherers*. New York: Harper & Row, 1988.

Graves, Robert. *The Greek Myths*. London: Penguin Books, 2011.

Hamilton, Edith. *Mythology: Timeless Tales of Gods and Heroes*. New York: Penguin Books, 1942.

Jóźwiak, Piotr, et al. "Taxonomic Etymology: In Search of Inspiration." *ZooKeys* 513 (July 2015): 143–160. doi:10.3897/zookeys.513.9873.

Macfarlane, Robert. *The Lost Words, A Spell Book*. London: Penguin Books, 2017.

Pliny the Elder. *The Natural History of Pliny.* Vol. 1, translated by John Bostock and Henry T. Riley. The Project Gutenberg Ebook. https://www.gutenberg.org/files/57493/57493-h/57493-h.htm.

Sherr, Lynn. *America the Beautiful: The Stirring True Story behind Our Nation's Favorite Song.* New York: Public Affairs, 2001.

Smithsonian's National Zoo and Conservation Biology Institute. "Guam Kingfisher." https://nationalzoo.si.edu/animals/guam-kingfisher.

Szabo, Ildiko. *Kingfisher: Animal Series.* London: Reaktion Books, 2019.

Watts, A. E. *The Metamorphosis of Ovid.* Oakland: University of California Press, 1954.

CHAPTER 10: SECOND SEASON, SECOND CHANCES

Ackerman, Jennifer. *The Bird Way: A New Look at How Birds Talk, Work, Play, Parent, and Think.* New York: Penguin Press, 2020.

Burgess, Thornton W. *Mother West Wind When Stories.* New York: Grosset & Dunlap, 1917.

Dawson, William Leon. *Dawson's Avian Kingdom: Selected Writings by William Leon Dawson.* Edited by Anna Neher. Berkeley: Heyday Books, 2007.

Hendricks, Paul, Deborah Richie, and Lisa M. Hendricks. "Aerial Ramming, a Burrow Excavation Behavior by Belted Kingfishers, with a Review of Its Occurrence among the Alcedinidae." *Wilson Journal of Ornithology* 125, no. 1 (March 2013): 197–201. http://wjoonline.org/doi/abs/10.1676/12-075.1?journalCode=wils.

Rowling, J. K. *Harry Potter and the Sorcerer's Stone.* New York: Scholastic Books, 2001.

CHAPTER 11: WORLD CUP FOR THE BIRDS

Ask Nature. "Strategy: Covering Protects Eye, Pied Kingfisher." http://www.asknature.org/strategy/81ce7bdb99e76d2e0d9dc2cbd01d21e4. Accessed Jan. 4, 2019.

Mandela, Nelson. *Long Walk to Freedom.* New York City: Back Bay Books, 1995.

Wanink, Jan. H. "Foraging Locations of Kingfishers and Cormorants Depend on the Distribution of Harvestable Prey." *African Journal of Ecology* 34 (1996): 90–93.

CHAPTER 12: GHOST KINGFISHERS

Islapedia: The Santa Cruz Island Foundation. "Townsend, Charles Haskin." https://www.islapedia.com/index.php?title=TOWNSEND,_Charles_Haskins. Last modified June 30, 2021.

Loss, S., T. Will, and P. Marra. "The Impact of Free-Ranging Domestic Cats on Wildlife of the United States." *Nature Communications* 4 (2013): 1396. https://doi.org/10.1038/ncomms2380.

Marks, Jeffrey S., Paul Hendricks, and Daniel Casey. *Birds of Montana*. Arrington, VA: Buteo Books, 2016.

Pyle, Peter. *Identification Guide to North American Birds, Part 1*. Point Reyes Station, CA: Slate Creek Press, 1997.

Richmond, C. W., and F. H. Knowlton. "Birds of South-Central Montana." *The Auk* 11 (1894): 298–308.

Scholander, S. I. "Land Birds over the Western North Atlantic." *The Auk* 72 (1955): 225–239.

Smithsonian National Museum of Natural History. "Division of Birds." https://naturalhistory.si.edu/research/vertebrate-zoology/birds. Accessed July 11, 2021.

Weidensaul, Scott. *Of a Feather: A Brief History of American Birding*. San Diego: Harcourt Books, 2007.

Winspear, Jacqueline. *Maisie Dobbs*. London: Penguin Books, 2003.

CHAPTER 13: SONG OF SHARPENING STONE

Henry, Marguerite, and Wesley Dennis. *Misty of Chincoteague*. New York: Simon & Schuster Books, 1975.

Nichols, Robert E., Jr. *Birds of Algonquin Legend*. Ann Arbor: University of Michigan Press, 1995.

CHAPTER 14: BIRD OF MYTH IN LONDON

British Broadcasting Corporation (BBC). "My Halcyon River." http://www.bbc.co.uk/programmes/b0078gk1. Accessed July 1, 2021.

Hopkins, Gerard Manley. *Gerard Manley Hopkins: Poems and Prose*. Edited by W. H. Gardner. London: Penguin Classics, 1985.

James, Charlie Hamilton. *Kingfisher: Tales from the Halcyon River*. London: Evans Mitchell Books, 2000.

Royal Society for the Protection of Birds (RSPB), "Kingfisher—Threats." http://www.rspb.org.uk/discoverandenjoynature/discoverandlearn/birdguide/name/k/kingfisher/survival_and_threats.aspx. Accessed July 1, 2021.

Santos, Sherod. *Greek Lyric Poetry: A New Translation*. New York: W.W. Norton, 2005.

Sappho. "Poetry Foundation." https://www.poetryfoundation.org/poets/sappho/. Accessed July 1, 2021.

Tate, Peter. *Flights of Fancy, Birds in Myth, Legend, and Superstition*. New York: Bantam Dell, 2007.

Woodall, Peter F. "Common Kingfisher (*Alcedo atthis*). Cornell Lab of
   Ornithology: Birds of the World. Version 1.0, March 2, 2020. Text last
   updated February 2014. https://doi.org/10.2173/bow.comkin1.01.

CHAPTER 15: RATTLESNAKE CREEK RETURN

Evans, Brock, with George Venn. *Endless Pressure, Endlessly Applied: The
   Autobiography of an Eco-Warrior.* La Grande, OR: Wake-Robin Press,
   2020.
Heinrich, Bernd. *White Feathers: The Nesting Lives of Tree Swallows.* New
   York: Houghton Mifflin Harcourt, 2020.
Hendricks, Paul, and Lisa M. Hendricks. "Context of Rattle-Call Use by
   Adult Belted Kingfishers (*Megaceryle alcyon*) Near Their Nests." *Wilson
   Journal of Ornithology* (in press, vol. 133, 2021).
Nelson, Richard. *The Island Within.* Albany, CA: North Point Press, 1989.
"Oregon's Ninth Poet Laureate Kim Stafford." YouTube video, March 12,
   2021, 6:13, Collin Serigne and Daniel Stumpf. Lewis and Clark College.
   https://youtu.be/5HcFlMGVX_E.

Index

Page numbers in italics refer to illustrations.